About the Author

C J Taylor began her career in journalism in 1961, spending over fifty years as a print journalist and feature writer in Sussex, Gloucestershire and South Wales.

Following her retirement, she embarked on an academic journey, achieving a first-class honours degree in Religion, Philosophy and Ethics, and then a master's degree focusing on eco-feminism and Goddesses at Greenham Common women's peace camp and in Extinction Rebellion.

She has four children, including the daughter who was adopted when she was an unmarried mother in the sixties, and with whom she was reunited in the nineteen-nineties: thirteen grandchildren and a great-granddaughter.

Her personal interests include learning Italian and playing the guitar. She also dedicates part of her time to volunteering with a group that provides breakfast for the homeless and those in need.

The first book in the series, *Perfectly Imperfect (The Story of the Two Js)* was published in 2024. *Living Live Backwards (The Continuing Story of The Two Js)* is the second book in the trilogy.

Also by C J Taylor:

Living Life Backwards
(The Story of the Two Js: Book Two)

Perfectly Imperfect

(The Story of the Two Js)

C J Taylor

First published in 2024 by C J Taylor
Second edition published 2025 by Fuzzy Flamingo
Copyright © C J Taylor 2024

Author photos: Paul Nicholls Photography

C J Taylor has asserted her right to be identified as the author of this Work in accordance with the Copyright, Designs and Patents Act 1988.

ISBN: 978-1-9192648-1-3

All rights reserved.
No part of this publication may be reproduced, stored in a retrieval system, or transmitted in any form or by any means, electronic, mechanical, photocopying, recording or otherwise, without the prior permission of the copyright owner.

Editing and design by Fuzzy Flamingo
www.fuzzyflamingo.co.uk

A catalogue for this book is available from the British Library.

*For John and Diana, who changed my life,
and Ray, who showed me how to live it.
Also, my granddaughter Jasmine, one of a new generation of strong
women fighting patriarchy, who read this book while I was writing it.*

While this book is based on the true stories of those who related them to me, many of the names, dates, and places have been changed and I must stress that this is essentially a work of imagination. Nevertheless, I hope it reflects an extraordinary time in women's recent history when so much heartbreak was caused by the whims of a puritanical society and in the name of religion. Although it seems so much has changed during the past century, scratch below the surface, you will find that many old attitudes and opinions continue. In the twenty-first century, misogyny seems more prevalent than ever. Patriarchy still rules.

C J T

> *"If a woman has sex with a hundred random men in a year, she can still only produce one full-term pregnancy. If a guy has sex with a hundred women in a year, he can produce a hundred full-term pregnancies. So why, exactly, do we only talk about regulating women?"*
> Maria Guido (scarymommy.com)

Preface

> "The memories of a man in his old age are the deeds of a man in his prime."
> "Free Four"
>
> Pink Floyd,
> on the album 'Obscured by Clouds' (1972)

MY NAME is Juliet and I'm an old woman. I've had my allotted three score years and ten and then some. It's been a good life, not without its trials and tribulations, but then, what life is? I find myself wallowing in the past a great deal nowadays. It creeps up on me. One minute I'm doing something totally mundane like brushing my teeth or walking to the shops when, in an instant I'm plunged deep into dreams. Into a life long ago, another world viewed in sepia, like those old photographs of our stiff and starchy forebears.

I frequently dream at night, too. Once, I hardly ever dreamt, or if I did I could barely recall them. Nowadays I tend to remember quite easily all those unbidden night-time visits to unconscious memory.

I've heard it said that when you die your life flashes before you. Can it be possible? That a whole lifetime can be conjured up so quickly? Or is life recalled by the constant dreaming that accosts us in old age? Glimpses of the past, things we did and things we wish we had not done. Forgotten memories dredged up from goodness knows where flitting through our minds.

So here I am, an old woman endlessly dreaming. A few of these trips into the past bring with them toe-curling embarrassment that I would rather leave buried; others usher in nostalgia, while some move me to tears for missed opportunities and love lost.

Life is a collection of memories, and staring into the past is one of the advantages of old age. While there are many happy memories, I can also see with clarity the mistakes I made and the chances I missed. We only get one go at life; how different would mine have been if I'd had such insight at twenty?

My name is Juliet, and my life has been both a gift and a blessing. I am thankful and content.

Part One
Juliet and Ted

(1964-1977)

Reflection

"Life can only be understood backwards, but it must be lived forwards."
Soren Kierkegaard, Danish theologian and philosopher

WHEN I met Ted, I had barely recovered from the end of a love affair. Not only a love affair but also the loss of an illegitimate baby I was forced to have adopted. Those were the days when being unmarried and pregnant was a sin, a secret to be concealed at all costs from an unforgiving society. The disgraced girl was hidden away until the child was born when it would be given to new parents, while the heartbroken birth mother would be sent back to her previous life, and her fall from grace would never be mentioned by anyone. It was as if nothing had happened.

Knowing I had to put the past behind me for the sake of my own sanity, I quickly embraced a relationship with Ted, and within a few months we were married. Was this marriage on the rebound? Probably. Nevertheless, it was a good marriage which lasted for half a century.

'Honesty is the best policy' has always been one of my rules for life, so I confessed all to my husband-to-be, not willing to go into marriage with a secret past that might quite conceivably pop up at some time in the future. I then discovered that Ted, too, was hiding a secret: he was quite recently divorced after a very short marriage had gone sour.

So, there we were, a young couple damaged by life, who eventually found each other and had a long and happy marriage. We were lucky, I think; many others like us were not as fortunate.

My mother threw me out when I became pregnant, desperate to protect our family name from gossip and social ruin. Even though she was anxious to get me 'off-hand' as she put it, she then found my marriage to Ted totally unacceptable on the grounds that he had neither money nor position and was not, therefore, good enough for her only daughter.

With the benefit of hindsight, I know that my life and that of my mother were based on mutual misunderstanding. We had never enjoyed an easy relationship. She was not brilliant at mothering and wanted an uncomplicated daughter who was a carbon copy of herself; I had no understanding of the strict Edwardian upbringing and patriarchy that ruled her life and made her the way she was.

Keeping an unswerving devotion to the standards of a fading age, she made every attempt to instruct me in the skills she fondly imagined all prospective husbands would look for in a wife. Thus, I was taught needlework, given piano lessons, and sent to tennis, dancing, and French classes. In theory, I have all these accomplishments at my fingertips; in reality, I am competent at none.

Nevertheless, my mother was convinced the skills she had given me would go a long way to securing a 'suitable' marriage. She was disappointed. Not only did I have a passionate affair with a man to whom I was not wed, but I produced an illegitimate daughter and then, to add insult to injury, married a man she considered unworthy.

I continued to frustrate her throughout the years, never reaching her exacting standards. Where I was concerned, my mother's glass was always half empty.

Chapter One

WHEN TED Jackson met Juliet Campbell in 1964, he had just been fired from a perfectly respectable and relatively well-paid job in advertising after a row with the senior partner.

"I'm sorry, Ted. You're a good worker and one of the most creative people here, but we just can't have brawls in the boardroom," the personnel officer said unhappily, trying to avoid his eyes. She liked Ted; she even fancied him a bit and couldn't shake off the memory of a random but sexy moment in the stationery room; nevertheless, she had her job to do and knew which side her bread was buttered.

Ted shrugged and packed his belongings into a cardboard box. He knew he could easily get another advertising job, but he wanted a change. He was fed up cow-towing to his boss and the agency hierarchy, planning to get an outside job for the summer and then go back into advertising later in the year. He was also bored with London and decided a few months by the sea was what he needed. Within days, he was hired as a brickie on a Brighton building site.

That evening, wandering around looking for somewhere to have a drink, he clattered down the metal steps of a basement club in Brighton's Lanes only to be stopped at the door and told he couldn't go in without a tie. Amazingly, he did not argue or give the doorman an abusive mouthful but simply walked back to his seafront digs, put on a tie, and returned.

As he walked into the bar in search of a pint, a pretty, red-haired girl rushed over to him, grabbed his arm, and said breathlessly: "Hello, darling, I've been waiting for you," and gave him a peck on the cheek. Gazing anxiously up at him, she murmured: "Please pretend to be my boyfriend, just for five minutes. Then I'll go and leave you alone."

This is the stuff dreams are made of, thought a startled Ted, but looking into the girl's silvery green eyes, his usual stock-in-trade Smart Alec reply died on his lips. Instead, he smiled and said: "Sorry I'm late, sweetheart, what can I get you to drink?"

"A glass of red wine, please. Chianti if possible." An unusual and rather sophisticated choice, thought Ted and was about to say so before remembering that if she were his girlfriend, he would know her taste in wine. "The usual then," he said and walked over to the bar.

When they were seated with their drinks, the girl grimaced and said: "Thank you so much. I am truly sorry to have grabbed you like that, but I was accosted by this man I couldn't shake off; he was very determined, and I got a bit panicky. So, I told him I was waiting for my boyfriend and then, miraculously, you walked in. I'm Juliet, by the way."

"How d'you do? I'm Ted, and before we go any further, I'll just go over and have a quiet word with him." Ted stood up with a pugnacious look on his face.

"He left just after you arrived," said Juliet, feeling relieved. Ted looked as if he might have hit the man, and she had no wish to be the catalyst for a fight.

As Ted sat down again Juliet took a proper look at this rather nice-looking fair-haired man, dressed in a fashionable collarless jacket with shirt and tie, slim-fitting trousers and black Cuban-heeled boots, who had so sportingly saved her from a difficult situation. "I'm really grateful."

Something of a Jack-the-Lad, Ted reckoned he was good with

women and never really considered rejection a possibility. Girls were usually more than eager to go out with him but as most of them bored him silly, he spent a day or two wooing them then took them to bed and immediately lost interest. He felt instinctively that this girl was different.

Juliet was certainly unusual looking with a quirky style that had grabbed Ted's attention immediately. Her short, spiky hair was marmalade red, reminding Ted of a ginger cat his grandmother used to have. She was wearing a short emerald tunic, black polo neck jumper and thick black tights with knee-high silver boots which, while very sixties, had an odd, folksy air about them. Her mouth was far too big for her face, but her eyes, her strange silvery green eyes fringed by thick dark red lashes, were magical.

Taking a gulp of his pint, Ted gave her a suggestive wink and purred smoothly: "I've seen gorgeous eyes like yours on an advertising hoarding in town."

Looking at Juliet's underwhelmed expression, he regretted the remark as soon as he had said it. This girl was better than that. A lot better.

Juliet, who despised obvious men with predictable chat-up lines, particularly those who knew they were good-looking, sighed and picked up her bag, ready to leave. Pity, he had seemed promising, and it had been a while since she had met a man she fancied, but she had absolutely no interest in someone who thought she'd fall for such puerile flattery.

Anxious to stop her running out on him, Ted quickly apologised, saying with a self-deprecating smile, "Sorry. I don't know why I said that!" and then suggested that they found a more salubrious place to have a second drink.

Juliet was about to refuse, but noticing a hint of mockery in his clear blue eyes, almost as if he was laughing at making a fool of himself, she said: "Good idea, where shall we go?" and walked out of the club. Later, she wondered why she had allowed it to happen. What was it about Ted that instantly overcame her usual caution?

After sauntering along the promenade chatting amicably, they eventually settled themselves on the window seat of a seafront pub with a view of Brighton's Palace Pier. The rest of the evening flew past while they gossiped away as if they had known each other forever.

Ted thought he had never met a girl who was so…he struggled for words, so content in her own skin. She told him she had lived in Italy for a while, and he supposed that accounted for her casual continental style, although surprisingly, she also had an attractive air of shyness. It was a potent combination, and he was enchanted.

"So why were you sitting unaccompanied in that club?" Ted enquired with interest.

"Oh, it was a silly thing to do, really. I was going with a girlfriend, but she got a last-minute date with a guy she had had a crush on for ages, so I got dumped. I decided to go anyway, and the inevitable happened. I got buttonholed by a very unsavoury man. My own fault, I guess, but then you came along like a knight in shining armour and rescued me." Ted patted her hand. "Always pleased to be of service."

Juliet had to admit she was rather smitten by this charming man. He was not conventionally handsome, but he had an attractive crooked smile and a slightly enigmatic air, which was very compelling. After spending time with romantic Italian men, Juliet recognised immediately that Ted enjoyed the company of women and knew how to treat them. He looked intently at her while she was speaking, really listening to what she was saying, and he even showed interest in her work as a florist, a topic of conversation that was often a big turn-off for many of the men she met. She had almost forgiven him for the fatuous comment about her eyes.

Ted offered to walk her home but Juliet said it was too far

and she would get a taxi. Walking up the hill to the rank of cabs outside the railway station, Ted reached out and folded his fingers around Juliet's hand; there was a slight jolt in his stomach as his skin touched hers. He looked down at her. Had she felt it, too? There was no indication she had, but she left her hand in his. Ted made an impulsive decision to see her home and then travel back into town by taxi. He just wanted to prolong the evening with this girl, feeling a deep, fizzing excitement at the possibilities ahead.

Sitting with his arm around Juliet in the back of the cab – the driver having diplomatically turned off the light and closed the sliding window between the front and back seats – Ted bent over and kissed her on the mouth.

"Phew," he said when she returned the embrace, "I've been wanting to do that all evening but I wasn't sure how you would react." As he kissed her again with more purpose, Juliet thought: Well, I like a snog with a good-looking man as much as anyone, and he certainly is a good kisser.

When they reached her home on the Downs, Ted asked the cab driver to wait while he accompanied her to the door. Kissing her lightly on the cheek he asked if he could take her to the cinema the following evening. Juliet agreed, and he wrote her phone number on the back of his hand. "I'll ring you," he said and climbed back into the taxi for the return trip to town.

Juliet was quietly happy. There had been boyfriends before, of course, and one particularly unforgettable liaison in Italy, but no one since then with whom she had felt so comfortable. No doubt her mother would have endless questions when Ted rang tomorrow but it would be worth it to see him again.

Would that connection – that beguiling sense of intimacy she had felt – still be there? It was. But it wasn't long before Juliet discovered that Ted was not exactly what he seemed.

Chapter Two

TED HAD, in fact, simply reinvented himself. Growing up without the father who had walked out when he was three, and with a mother who cared little about him, Ted had an impoverished and rather rough childhood, playing truant from school so often that his education was almost non-existent. In his teens, realising that the stylish, upmarket girls he fancied would never give him even a passing glance, he decided to kill off his old life and create a completely new one.

He had left home at sixteen, moving into a YMCA hostel and taking on a succession of labouring jobs until he could afford a room of his own. Once settled, he began to work on his fresh identity.

Compensating for his lack of schooling, he read copiously everything he could lay his hands on, from Greek myth to Russian novels. He also attempted to improve his general education, making two surprise discoveries in the process: he had the ability to soak up information like a sponge, and he was a natural at mathematics. He also refined his elocution, quite easily dropping his sloppy London street talk for a posher, more classless accent.

By the time he moved into his twenties, Ted had become a self-assured and confident man who knew how to conduct himself and could handle most situations. Girlfriends were impressed by his poise in restaurants, knowing which wine to drink and how to deal efficiently with patronising head waiters. Since he was always as willing to make up a four at bridge in a gentleman's club as he was to play snooker in a pub or the slot machines in an amusement arcade, Ted also had a wide circle of male friends.

Although he never actually lied about his past, Ted gave the impression he was from a well-to-do background. For obvious reasons, he never took girls back to his attic room but referred to 'my flat,' making it sound like a penthouse apartment rather than a small room in a shared house, and the slight air of mystery that surrounded him drew women like a magnet.

Personable and charming, with a good sense of humour and an instinctive fashion sense, Ted soon discovered that the type of girls who had ignored him in his teens were now queuing up to go out with him. Hanging out with the right people in the right places landed him a job as a junior in an advertising agency, where it was quickly discovered he had a raw creative talent and was particularly good at impressing clients who started asking for him by name. Very quickly, he managed to progress and charm his way up the corporate ladder.

So, Ted Jackson landed in Swinging Sixties London as an engaging young man with well-heeled friends willing to occasionally lend him their swish bachelor pads for an evening if he wanted to take a girl to bed. This he did as often as he could, gaining the reputation of being a bit of a stud.

However, his deprived past, which had left him with a slight chip on his shoulder and a hot temper, surfaced every so often, and he would fight aggressively to protect his fragile ego if he thought his credibility was being questioned or if he suspected, as he often did, that someone 'posh' was looking down on him. He worked tirelessly to preserve the mask of respectability and social standing he had woven around himself.

★★★

With Juliet, it was different; Ted discovered with surprise that he was able to relax. After that first gaffe about her eyes, he gave up trying to flirt and just became himself, never feeling the need to impress.

"I rarely use the word love," he told her one evening shortly after they met when they were sitting in a seafront shelter watching the twinkling lights of the Palace Pier, "but I'm beginning to feel more and more that way about you."

A warm glow of satisfaction spread through Juliet. "That's just how I feel," she said. Ted gave her a long, slow kiss. Funny, but he had no desire to push sex with Juliet as he had with every other girl he'd gone out with. He knew he could wait for her; this was the girl he was going to marry. When you found something good, you just held on tight until it was time to let go, and he had every intention of holding on to her forever.

Three weeks after their accidental meeting in the nightclub, having spent every evening and weekend together, Juliet moved into Ted's tiny, rented seafront room. Gloating over their good fortune at finding each other they formed a kind of mutual appreciation club, almost grateful to the man who had made unwelcome advances to Juliet and constantly wondering what would have happened if Ted had told the doorman to take a running jump and had gone off without a tie to the nearest pub.

As she grew to know Ted better, Juliet got past the public persona and realised with growing pleasure that he was unconventional, a free spirit who shared many of her beliefs and convictions. They were both drawn to the slightly hippy Flower Power movement, admired Bruce Kent, joining the Campaign for Nuclear Disarmament, and enjoyed an eclectic taste in music ranging from Mozart to The Beatles, as well as jazz, with a bit of heavy rock, folk and blues thrown in for good measure.

The only downside for Juliet was that Ted wasn't a fan of Elvis Presley, whom she had idolised since she was thirteen. Oh well, no one can have everything, she told herself with a forgiving smile; at least he liked Bob Dylan.

"It was obviously meant to be," said Juliet, squashed into the single bed they now shared. "I mean, who else could I have found who was so like me? Maybe it was the coins I threw into the Trevi Fountain when I was in Rome. It's said you meet the man of your dreams after doing that."

It didn't take long for them to decide to get married. "We might as well, we spend all our time together anyway," said Ted. "How about a real sixties Flower Power wedding? You in a long white dress with flowers in your hair, me in a white suit and both of us with bare feet. I could even play my guitar."

"Do you play the guitar?" asked Juliet with a sudden spark of interest.

"Not at all," replied Ted, "but I could learn." They went into a paroxysm of childish giggles as Juliet said: "Oh, I would so love to see my mother's face if we did that."

Pulling herself together, Juliet pointed out that Ted hadn't even proposed to her. "All girls want a proper proposal…" She paused and said frowning, "Also, I haven't told you anything about my past, you know, other boyfriends and stuff. It's quite important you know about that before taking me on."

Ted averted his eyes and crossed his fingers behind his back. Revealing his rather chequered past was one conversation he didn't particularly relish right now, although he knew it was something he couldn't put off forever.

Ted shook his head. "Oh, no need for that conventional twaddle," he retorted with more force than he intended. "I don't need to know who else there was before I met you. It's not important. It doesn't affect how we feel. We know we love each other and want to be together, and that's enough. No need for pointless gestures. Surely you don't want a huge swanky engagement ring to flaunt and make your girlfriends jealous?"

"No-o-o," said Juliet hesitantly. Ted laughed and gave a huge mock sigh: "Just as well, sweetheart, because I can't afford one – *we* can't afford one. When I've made my fortune, which I will do, I'll buy you the biggest diamond ring in the world, until then…" he kissed her, picked her up, and carried her over to the bed. "Come on, Mrs Jackson-to-be, let's do what we do best. I'm going to make love to you from head to toe."

"We need to talk about names," said Juliet, shuffling across the bed to make room for him. "I'm thinking of staying as Juliet Campbell. Taking the man's surname on marriage is very patriarchal, you know."

Ted wasn't listening. His whole being was already firmly focused on making love to her. The thing he enjoyed doing most in the world.

★★★

Sex with Ted had been a bit of a concern for Juliet initially. She had slept with only two men previously – the second time had been a fiasco, but the first was when she fell in love, and it had set an enormously high bar for perfect lovemaking. She was apprehensive that Ted might turn out to be a disappointment in bed. Her fears were unfounded. Ted passed, if not with flying colours, then pretty close.

Juliet knew she was never going to be able to repeat the experience she'd had in Italy. In the circumstances, Ted was perfect. Not only was he an emotive and confident lover, but there was an undeniably strong erotic pull between them.

As for Ted, he was amazed and delighted to discover that Juliet was what his more ungentlemanly friends, indulging in locker-room talk, would call 'a good lay.' She was, quite simply, very good at making love, and what's more, she clearly enjoyed it. This was so unusual for a young English girl that Ted was taken aback, wondering with slight alarm how his performance measured up for her.

She's obviously had an experienced partner, he thought with a twinge of envy for the man who'd had the pleasure of teaching her.

★★★

Despite Ted's vehement assertion that what had happened before they met was of no importance, Juliet insisted that she told him about past affairs. She was scrupulously honest.

"You have to know that I have had a few boyfriends and one serious relationship, which really did not end well," she confessed. She then recounted her life story to date leaving out none of the more distressing details.

That explained so much, thought Ted. Juliet's impressive maturity, composure and acceptance of life was a result of all that had happened to her while she was only just out of her teens. It had been a lot to deal with but she had coped and emerged optimistic and relatively unscathed. Ted was proud that she was going to be his wife.

After Juliet's candour, Ted was forced to admit that, as well as numerous affairs over the years, he had also been married before. His face was deathly pale and his body rigid with tension as he gabbled: "She left me after a year, and we are divorced; there were no children," looking, thought Juliet, like a small boy expecting a severe scolding.

"I'm honestly sorry I haven't told you this sooner, I should have done, but I was worried you'd throw me over."

Juliet put her arms around him and kissed him. "It's not a problem," she said. "We all make mistakes. Don't let's brood about the past any longer. We must look towards our future together."

Ted felt an enormous weight lift off his shoulders. "You're just amazing," he told her with gratitude.

Acknowledging his previous life had been a worry for several weeks. Ted had every intention of admitting his catastrophic previous marriage before the wedding, but finding the right moment had proved difficult. With astonishment, he realised that he had been terrified of Juliet's reaction to the news. It was the first time he could remember when he had cared about what someone else thought.

Chapter Three

THERE WAS a lot of opposition to their marriage. Juliet's parents were horrified that their only daughter was proposing to wed someone she had only just met, someone without position or prospects and probably very little money. She could do much better than that. They had turned a blind eye to the fact that she had moved in with this man so quickly after meeting him. No point in trying to stop her, it was just a flash in the pan; she'd soon be back home, they told each other without conviction. Now look what had happened and so quickly after her previous love affair and its tragic consequences. Was this marriage on the rebound?

"Goodness knows we've done our best," Mary Campbell wailed to her daughter during one of their interminable rows on the subject. "Your father and I have supported you through all your scrapes, you know what I mean without me spelling it out, and you've thrown it all back in our faces. I just don't know what we did wrong. Other people's daughters don't behave in this cavalier fashion without a thought of what their parents are going through."

Juliet glanced across at her father, who had his head buried in the *Daily Telegraph*. His toe was tapping restlessly against the table leg.

"Daddy?"

"Well." Dennis Campbell was obviously uncomfortable at being dragged into the quarrel. Of course, he wanted Juliet to be happy; even so, he would have liked her to marry someone who could look after her and he wasn't at all sure that this Ted could, or would, do that. He seemed a bit wild, although Dennis had to admit that Juliet had had her moments. He also had a sneaking suspicion that not only was he unconventional – Ted certainly hadn't asked for his daughter's hand in marriage – he was also penniless.

Before he could say anything, Mary continued her rant. "We did consider getting you made a ward of the court, but unfortunately, it seems you are too old, although, may I point out, not yet at the age of majority."

Juliet, who was twenty, knew full well that to be made a ward of the court she had to be under eighteen, but until she was twenty-one, she still needed her parents' consent to marry.

"I will be twenty-one in a couple of months, so you might as well accept it with good grace," snapped Juliet. "And whatever you say, I will still get my inheritance from Granny then."

Her mother gave a howl and burst into tears. "When I think of all the plans we made for you."

"Yes, but Mum, they were your plans, not mine. This is my life, and I want to marry Ted. I'm going to marry Ted. Please be pleased for us."

Mary stared at Juliet with wild, red-rimmed eyes. "You were proposing to marry someone else not so very long ago, and look what happened then; there was also another man before that. Have you no self-respect? I really don't know what's happened to girls these days."

Turning her back on Juliet, she said: "You're a selfish, spoilt girl, and given time you'll realise that we are right to try and make you see sense. Don't even think of having children because they will break your heart every time." She was so upset that she gave no thought to her twin sons, who were dutifully following the parental plans drawn up for them.

"May I remind you, Miss," she continued, her voice rising with emotion, "that when it all goes horribly wrong, as it almost certainly will, you need never come back home and hope that we will get you out of this scrape. We are finished with you, your father and me. You have hurt us once too often. This time, you have made your bed, and you must lie on it."

Juliet left her childhood home, a comfortable detached villa on the Downs above Brighton, feeling resolute but churned up inside. Blast everyone; why couldn't anything in her life go smoothly? Her throat tightened as she fought back the tears which threatened to spill down her cheeks. She would not cry. True, her parents had eventually agreed to give their consent to the marriage, but the parent-daughter relationship was decidedly frosty.

Juliet had already spoken to her brothers. Alan working round the clock as a trainee farrier deep in the Cotswold countryside, was far more worried about treating a lame equine patient than his sister's romance. "Sounds great, Smudge," he said, reverting to her childhood nickname. "If it's what you want to do, go for it, but are you certain he's the right one this time?"

Bertie, in his fresher year reading English at Oxford, immediately wished her luck and said: "He'd better be good to you, or I'll send the boys round!" Because he had an essay to write, exams looming, and the promise of a free pint at The Mitre, Bertie was anxious not to prolong the call but added: "Bet the parents aren't overjoyed, but you do what's right for you."

★★★

Ted fared only slightly better with his mother, who, frankly, had little interest in what her son was doing provided it didn't cause her any hassle, but she, too, showed no enthusiasm for the proposed union. He trekked up to London to see her, feeling he at least owed her the courtesy of telling her his news face-to-face.

Sitting on an uncomfortable wooden chair in her messy sitting room, he watched his mother lighting a fresh cigarette from a dying stub. "Marrying a posh girl never works out," said Alma Jackson. "Can't think why you want to get tied up with people like that. Still, I suppose there might be some money coming your way, which you might consider sharing with your loving Mama."

She stared at him, screwing up her eyes against the smoke spiralling from her cigarette. Years of chain-smoking had left her skin wrinkled and leathery and she looked much older than her forty-eight years. "This marriage feels a bit like history repeating itself, and I think we've been here before, although *that* girl was anything but posh."

She ground out her cigarette on a chipped saucer and regarded her son. "She was undoubtedly a bit of a brazen hussy by all accounts. I hope you learned your lesson and now know what you're doing, although I doubt it. You're like your father, led by your dick."

Ted was furious. She had no right to talk to him like that. Okay, she was his mother, but only technically. She had never shown any mothering instincts towards him or his sister Clara. "You really have become a miserable old woman," he seethed. "You manage to suck the joy out of everything."

Dragging on her cigarette, Alma gave no sign that she had heard him. "Anyway, even if she is posh, this one sounds like a step in the right direction, especially if she has money." Looking at the rather tired cellophane-wrapped supermarket daffodils Ted had given her, she added: "And at least she has taught you some manners."

Ted ignored the dig. "My God, is money all you ever think about? You might consider offering your congratulations if nothing else. I don't expect a wedding present."

Alma sniffed: "I gave up hoping for the best a long time ago.

My life has been nothing but disappointment. Why should it be any different now? What have any of you ever done for me, you or your conniving father, or your sister, come to that? Why shouldn't I hope that your rich girlfriend might spare a thought for her future mother-in-law?"

Ted looked at her with loathing as she chuckled to herself, striking a match to light a fresh cigarette, holding it carefully between long, nicotine-stained fingers. "Now that's quite a thought, isn't it? Let me think, what would I do with a few hundred pounds…?"

Ted had had enough. "Well, you just keep on thinking. I'm off. Oh, and by the way, she's not rich. Far from it. Bye." He slammed out of the drab flat in Victoria and caught the next train back to Brighton. "Waste of time and a train ticket," he muttered.

He had no intention of trying to contact his father, whom Alma had divorced for adultery and cruelty when Ted was a toddler and Clara a babe in arms, and was now living somewhere in Kent with his second wife and a whole new family.

Chapter Four

IN THE end, they married in the local register office with Clara, anxious to meet the girl who had managed to tempt her wayward brother so quickly into marriage, and Roger, Ted's boss at the building site, as the only witnesses and guests.

Relations between Juliet and her mother were still strained. Although her father kept in touch and had sent her a cheque as a wedding gift, they rarely met.

"Ridiculous when you consider they only live a few miles up the road," said Juliet. "But if that's the way Mum wants it, that's fine with me. We'll tell her we're married afterwards. It's not my fault she's missing the wedding of her only daughter."

The one person Juliet really missed at her wedding was her best friend, June. She was in America where her lawyer husband Brian Turner was on a year's job exchange.

"I'm so pleased for you, darling," said June in a long transAtlantic phone call. "Sorry I can't be with you, but I'll be there in spirit, and there will be something lovely in the post for you. Although, given the length of time it takes for parcels to get across the Atlantic you'll probably be celebrating your first wedding anniversary by the time it arrives."

The girls, who had been firm friends since infant school, chattered on until Juliet, mindful of the time, gasped: "June, this call must be costing a fortune. We must ring off."

June laughed. "Oh, don't worry, Brian's firm will pick up the tab. Oh, the joy of having a rich husband!"

Joy, indeed, thought Juliet, who had never been rich. Comfortable, as her parents would say, but not wealthy. She and Ted were now much further down the financial ladder, not quite on the breadline but almost.

Ted had considered going back into advertising to earn more money, but he was enjoying his job on the building site and didn't want to leave it unless he had to. Juliet was working in a flower shop in Brighton's Lanes, trying to progress her floristry career, but it didn't pay well.

"We're managing at the moment, so let's continue as we are for the time being," suggested Ted.

Juliet decided she didn't need a new dress for the wedding, she couldn't afford one and there was no way she was going to ask her parents for money. The idea of a Flower Power wedding had been abandoned, with even Ted accepting that it would be unusual enough in Sussex to cause far more publicity than either of them wanted.

Ted was going to wear his only suit, a remnant from his advertising days. Juliet riffled through her wardrobe and selected her favourite black chiffon dress with a billowing gypsy skirt, which came down to her ankles, paired with her silver boots.

"Black for a wedding?" queried Roger, pausing on the register office steps. "You look as if you're going to a funeral. Don't get me wrong, you look beautiful, but it's hardly conventional attire for the happiest day of your life!"

"But that's it," said Juliet earnestly. "We're not conventional, Ted and me. Anyway, what's the point of spending money we haven't got on a wedding dress I don't really need and will never wear again?"

Ted ruffled her spiky hair. "That's my girl." Now, come on. Let's go and get hitched before I change my mind!"

The young couple had also had a conversation about rings.

Ted didn't wear jewellery and flatly refused to wear a wedding ring. Juliet worried about the cost of buying a new ring for herself, dug out her grandmother's Victorian wedding band and handed it over to Ted. He looked at the smooth, thin circle of old gold lying in the palm of his hand.

"Are you sure you don't want a new one?" Juliet nodded. "Absolutely. Anyway, Granny would be thrilled to think we are using it."

When they came out of the register office and into the bright afternoon sunshine after the simple fifteen-minute ceremony, the pubs were closed, so the wedding party had tea and currant buns in a café and then went their separate ways.

"Have a good evening," said Roger with a suggestive leer. "Let me know if it's any different when you're married!"

"That was so quick," said Ted. "Are we really married, d'you think?" Juliet laughed. "Well, we have the certificate to prove it, and it was the perfect wedding. Absolutely no fuss and nonsense. I could never imagine myself walking down the aisle in a big, flouncing dress in front of loads of people. Even when I was a little girl, I couldn't picture my wedding day; it was always hazy. June used to have bride and groom dolls she played with; she was always planning exactly how her wedding day would be. I never did. Seemed pointless."

She had eventually talked Ted around to the idea that a woman taking a man's name on marriage was patriarchal and old-fashioned. Ted hadn't been sure. He wanted Juliet to have the same name as him, he wouldn't feel they were married otherwise. After some resistance from Ted and a bit of pleading from Juliet, they compromised. Juliet would use the name Campbell-Jackson.

As soon as they arrived home, Ted dragged Juliet over to the bed. "I was thinking about this all through the ceremony," he told her, pulling her dress over her head and trying to kiss her at the same time.

They made love twice. The first time slowly and gently, joyfully celebrating their very first coming together as a married couple; then more roughly and vigorously, sex pure and simple with an animal passion, mating in its most basic form. Afterwards, sated and completely exhausted, they slept closely wrapped in each other's arms. Ted, totally ecstatic that this remarkable girl was now his wife, felt safe and secure for the first time in his life; she was the best thing that had ever happened to him. Juliet was content and relaxed, knowing that Ted loved her and would always be there for her.

"Wow, oh my goodness!" she said when they eventually surfaced. "That was love-making in a league of its own. Off the scale! You can tell Roger sex *is* different when you are married."

The newlyweds giggled like a pair of schoolchildren as they sent a telegram to Juliet's parents to tell them the good news.

"Well, that's that," said Mary, tearing up the message and letting the pieces flutter to the floor, "no good will come of it, you can be sure of that, and to think of the wedding she might have had. We could have booked the church for midsummer; it always looks lovely when all the flowering cherries are in bloom, and that new room at the Country Club would have been ideal for the reception. It's just so thoughtless of her to go off and do her own thing, but then, I suppose that's what I've come to expect."

Dennis was silent. Thirty years of marriage had taught him that when Mary was like this, no answer was necessary nor wanted. She would calm down eventually and be thankful that her only daughter was married and off her hands.

He was, however, pleased that Juliet was keeping her maiden name. Campbell-Jackson sounded good. Dennis poured himself a large Scotch and took it into the garden for some peace and quiet before supper.

Clara phoned her father. She had kept in touch with him in a casual way through the years. A baby when he walked out on

Alma, and with no childhood memories of him, Clara had no idea why she needed to maintain the contact; she just did.

Jackie Jackson had not seen Ted since he was three, but thanks to Clara, he had kept up to date with what was going on in the life of his first born. "So, what's she like, this girl?"

"Seems okay," said Clara, twisting the phone cord around her finger. "She's quite up-market in an understated sort of way. Very alternative, you know, Ban the Bomb, Save the Whale, a bit of a hippy, I think, like Ted. She's a florist, well, she works in a flower shop, and it's strange for someone with her background; her parents are well-off, so Ted says, but she's quite shy."

"Hmm." Well off. For a fleeting moment Jackie Jackson considered the prospect of a rich daughter-in-law and then dismissed it completely. "Well, I'm pleased the lad has settled down. I had a feeling he might go off the rails. Give him my best when you speak to him."

Chapter Five

JULIET AND Ted continued to live quite happily in the cramped attic room until Juliet found she was pregnant, and they used the tiny inheritance from her grandmother for a deposit on an odd slice of a house on a crumbling terrace behind Brighton's Lanes. Ted had been promoted to foreman on the building site, and his bigger pay packet helped considerably with the mortgage repayments.

It was his boss, Roger, who suggested Ted should join the local men's club, Band of Brothers, which mixed having a good time with charity work. Since Juliet had given birth to Rosie three months earlier, Ted had been feeling pretty fed up and frankly unwanted. Everyone told him that this was quite usual and normal service would be resumed shortly. Ted was not amused nor convinced. His lovely Juliet was now totally absorbed in their baby daughter. He loved them both dearly, but he had been totally unprepared for the way Juliet had turned from him and now seemed to be bound in a special relationship with a screaming scrap of humanity. It seemed that Juliet and Rosie were locked together in a place he couldn't reach.

Band of Brothers, based in the back room of a Brighton pub, was a lifeline. "It's good fun. You can have a drink and a laugh, and even the charity events are worthwhile. Come and see what you think," said Roger.

Ted went and liked it. Although most of the members were

young professionals, solicitors, estate agents or accountants, Ted did not feel excluded, and his obvious ability and good humour soon made him popular. He was occasionally knocked back by the chip on his shoulder, which still surfaced when he felt wrong-footed, but his natural intelligence and common sense pushed such misgivings to the back of his mind. Marriage to Juliet and the birth of Rosie had given him a shot of much-needed confidence. After all, he was only doing a labouring job by choice, he told himself. He could always go back to advertising if he wanted to.

Being the sort of person who threw his heart and soul into everything he did, it wasn't long before Band of Brothers threatened to take over his life. He served on committees, used his advertising skills to help publicise events, and his building skills to restore a garden wall at an old people's home.

While Juliet was pleased Ted had found something into which he could put his energies, she was worried that her free-spirited husband should join such an organised group. She was also mildly concerned that all his spare time was spent away from home. When she eventually returned from the exclusive love affair enjoyed by all mothers with their newborn babies, she found her husband was off on a jaunt of his own.

"You can join Girls Together," said Ted one morning as he dodged the paraphernalia needed to produce Rosie's breakfast. "In fact, I'd really like you to. All the other wives go, you'd have fun."

"You must be joking. I'd absolutely hate it. All those ghastly women, not to mention an unbelievably awful name. Girls Together, indeed. Girls in a group are far nastier than men, you know. I bet they're all back-biting and catty."

Just listen to me; I'm beginning to sound like my mother, thought Juliet with a pang of guilt. They say all girls turn into their mothers in the end; perhaps it's happening to me already, and I'm only twenty-three. What will I be like at fifty? A vicious shrew, most likely, and Ted will have divorced me.

Ted decided to abandon breakfast at the table. Gulping the remains of his coffee and clutching a slice of toast between his teeth, he mumbled: "We all have to grow up, Smudge." He had picked up her nickname from Alan. "That hippy love and peace stuff is for kids. This is the real world." He dropped a kiss on the top of her head, still spiky and still marmalade in colour. "Give it a go and see how you feel. You may like it."

Chapter Six

FROM THE moment she walked into the lounge bar of the Red Lion, set aside each Thursday evening for the Girls Together meeting, Juliet knew she was in alien territory. She considered turning tail and rushing back to Ted, who was babysitting Rosie, and telling him he could have a night at the pub instead, but knowing how disappointed he would be at her lack of effort, she forced herself to carry on.

Oh June, where are you when I need you, thought Juliet. The Turners had no sooner returned from the States than Brian was offered a permanent job in New York. "There's no stopping him," June had stormed. "I don't want to live in America, particularly not New York, but Brian says we must. So, we are going. But I've told him two years max. Any longer, and I'm coming back, with or without him."

Juliet took a deep breath and introduced herself to the Girls Together group. The women were friendly enough. Someone bought her a drink, introduced her to members of the committee and explained how the meeting worked. "Chat and drinks, important announcements, a speaker or demonstration, coffee and more chat," said Cherry, a slim dark-haired beauty who had been chosen as Juliet's 'buddy' for the first few meetings.

Despite Cherry's best efforts, Juliet remained uneasy. She felt like a fish out of water. For a start, she looked all wrong. Her spiky orange hair, decidedly plump figure and ethnic clothes were in complete contrast to these smart, immaculately groomed, and, it had to be said, skinny women. They all looked like Hollywood stars with tanned skin, long, beautifully styled hair, and expensive clothes. Juliet, horribly aware of a stain from a patch of baby sick on the right shoulder of her Indian cotton blouse, was reminded of the Beach Boys' song *California Girls*.

Cherry, having had little success with conversation after asking Juliet if she played tennis or went horse riding, both with negative replies, was unsure what to say to this strange, shy girl, so she passed her a willow basket crammed with dress-making patterns.

"One of the things we do is pass on patterns of successful dresses and skirts. You can just take one you like and bring it back when you've finished. Or if you have any of your own you don't want anymore, just add them to the basket." She smiled carefully and said: "There are just a few people I need to catch up with. Back in a mo."

Juliet sifted through the basket. There was a huge variety of patterns, but they weren't the kind of clothes she would wear, and anyway, she didn't really sew and was totally incapable of making a garment that could be worn. Sewing on a button or turning up a hem was about the limit of her ability. Her mother, who had attempted without success to give Juliet needlework skills for just such a social occasion, would be dismayed. The other thing she noticed was that all the patterns were to fit a size 10-12.

When Cherry returned from her wandering, Juliet said: "Most of these patterns are in very small sizes; how many people d'you know who are a size 10?"

"We all are darling." Cherry didn't say, "My God, you're fat," but her eyes expressed her thoughts as clearly as if she had spoken. At that moment, a glass was thumped on the top table, and the meeting began. Saved by the bell, thought Cherry, slightly regretting her careless remark.

Realising she had been snubbed and feeling like a beached

whale, Juliet sank back into her tub chair, which suddenly seemed a bit of a squeeze around the hip area, when she heard the word "Bitch!" whispered over her shoulder. Turning, she saw a head of wild blonde curls and laughing blue eyes. "Talk later," said the girl with a wink. Juliet settled into her chair, feeling distinctly cheerier.

After numerous announcements of the coffee morning on Tuesday and tennis match on Saturday variety, there was a talk on a children's hospice that was being set up by local nuns, followed by various arrangements to hold fund-raising events to aid the hospice appeal before a refreshment break was called.

Juliet was about to turn around to see if she could spot the owner of the curly hair and blue eyes when a willowy blonde with a minute suede mini skirt and endless brown legs encased in long leather boots sashayed up to her and said: "Hi, I'm Paula. I didn't realise that gorgeous man was *yours*!" Startled, Juliet looked blank. "I beg your pardon?"

"Ted Jackson. The builder. I didn't realise he belonged to you!"

"Well," Juliet wasn't quite sure what to say, "he's my husband."

Paula looked mildly irritated. "I know, sweetie. All I'm saying is I hadn't put you two together…you're so… um…so different." Pulling herself together, she added lamely: "Different sorts of people, I mean." Seeing Juliet's surprise, she added: "I've met him a couple of times at some of the Band of Brothers' fund-raising events. A bit of a dish!"

Having dropped her bombshell, Paula sashayed off again with a satisfied smirk on her face, confident she had put the cat among the pigeons. She rather fancied Ted Jackson and there was a Band of Brothers social evening coming up; she might try her chances. His drab wife wouldn't offer much competition.

Juliet was digesting Paula's remark when an arm snaked around her shoulder and a voice whispered in her ear: "Ignore her. She's the well-known man-eater. All the lads know about her, so I shouldn't worry too much about yours."

The voice revealed herself as the wild-haired, blue-eyed girl who had been sitting behind her. She stuck out a hand, "I'm Cindy, pleased to meet you. I'm new too, like you. Well, this is my third meeting, and I must say I was beginning to think I'd not bother again, but you look as if you might brighten things up. Love your skirt by the way. Gorgeous colours. I really like that gypsy style. Is it Indian cotton? Ah, yes, I thought so! Very nice."

Juliet relaxed. With Cindy on her side she felt she might just be able to cope. She looked towards Paula, who had moved over to the other side of the room and was patently gossiping, and not in a nice way. "Are they all like that?"

Cindy considered. "No, most of them are quite jolly. I know a lot of them look like Barbie dolls but they're generally okay. And there are some girls who are almost normal, although not quite as normal as you and me."

★★★

As Juliet and Cindy got to know each other better, discovering they had much in common, life took on a satisfying rhythm. Cindy and her husband Dave had three-year-old twin boys, and the two young couples soon became firm friends. Rosie's birth was followed by two sons, Felix and Michael. Life was hectic but good.

Chapter Seven

JULIET OFTEN thought about those early days and wondered where they had gone. What had happened to all those hopes and dreams? What had a decade of living done to turn a bright-eyed twenty-year-old into a middle-aged misery who was tired of life? Well, not middle-aged, just in her thirties, and maybe not a misery, at least she hoped not. But she wasn't the girl Ted had fallen for all those years ago. Life itself, that's what had done the damage. A husband who she often felt she didn't really know anymore, and three children who ran her ragged.

She loved them all to bits, of course she did, but things had not been easy and Juliet sometimes allowed herself the luxury of wallowing in 'what if.'

What if she had finished her A-levels and gone to university instead of becoming a florist? What if she and Ted hadn't had children and had gone on the backpacking world trip they had planned when they first met? What if she hadn't met Ted and had gone down the path prescribed for her by her mother? Memories of her time in Italy tiptoed through her mind. At this point, Juliet always gave herself a shake and jerked herself back to the present. Too dangerous to go along that route.

The evening they had just spent at one of the regular Band of Brothers' dinner events was an example of Juliet's frustration. With Cindy and Dave away on holiday, Juliet had spent the whole evening feeling thoroughly uncomfortable, self-conscious about her clothes and aware that she was still the subject of gossip.

It had been a horrible dinner, not just the food – which, like all mass-produced catering, had been bland, tasteless, and predictable with a passable prawn cocktail, coq au vin with indifferent coq and questionable vin, plus a particularly messy trifle – but also the company. Spending what should be pleasurable time with people she didn't care about or even like was a nightmare. Not just people, dozens of people; hordes of chattering smug couples who spent their time gossiping.

Juliet knew she stood out like a sore thumb, completely devoid of any camouflage, unable to force herself to make the unimportant small talk required on such occasions. She found it hard to pretend she was interested in who had won a recent tennis match or who was having an affair with whom. Most of the women thought she was stuck-up and she knew all of them felt sorry for Ted.

"My clothes are all wrong," she had whispered anxiously to her husband as they arrived at the seafront hotel where the dinner was being held. "Nonsense," Ted replied, giving her shoulder a comforting pat. "You're always saying that. You look fine."

Juliet knew that the long plaid skirt with the matching waistcoat she was wearing was…just not right. Most of the other women were in floral print mini dresses with feminine flounces and ruffles, the kind of clothes that just didn't suit her. She took a deep breath and walked into the dining room, aware that she, as well as Ted, was an object of pity. She didn't fit in. Frankly she would rather have spent the time in front of the television or curled up with a good book rather than in a second-rate hotel with indifferent food and disagreeable company.

Ted, of course, really enjoyed the evening. Something of a chameleon he had the enviable ability of being able to adapt to whatever group he happened to be in. This allowed him to wallow in popularity, which fed his fragile ego and made him happy.

He was very gregarious and uninhibited, with a forceful opinion on almost everything, including subjects about which he knew very little. On one memorable occasion he had confidently given his thoughts on brain surgery to an eminent neurosurgeon. This total, but often misplaced, self-assurance gave Ted a certain standing among the men, while the women found him attractive and desirable and openly flirted with him.

None of this was lost on Juliet, who knew that such admiration and acclaim was exactly what her husband needed. She also knew that his love and need for her and their children kept him grounded. She was not in the least concerned about him straying with one of the 'California Girls,' she told herself, although she did sometimes wonder if he could be tempted.

When she once shared her thoughts with Ted, he had looked genuinely astonished. "I'm never aware of women trying to flirt," he had said. "I just don't notice them. I only notice the person I want to be with – and that's you." Gathering her into his arms, he stared into her eyes and sighed: "You're so beautiful, my darling."

"I'm not really beautiful," she protested.

"You are to me," Ted replied, "and even though we're an old married couple now, I still fancy the pants off you. Why would I want to look anyone else?"

Pulling herself back from the memory, Juliet turned to look at Ted, who was already in bed with his eyes firmly closed. "Hurry up, Smudge, it's late, and I've got an early start in the morning. Turn off the light, my headaches, and I'm farting like mad. I'm sure that red wine was a bit suspect."

Very romantic, Juliet thought sourly, looking at her recumbent husband with irritation. It always annoyed her that he could fall asleep instantly. Just like that, as if he didn't have a care in the world, which knowing Ted, he probably didn't. Nothing really fazed him, whereas Juliet worried about everything. Even if there was nothing to worry about, she worried that she had forgotten something she should be worrying about.

Currently, she was worrying about her mother. A shiver of guilt crept through Juliet; she hadn't really given Mary a thought since that morning when a phone call from her brother Alan informed her that their mother was seriously ill.

"She's not been well for ages but made light of it, of course, and really didn't talk about it. Now it's suddenly hit her. Dad's distraught."

Juliet rang her father, who spoke quietly and calmly. Everything that could be done was being done, he assured Juliet.

Her parents had sold the big old family house on the South Downs and moved to a cottage in Cornwall when her father retired. Her brothers went down regularly, but Juliet only managed the trip about twice a year.

While the passing of time and the births of Rosie and the boys had healed the rift over Juliet's marriage to Ted, trips to Cornwall took second place to hectic family life in general. The children loved visiting their grandparents, of course, and Mary was much more easy-going with them than she had ever been with Juliet and her brothers.

"I know how busy you are with the family, don't come rushing down. It's a long way. If anything changes, I'll call you immediately. She's fine right now, sleeping a lot, but the doctor says there is no immediate danger," said her father reassuringly.

Comforted, Juliet got on with her day. She sent flowers to her mother and decided that if nothing had changed, she'd visit next weekend.

Juliet allowed her mind to range over her childhood; comfortable, certainly, but there had always been a stilted quality to it. She knew her brothers had romped through their early years and both had a close relationship with their parents. Juliet, the only girl, had always felt she failed to meet some invisible goal, that she was never good enough. She always knew she was a great disappointment, especially to her mother.

The clock struck midnight, and Juliet gave herself a shake. No point in raking over the past. It had taken her a long time, but she had grown up a confident, happy woman – despite her mother. She still tended towards shyness with people she didn't know, but she managed to hide it quite well. She was, as Ted had first thought all those years ago, comfortable in her skin. Juliet hopped into bed and snuggled up against Ted, who was snoring gently. "All water under the bridge," she muttered and fell asleep almost immediately.

★★★

It was pitch dark when Juliet woke up. She glanced at the bedside clock – three o'clock. Her head ached, and her mouth was dry. Ted must have been right about that wine; there had definitely been something wrong with it.

She climbed carefully out of bed and padded softly across the room, narrowly avoiding collision with a chair piled high with Ted's discarded clothes. She quickly pulled on her comfortably old dressing gown and fluffy slippers, then carefully negotiating the steep Victorian stairs, went into the kitchen for a glass of water.

Juliet sipped her drink standing by the sink, turning to stare out of the un-curtained window. She gave a start. There was someone looking in, a woman's face at the window. Panic rose in her throat and she stifled a scream. Then she relaxed. How ridiculous; it was her own face reflected in the glass. She was watching herself. How Ted would tease her when she told him in the morning.

She gazed at her reflection a bit longer. Funny how much she was beginning to look like her mother, especially around the eyes and mouth. Was she going to turn into her mother? Absolutely not! She lived a completely different life to Mary Campbell and was her own person, not a copy of the woman who had given birth to her and brought her up.

Juliet loved her mother…well, everyone loved their mother…but she would never inhibit Rosie, Felix, and Michael or cause them to grow up with the deep fear and embarrassment of being not quite good enough as she had done.

Juliet drained her glass and returned to the bedroom. Three-thirty read the luminous hands of the clock. She slipped into bed beside the still-snoring Ted, her head crammed with thoughts about her mother. She shook her head wearily; the early hours of the morning were not the right time for brooding.

Part Two
Juliet and June

(1948 onwards)

Reflection

"A friend is someone who helps you up when you are down, and if they can't, they lay down beside you and listen."
A.A. Milne, 'Winnie-the-Pooh' (1926)

JUNE WAS the sister I never had. We did everything together and I would quite happily have foresworn all boyfriends in favour of a life with June. She was my best friend, my perfect person.

As we moved into our teenage years we spent hours and hours closeted in either her bedroom or mine – although mostly hers, as my mother tended to be very intrusive and pop into my room without warning on the pretext of offering drinks and biscuits. I'm pretty sure she eavesdropped at the door as well, always convinced that we were up to no good and I was keeping secrets from her.

She even opened my letters, not that I received many, saying that if I had nothing to hide, there wasn't a problem. This always made me boil with indignation and the unshakeable conviction, even as a child, that it was *just not right*. It took years before I had the courage to rebel and tell her firmly that I would prefer she didn't open my private correspondence.

All this resulted in me becoming very secretive indeed, and sadly, throughout my life, it never occurred to me to share any of my thoughts or worries with her. She was my mother and I loved her, but I don't think I ever really *liked* her.

So, June became my best friend in the world. Although we both had other friends, of course, boys and girls whom we spent time with together and separately, none could supplant the intimacy and understanding I shared with June.

We learned, years later, that there were those among our more worldly acquaintances who had whispered that June and I might be lesbians. To be honest, in those days we were so naive neither of us would have known what that meant. We were both fans of the Bloomsbury Group and fancied ourselves as Vanessa Bell and Virginia Woolf, sisters and lifelong friends.

So what did we do during those endless afternoons and weekends closeted in bedrooms? We gossiped about people we knew at school or youth club, compared our naked bosoms in the mirror to see whose was the biggest, tried on each other's clothes, discussed in the most intimate terms what we thought sex was like and the merits of French kissing – rating the boys we fancied out of ten.

It was all a very innocent part of growing up and learning who we were. How disappointed my mother would have been to find out it was nothing more salacious.

Chapter One

JOINED AT the hip. That was what the boys at the youth club used to say about Juliet and June. The Two Js. When you saw one, the other was always close by. All very well, but not so good when you wanted to take June Barker out on the cricket field in the dark for a quick kiss and a cuddle and, with luck, a bit of a grope. She was a good sport, June, and a real looker, too. All the lads vied to get a date with June.

Problem was, you had to siphon her away from Juliet Campbell because they were always together, and no one really wanted to get off with Juliet. Not that there was anything wrong with her except that she was a bit on the plump side. She just didn't have any charisma, no sex appeal. She wasn't that sort of girl.

Juliet and June had been firm friends since their first day at school aged five. They were put on the same worktable and sat close together for mutual comfort in a strange environment. Their friendship was cemented early on when Juliet, who hated milk, was sick on the classroom floor after being forced by a well-meaning schoolmistress to drink the daily third-of-a-pint provided for pupils by the government.

It was a frosty day and the crate of half-frozen bottles had been brought in and left beside the radiator all morning. Juliet's nervous whisper of "I don't drink milk" was completely ignored by the teacher, who insisted she drank it, pointing out that all her classmates were happily slurping up lukewarm milk through their straws.

"Your father has paid for this milk with his taxes," she said firmly, ramming the straw into the child's protesting mouth.

It was all too much for Juliet, and after a couple of swallows, she threw up the curdled milk along with her half-digested breakfast. Before anyone could move, June rushed to Juliet's side, put her arm around her and said loudly and defiantly: "And I don't drink milk either. Ever!"

The hapless teacher was about to protest – how was it possible to be trounced by two five-year-old girls? – but faced with such unity, she reluctantly admitted defeat and went off to find a floor mop and some hot, soapy water. Juliet and June, hands gripped together, stood solidly in the middle of the classroom, beaming at each other.

Chapter Two

JULIET'S GRATITUDE for June's support knew no bounds, and in years to come, she marked the start of their long friendship from that point. All through primary school and into their teens, they were always together. They were as close as sisters, closer than sisters. And they told each other absolutely everything.

The fact that as June grew up, it became increasingly obvious that she was going to be a beauty, while Juliet with long marmalade red hair and unusual green eyes, was quirky but certainly not pretty, made no difference to their friendship.

"She looks like Elizabeth Taylor," Mary Campbell used to say to Dennis when June had cycled home after an evening spent whispering, laughing, and trying on clothes in Juliet's bedroom. "I wouldn't be surprised if she ended up as an air hostess or a model. She's certainly got the figure for it. Such a pity Juliet isn't more like her."

There was no doubt that June was a stunning-looking girl. Her smooth black shoulder-length hair, never out of place, bright blue almond-shaped eyes, a smooth, creamy complexion and fabulous figure with seemingly endless legs drew admiring glances wherever she went. But she appeared completely unaware of her good looks or that she was causing such a stir.

It was this very insouciance that drove the boys wild. She smiled her enigmatic smile and swiftly whisked herself out of range when a lad tried to become romantic. She laughed aloud at clumsy teenage manoeuvring as a young stud tried to get her alone so he could ask her on a date. Linking arms with Juliet, she would skip off, leaving would-be suitors spitting with frustration.

Attracting boys so easily, June had perfected the skill of running away yet egging them on at the same time. It was tantalising and she instinctively knew it. It wasn't that June didn't like boys; she did. She was just very fussy about those to whom she granted her favours.

Pete Hammond was a case in point. Tall, blond, and conventionally handsome, in the top sets at school and an all-round sportsman, he pursued June relentlessly. He was used to getting his own way, used to all the girls sighing after him, and certainly not used to being ignored.

When all his usual ploys failed to bring June to heel, he decided to change tactics. He went to see his best mate Garry Smith and offered to do his maths homework if he would join him on a double date with Juliet and June. "You have to be joking," growled Garry. "I wouldn't mind having a bash at June myself, but the other one…"

"Nothing wrong with Juliet," said Pete encouragingly. "Go on. Once I get June on her own, I'll have cracked it and you won't have to go out with Juliet again. I'll do your maths for you," he promised temptingly.

Garry considered. "Maths homework for a week," he said firmly, knowing he had the upper hand for once. Not often, you got one over Pete, but this time it was obvious that June was a quarry his friend could not resist. "Okay," said Pete with the lop-sided grin that set the girls' hearts fluttering. Doing Garry's homework for a week would be a doddle and he was supremely confident that just the one date was all he needed to hook June and be the envy of his peers.

As it happened, June was more than happy to go out with Pete Hammond. He was the type of boy she liked: good-looking, popular, clever, and from a well-off family who lived on the right side of the park; she just enjoyed keeping him dangling for a while.

"Boys are always so grateful when I eventually say yes," she giggled to a slightly disapproving Juliet. "It's always worked in the past, and it's working with Pete. Just wait and see."

When Pete rang and asked her to go on a double date with Garry and Juliet, June had stayed silent for a few moments before saying: "Oh, okay," very casually, just in case he might think her too keen. Garry had already asked Juliet, and in true Two Js fashion she had immediately phoned June. "He said it was a double date with you and Pete."

"I've been expecting it," said June. "You don't mind, do you? Garry's quite nice, in some ways nicer than Pete, although nowhere near as good-looking, of course, and it's all for a good cause. My happiness; as you know, I've fancied Pete for ages." Juliet laughed. "In that case, good job, I didn't refuse. Double date it is. The things I do for you."

"Don't pretend that going out with Garry will be a hardship. You may eventually be grateful to me; perhaps we'll have a double wedding." Juliet snorted down the phone. "Steady on. It's only a date, my girl. One date, and we both know that Garry has only asked me out because Pete wants to go out with you and thinks you won't go on your own."

June gave her sexy, gurgling laugh, which drove the boys mad. "True. Well, I do appreciate your support, Jules; I'll do the same for you sometime."

"Huh," said Juliet, and put down the phone.

★★★

The date ran true to form. They went to see the latest Elvis Presley film at the Odeon. Garry was all for going down to The Regent, where *Bridge on the River Kwai* was showing, but he was dissuaded by Pete, who kicked him on the ankle and hissed: "A war film is hardly going to set the scene for romance. Are you on my side, or what? Maths, remember." Garry recalled the particularly tricky algebra homework that Pete was going to do for him and quickly agreed that he had no problem with watching Elvis.

Both girls were devoted Presley fans, so Elvis it was. All the seats in the back row of the Odeon were doubles, and once the lights went down, June and Pete were glued together in a passionate embrace.

Garry thought bitterly that they could have gone to see *Bridge on the River Kwai* after all. Pete and June obviously had no intention of watching the film and were quite likely to be otherwise engaged throughout. They were far more interested in snogging and groping than in Mr Presley's absurd gyrating.

Juliet was uneasy, feeling she was there under false pretences; Garry clearly wasn't interested in her. Garry was frankly bored; he didn't find Juliet particularly attractive and he considered Elvis Presley ridiculous.

After a while, Garry thought he had better show willing, so he half-heartedly reached for Juliet's hand and when she passively allowed him to hold it, he slid his arm along the back of the seat and ruffled her marmalade hair, which was piled into an untidy beehive.

Juliet stifled a sigh. How annoying! All the grips will fall out if he fiddles with my hair much longer and it had taken ages to put it up. She just wished she could watch Elvis in peace; she was far more thrilled by him than by Garry but she knew the rules. When a boy took you out, paid for a cinema ticket plus a bottle of pop and maybe a trip to the Linger-Longer coffee bar later, he expected a return on his investment, and if that meant kissing someone she didn't fancy, well, so be it. Without enthusiasm, she leaned in towards him and rested her head on his shoulder. "Never look a gift horse in the mouth," muttered Garry insolently to himself, and as he bent over to kiss her Juliet thought: June owes me big time.

***

June was always in debt as far as Juliet was concerned. After the cinema trip she started going steady with Pete, but because her rather old-fashioned parents thought she was far too young for dating, Juliet was always used as a decoy.

"Pete and I are going to a dance at the University," June would ring to say. "I've told the parents I'll be at your house. Cover for me if necessary."

Another time she asked Juliet to walk home with her after youth club. "But it's half a mile in the opposite direction," protested Juliet.

"Yes, silly, but Pete's coming with us and just in case my parents are looking out for me, they won't suspect anything if you are there too."

The slow route home took them across the pitch-dark cricket field where June and Pete slipped off into the bushes for a cuddle, and Juliet was left standing alone in the gloom, holding Juliet's coat and bag.

What on earth am I doing? Juliet asked herself crossly. I must be mad. June's just taking advantage.

By the time the young lovers emerged, it was almost ten o'clock, and when Juliet eventually arrived home she had to face the fury of her mother, who was worried because she was so late.

"Where have you been," screamed Mary, out of control with worry. "You've been up to something."

Juliet allayed her mother's suspicions by explaining she was with June. "We were chatting and lost sight of the time. I'm sorry."

Mary relaxed. "Well, I'm sure the Barkers were equally worried about June. You two really need to think a bit more about other people. Chatting indeed, that's all you girls ever do."

Never again, said Juliet to herself as she escaped thankfully to her bedroom. In the future, June is going to have to sort out her own love life. But such was the nature of the girls' relationship that Juliet could never say "No." If June needed her support, she gave it.

A succession of boys followed Pete, but June never seemed to take any of them seriously and the tie with Juliet remained as strong as ever.

Chapter Three

JULIET WAS about to leave school for a college course in floristry when she started going out with Rob Spicer. He was at the local boys' grammar doing A-levels, and although she'd had friendships with boys before, this was first love for both of them.

"I can't see what you see in him," said June sniffily. "He's not at all good-looking; he's younger than you, his parents are divorced, and his mum works as a char."

"She's not a char," retorted Juliet. "She's a housekeeper at the Grand Hotel, so don't be such a snob. Anyway, I like him and he's only a few months younger."

Because June was so critical of Rob, Juliet didn't tell her that he was surprisingly exciting and more than happy to experiment in all sorts of ways. On their last date, they had spent a lot of time trying to French kiss which, instead of increasing desire for each other, had ended with them gasping for breath and collapsing in hysterics.

"It's a really weird thing to do and definitely unhygienic," said Rob when he had stopped laughing. Juliet thought it would probably be more thrilling if you did it with someone who really turned you on – Elvis Presley, for instance; I bet he can French kiss perfectly. She really liked Rob, but she wasn't desperate to spend time with his tongue in her mouth, or her tongue in his, for that matter.

Juliet eventually relented and told June about practising

French kissing with Rob. "It wasn't that successful because we kept forgetting to breathe. And he thought it was a weird thing to do."

June shrugged. "I told you he was pathetic and too young for you. You need to get yourself a grown-up boyfriend."

"Like your American sailor, Riff or Biff or whatever this one's called. And if Rob is too young for me, then Biff is too old for you!"

"He's called Griff, and he's great fun. And yes, he's twenty-four, a man, not a boy like all the others. I really like him, and he does French kissing brilliantly." June's blue eyes sparkled and Juliet smiled. She couldn't stay cross with her for long.

"So, what are the latest birthday plans?" asked Juliet, determined to turn June's thoughts away from Rob's supposed shortcomings and her enthusiasm for Griff.

June's wealthy father had offered her a succession of ways to celebrate her eighteenth birthday, although the big event would be her twenty-first, of course.

"Well, I don't really want a party because Mum would insist on vetting the guest list, which would mean I couldn't invite any of my friends, apart from you and my horrible cousins.

"Families really are the end, aren't they? You are so lucky to have two lovely brothers and only a handful of cousins. My parents have an endless number of relations."

Knowing that June was fond of most of her cousins, Juliet laughed. "Well, at least you're an only child, and your parents are devoted to you. My mother isn't that keen on me at all, and I also have Alan and Bertie to put up with, and they're a real pain, I can assure you.

"It must be nice to have brothers, though," said June wistfully. "Or a sister, although I have you, so I don't need a sister. I've always wondered why Mum and Pops, who both come from big families, never had another child."

Juliet was in no mood for soul searching. "Well, ask them, but come on, tell me, what are the other birthday options?"

"Oh, a holiday, Pops thought Spain or Italy might be nice, or some money. I think I might go for the cash."

The girls casually discussed how much June's father might give her and what she would do with the money. "Clothes, of course," said June. "And I saw some sensational boots in Hannington's window the other day. Pricey, but with some of the money from Pops, I could afford to get them."

★★★

On the morning of her eighteenth birthday, June went down to breakfast to find two white envelopes lying on her plate.

"A cheque and a surprise," said her father with a cheery smile. "One you asked for and one we thought you should have," said her mother.

June opened the first – a cheque for fifty pounds. "Thank you, Pops," she said, going round the table and kissing his bald head. "Very generous; I will spend it wisely."

Her father patted her hand. "I should spend it frivolously if I were you. You're a good girl, and you've made your mother and I very happy."

June ran her thumb under the flap of the second envelope and drew out a piece of thick paper. She read it in stunned silence. It was her birth certificate.

"Now you are eighteen we thought you should know that you are adopted," said her father, gazing at her over his half-moon spectacles. "You have the right to know where you have come from."

He shook out his newspaper and returned to reading the stock market reports. June stared at him with blank astonishment, then dropped the certificate on the table, rushed into the downstairs cloakroom and was sick.

Everyone was told that June had flu – a sudden bout that had caused her to take to her bed and stopped all birthday celebrations.

"Such a shame," said the aunts, uncles, and cousins. "Too much excitement, the thrill of getting all that money," said her friends. "The result of over-indulgence," said Juliet's parents sagely. Only Juliet knew the truth; she sat on the bed in June's frilly pink and white bedroom and held the weeping girl in her arms.

"How could they?" June sobbed over and over again. "How could they keep such a secret for so long? For eighteen years, I thought they were my parents. Eighteen years! And now I find out that my mother isn't Barbara Barker, nor is my father Dickie Barker. I don't know who these people are anymore. They are strangers.

"My real mother – birth mother, they call her – who is also a stranger, is a woman called Annie something or another. Nelson, I think it is. And my father is," she gave a shuddering sob, "my father is unknown. I wish I was dead.

Chapter Four

SURPRISINGLY, IT was Mary Campbell who eventually filled in the gaps for Juliet. June's mother, distraught at her beloved daughter's distress, had appealed to Mary, one of the few people who knew June's history, hoping that Juliet and the Campbells could help to lessen the blow.

Mary sat Juliet down and started to relate to the Barker family's secret.

Barbara and Dickie Barker had married late in life, and because Barbara was nearing forty, there was no expectation that their union would be blessed with a child. So it was a huge surprise when Barbara, after a few weeks of feeling off-colour, went to the doctor and discovered she was pregnant.

"There was great rejoicing," said Mary, "especially as both Barbara and Dickie came from large families themselves. Every care was lavished on Barbara. Dickie treated her like a piece of fragile glass and elaborate preparations were made for the coming child.

"When the time came, Barbara went into a private nursing home and there was no indication that anything would go wrong. But the baby, a little girl, was born with the cord wound tightly around her neck and was strangled at birth. As you can imagine, Barbara and Dickie were inconsolable. All their dreams for the future seemed dashed.

"Then a midwife told them that in the same nursing home

was a young unmarried mother who had given birth to a daughter she was unable to keep. So the Barkers arranged to adopt the child privately, and Dickie paid good money to ensure that the whole thing was kept a closely guarded secret.

"Of course, you couldn't do that sort of thing nowadays. The Welfare people would be down on you like a ton of bricks. But remember, this was nineteen-forty-three, in the middle of the Second World War, which blurred the edges of what was permitted considerably."

Juliet's eyes were like saucers. There were so many questions she wanted to ask, but she was stopped by the thought that Mary might not continue if she butted in. Her mother was unusually forthcoming and Juliet didn't want to break the spell.

"So Barbara went into the nursing home pregnant and came out two weeks later with a baby girl," continued Mary. "What could be more natural? Who would think anything was amiss? The baby, of course, was June. I suppose if I were being uncharitable, I would say that June was bought with Dickie's money!"

Juliet was stunned. "But how do you know all this? And who else knows?" she demanded when she had caught her breath.

"I don't know who knows, I have certainly never mentioned it to anyone, apart from your father, until now. It's not my secret to tell," said Mary piously.

"But Mum! *How* do you know? How did you find out?"

"Well." Mary paused and eyed her daughter, "This isn't something to gossip about; I'm only telling you because you are June's best friend and the Barkers have asked for our help."

"Yes, yes, I know," said Juliet impatiently. "You can't stop now. I really need to understand. It's important."

Mary settled back in her chair and prepared to unburden herself of a confidence she had kept for almost two decades.

★★★

June's mother was a teenage girl called Annie Nelson who had an affair with an American GI stationed at a camp on the outskirts of Brighton during World War Two. For the best part of a year, they were together, and the soldier, who was called John Studbecker Junior, asked Annie if she would marry him when the war was over. Annie accepted his proposal and a small garnet ring and started to make plans to move to America to start a new life as a GI bride.

"How strange," interjected Juliet, "that Annie Nelson went out with an American serviceman just like June is now going out with Griff. Like mother like daughter."

Mary tutted and said: "Shush, child," before continuing the story.

At the beginning of nineteen-forty-three, Junior, who had been sent north with his regiment, wrote to tell Annie that news of their engagement had not gone down well with his family. He was, he admitted, expected to tie the knot with his American girlfriend Mary-Jo, whose father and brothers ran a ranch that adjoined the Studbecker property in Oklahoma. It was a good match and would more than double the family landholding. He was sorry, but his parents would not countenance him taking home an English bride.

Junior was horrified to learn that Annie was pregnant and immediately obtained compassionate leave to visit her in Brighton. Realising how difficult it would be for her to be an unmarried mother, he gave her money with strict instructions to book herself into a private clinic before having the child adopted. The only other proviso he made was that he should not be named on the birth certificate. Annie was to state that she did not know who the father of the child was.

"That was one of the hardest things for her," said Mary. "It looked as if she was a loose woman who went with loads of men, which she certainly did not. Junior was her first and only one. But nevertheless, Annie did exactly as he wanted."

"But how do you know all this," Juliet wailed. "You still haven't told me that."

"Annie Nelson was the kid sister of my best friend Ella," said Mary. "Ella and I were as close as you and June. So, as you are one of the few people to know that June is an adopted child, I was one of just a handful of people who knew what happened to Annie's baby."

"So where is Annie now? Is she still alive? Juliet asked.

"She is, as far as I know, but she left Brighton after the baby was adopted and went to London. Ella and I obviously kept in touch, and I know Annie eventually married and, I believe, had other children. But sadly, Ella died of cancer in the fifties, and I haven't heard from Annie for ages – not even a Christmas card. So, she must have moved on. Let's hope June can."

Chapter Five

JULIET WAS more than a little concerned about seeing June again. For the first time ever, she had a secret she could not share with her best friend. She knew who both June's parents were, and she was not allowed to tell her.

"Don't you dare repeat to anyone what I have just told you," Mary had said firmly. "And you must promise me that you won't speak to June about it. No doubt the Barkers will tell her what they want her to know. It's not for us to interfere." With a heavy heart and much misgiving, Juliet promised.

The Barkers, it seemed, did not want June to know anything apart from the details that were on her birth certificate. They were devastated that the daughter they loved so much had taken their 'surprise' so badly. "We really didn't expect her to react like this," Barbara Barker told Juliet, her round, rosy face puckered in distress.

"We just thought she ought to know the facts." June's father, who seemed to have turned into a shadow of his former jovial self, begged for Juliet's help. "Talk to her," he pleaded. "See if you can make her see sense; she won't even speak to us."

Despite the Barkers' confidence in her ability to pacify June, Juliet had little success. June didn't want to talk. She didn't want to go out or speak to any of her friends. Griff, it seemed, had been posted somewhere or another; June said she didn't know where, and she didn't care. "I don't fancy him anymore; I don't fancy anyone. In fact, I doubt I will ever trust anyone ever again."

Juliet went home sick at heart. What a thoughtless thing the Barkers had done, thoughtless and cruel. How much easier it would have been to have told June the truth when she was a little girl, so she grew up knowing she was adopted.

"It was Barbara who wanted to keep it quiet," said Mary when Juliet told her. "By sweeping everything under the carpet, she fooled herself into thinking that June really was the daughter she gave birth to. The fact that June looked absolutely nothing like anyone in her family or Dickie's never occurred to her. After all, June really is a beauty and with the best will in the world, no one can say any of the Barkers are good-looking."

★★★

After a week of staying in her bedroom and refusing to emerge, even for meals, which she ate alone in her room, June got up, put on her new pink circular skirt with its four paper nylon petticoats, and a white frilly blouse, tied a bright cotton scarf around her neck and announced that she was going to get a job.

"A job," cried her parents in disbelief, "but what about college? We thought you were taking up that secretarial and language course in September."

"Well, I'm not," said June. "I've changed my mind. I'm getting a job and I'm going to earn my own living. After all, I can't expect you to provide me with everything."

"But why wouldn't we?" said her father. "You are our daughter. We love you, and we want to care for you. There is no need for you to get a job." June's bright blue eyes looked almost steely. "But I'm not your daughter, am I? Not really." And she slammed out of the house.

June was as good as her word, and before long, she was working as a postroom clerk at a local solicitors' office. She never mentioned the events surrounding her birthday, and gradually, life almost returned to normal. Almost, but not quite. The Barkers were relieved; it looked as if the storm was over. Although June still refused to take up her college course and insisted on giving Barbara a weekly sum, which she said was 'for my keep,' she seemed to have settled down.

Barbara was horrified by the brown envelope containing two one-pound notes that June left on the kitchen table every Saturday.

"I can't take money from my own daughter," she protested to Dickie. "It's ridiculous." Dickie gave her a comforting pat on the shoulder. "June's just making a point," he said. "Take it, say nothing, and put it in a savings account for her. She'll be grateful for it one day. Things will settle down, you'll see, my dear. Don't fret. We'll soon be back to normal."

If Dickie and Barbara were unhappy with the lowly job June had found herself, they had the good sense to keep it to themselves. They both clung to the hope that June would quickly see the error of her ways, realise she had overreacted, resign from the office, and take up her college place. Then, life would return to how it was before the ill-fated birthday surprise.

Chapter Six

ONLY JULIET knew that June was determined to track down Annie Nelson, and the knowledge that she had information that might help June's quest weighed heavily on her conscience.

"I've got to find her; I've just got to," said June during one of their regular girly get-togethers. "I need to know what she is like and to find out something about my father."

Juliet spoke to Mary, begging to be allowed to put June in the picture. Mary remained adamant that Juliet must keep her promise and that the information she had must stay confidential.

"It's not fair to the Barkers," said Mary. "It's up to them to give June that information and if they decide not to do so, then it's not for you to step in. I know June's your best friend, but let things be. Least said, soonest mended." Mary had a platitude to suit every occasion.

June spent every moment she could spare on her 'detective work,' as she called it. There were several false leads, like the time when she found the name Annie Nelson in the London telephone directory. "It's an address in Camden Town, I think I might go and find it and see if it's her. Okay, I know it's a long shot, but just imagine, she may have had her name put in full like that in the hope that one day I'd see it and contact her. A sort of message. Otherwise, she would have just put A Nelson or Miss A Nelson."

Juliet urged her to phone first. "You can't just turn up on the doorstep. Camden Town might be a rough area and goodness knows what kind of risks you'd be taking. Do be sensible."

"I don't feel like being sensible," said June sulkily, but she eventually agreed to ring the London number before doing anything else. It was a red herring and the Annie Nelson who put her name in the telephone book no longer lived there.

"From what the woman I spoke to said, she couldn't possibly have been my Annie Nelson, so it would have been a waste of time and money to go there," she admitted to Juliet some days later.

Juliet breathed a sigh of relief, but there were several similar incidents before June gleefully announced that she had found her mother at long last with the help of a rather seedy private detective.

"Well, the good news is that she isn't a million miles away," she said with a touch of her old enthusiasm. "The bad news is that she lives in Essex." Juliet laughed. "And just what is wrong with Essex? Who's being a snob again?"

"Oh, nothing is wrong with Essex, not that I know much about it. I've only been to Southend – do you know it's supposed to have the longest pier in the world? – but I wasn't being snobby about it, it's just a really awkward place to get to."

However, it turned out that a trip to Essex, awkward or not, was not immediately on the cards. The detective, who furtively pointed out that his investigations were, strictly speaking, not exactly legal, insisted that he should take the first step by writing to Annie Nelson and informing her that the daughter she gave up for adoption wanted to contact her.

June was not best pleased with this arrangement and said so very forcefully. But the man was unmoved. Because the law ruled that when a birth mother and child were separated by adoption, it was forever, everything had to be done very carefully. Argument was fruitless. "Or we could both end up in court," he warned.

June eventually agreed to wait and spent the next week in a state of bad-tempered suspense. "I hate all this waiting around," she told Juliet. "I could have been there and met her by now. I have so many questions to ask. This is such a waste of time."

Juliet calmed her down and did her best to keep her mind off Annie, but June was not good company. She was completely disinterested in parties, music, boys, clothes, make-up, or any of the day-to-day events that make up a teenage girl's life. Even the prospect of going to the cinema to see a long-awaited Elvis Presley film could not tempt her. She just wanted to go and meet the woman who had given birth to her.

Eventually, the detective phoned. It was not good news. Annie Nelson, who now had the married name Annie Brent, did not want any contact with June. She didn't want to know about her, and she most definitely didn't want to meet her.

"I understand," said the detective in a sympathetic voice that made June want to slap him, "that Mrs Brent has not told her husband or subsequent children about you. She is worried that it will be a terrible shock for them."

June was distraught. "But she must see me. I must meet her. I must." She suddenly remembered just how much the man had charged her for tracking down Annie. A small fortune, and for what? Nothing! "You must get her to see me," she screamed hysterically down the phone. But the man was unmoved. "Sorry, m'dear. That's it. Job done." He hung up.

★★★

June, knowing she was beaten, took herself back to her pink and white bedroom. The Barkers stood by and watched helplessly, totally out of their depth. They were at last beginning to blame themselves for the nightmare in which they and June were trapped.

Two days later, June phoned Juliet at work. "I've decided. I'm going to Essex to see her."

"June, you can't. You know what the detective said."

"I don't care I'm going. This is ridiculous. She is my mother. She's got to see me."

With a shop full of customers, Juliet was unable to continue the conversation. "Look, I've got to go. I'll ring you back at lunchtime." But when Juliet rang the solicitors' office at one o'clock, she was told that June had taken two days' holiday. "She rang in and said she needed it for personal reasons," said the girl on the switchboard. A subsequent call to the Barkers revealed that June had set off for Essex a few hours earlier using her mother's car.

"She wouldn't listen to reason," Barbara said miserably. "And she wouldn't let Dickie or me go with her. She just drove off in my car. Perhaps it's for the best. She's not going to settle until she has sorted this out."

Juliet, who had heard nothing from June all day, was just preparing to go to bed when the bedraggled-looking girl turned up on the doorstep. "I need to talk," she said simply. "It's no good. She just doesn't want to see me."

Holding both of June's cold hands in hers, Juliet listened in sympathetic silence as June related her story.

She had found the house quite easily and went and knocked on the door. Annie Brent was visibly shaken when she realised who her visitor was, but she pulled herself quickly together and told June in no uncertain terms that she was not prepared to have any discussion with her. She had given her for adoption eighteen years ago and had not expected to hear from her ever again. And that's the way she wanted to keep it.

"She shut the door in my face," whispered June. "I knocked on the door again, but she called out of an upstairs window, telling me to go away or she would call the police."

June had returned to the car and sat outside Annie's house for several hours before reluctantly deciding to leave.

Chapter Seven

THIS SECOND rejection by Annie affected June severely. She went back to work the following day but then called in sick and once again took to her bed. The Barkers called the family doctor, who said June was thoroughly worn out and run down, emotionally and physically, and prescribed a complete change of scene. A holiday would be good, he said. Abroad, somewhere warm, where she could relax and regain her strength.

Barbara and Dickie, relieved there was at last something they could do to help, immediately arranged a trip to Spain.

Juliet, who had just started going out with a new boyfriend, waved them goodbye. "It's only for two weeks," called June as the car drove off. "See you as soon as I get back. I want to hear everything about your new bloke, and I'm sure I will have lots to tell."

Lots to tell there was, for both Barbara and Dickie were horrified by their daughter's behaviour abroad. "She set her cap at every man going," said Barbara when she met up with Juliet's mother on their return. "I was thoroughly ashamed of her. Goodness knows what Dickie thought. I've been far too embarrassed to ask him.

"She wasn't bothered what nationality they were either. Spanish, French or English, it was all the same. She flirted with anyone in trousers. I don't know what she was thinking; we brought her up better than that. I don't know where we went wrong. She behaved just like a tart."

Barbara was in tears of mortification, and for once, Mary Campbell was lost for words.

"I just didn't know what to say to her," she told Juliet. "I mean, what can one say to a mother whose daughter has behaved like that? Right under her parents' noses too!"

★★★

Closeted in the pink and white bedroom, June told Juliet her version of events. "I had an absolutely brilliant time," she said. She unwound the floral-patterned chiffon scarf from around her neck and showed Juliet three large purplish-yellow bruises.

"Love bites. I must say those Spanish boys are wild. I met the most gorgeous Spaniard called Pedro. Well, I met quite a few dishy boys, but Pedro was the one I liked best.

"Pedro the fisherman?" asked Juliet facetiously.

"Huh, very droll! No, Pedro, the bank clerk, but he was fabulous, very sexy, and" she paused… "And we did it on the beach in the moonlight. It was very romantic."

"Did it? Did what?" asked Juliet perplexed.

"You know IT," said June impatiently. "Went all the way; made love; fucked. It's certainly everything it's cracked up to be, and I can absolutely recommend it. Wow. I had no idea sex was such fun! Much better than the pathetic petting I've had from boys before."

"June! You didn't," cried Juliet in horror. "Weren't you worried about getting pregnant?"

As June gave an inscrutable smile, Juliet added: "And you know I don't like hearing you use the F-word."

"Nothing wrong with a good old Anglo-Saxon expression," said June defiantly. "You're beginning to sound like my mother… and yours!"

"Actually, it's a word that came from Germany in the Middle Ages," said Juliet.

"Oh, stop being so bloody annoying, Jules," retorted June. "You're too fucking clever for your own good. Men don't like clever women, you know."

She moved over to the dressing table to fix her eye makeup, spitting onto her cake of mascara to make a paste. Staring defiantly at Juliet in the mirror, mascara brush poised, she said: "And to answer your question – No, I was not worried about getting pregnant. Not in the least; Pedro seemed to know what he was doing. Anyway, my mother obviously wasn't bothered, was she, so why should I be?"

Juliet bit her lip. "But that was different, sweetheart. Go on, tell me more. Are you and Pedro engaged? Will you have to go and live in Spain?"

"What?" shrieked June. "Engaged? Oh no! I'll probably never see him again, but I'll always remember him. You never forget the first time you have sex, the memory stays with you for life. But then, there's plenty more fish in the sea. I've got a date for tomorrow night as it happens with a guy who works in the same office as me. He's a trainee solicitor, and he's got an MG sports car. His parents are incredibly wealthy. We're going up to Devil's Dyke for a drink, and then, well, who knows."

She gave her throaty laugh. "The MG's a bit small for a passion wagon, but I suppose we can always lie on the grass; there are no streetlights up there. I'm pretty sure he'll want to. We get on incredibly well."

She put away her make-up and turned round to look at Juliet, the smoky liner and black mascara making her eyes appear enormous.

"I'm feeling quite hopeful about Brian, actually. When he asked me out, he said: 'Are we just going to fool around or do you fancy getting serious?' so that sounds more than promising." Juliet was silent, shocked at June's behaviour and her reckless talk.

A couple of months later, she was even more dismayed when, after a succession of one-night stands with various young men, June announced that she and the trainee solicitor, who was called Brian Turner, were engaged to be married.

"Look at my lovely ring." June held out her left hand with an enormous diamond twinkling on the fourth finger.

"My God, that's not a ring. That's a rock!" cried Juliet.

"I told you his parents were loaded," said June smugly.

Juliet refused to be sidetracked by a diamond. "What d'you mean married? You hardly know him. You've been out with loads of boys since you met him. Plenty more fish in the sea, you said."

Juliet was amazed that June hadn't mentioned the blossoming relationship with this guy called Brian. After all, they told each other everything, didn't they?

June looked slightly embarrassed. "Actually, Jules, I've known him for ages and all the others meant nothing. I was just testing the water and it's good to get a bit of experience before you make a commitment. I've known Brian since I went to work in that god-awful office and frankly, it's the answer to prayer.

"You know we all must get married sometime. It's what is expected of girls like us, so the sooner the better really. I like Brian; he's good-looking, kind, clever, his parents have got pots of money, he's in love with me and good in bed. Tell me, Jules, exactly where am I going wrong?"

"But do you love him? It all seems so quick. It's a big decision, getting married. So... well, so final. Do think about this. It's not too late to change your mind."

June thumped her fist on the bed. "I don't want to change my mind. I am marrying Brian, and yes, of course, I love him." But staring down at the carpet, she avoided Juliet's eyes. "Please, Jules, don't judge me. I know what I am doing."

She jumped up off the bed and smiled. "Now, enough about me; tell me what you've been up to. I want to hear about this new fellow of yours. "What's he like? Is he more fun than that pathetic Rob? And, madam, I hear he's a lot older than you. When I think of all the fuss you made about Griff being twenty-four when I was seventeen!"

After going out with Rob for several months before becoming bored, Juliet had a few unremarkable dates with a couple of other boys before meeting Mike Bennett, a landscape gardener who was thirty-two.

"Well, I admit he's thirteen years older than me, but a bit of experience isn't a bad thing. He was engaged to a girl for a couple of years, but then she left him for someone else and he didn't go out with anyone for absolutely ages. Now he's met me and it's all systems go again."

"So-o-o? June raised her eyebrows. "Anything to confess to your Auntie June? How far have you gone? Have you climbed on the merry-go-round? Any fucking you want to tell me about? Older men are much more experienced, so that makes it all a lot easier." She smiled, knowing the answer.

"No! Certainly not. No, it's not that kind of relationship."

"So that would be a no, then?" June teased.

Juliet frowned. "Mike's very nice, very…charming but I have no intention of going to bed with anyone who is not my husband. I don't think Mike is up for marriage quite honestly, well, not yet anyway."

"Oh! I have no intention of going to bed with anyone who's not my husband," mimicked June naughtily. "How prissy you sound. This is the swinging sixties, you know; it looks to me as if you're being left behind when it comes to sex, drugs, and rock 'n' roll."

June knew only too well that none of Juliet's relationships had progressed further than necking, a bit of French kissing, and the occasional fondle, quite old-fashioned in the promiscuous sixties.

Juliet laughed. It was good to see the old June back again. "Well, I love rock 'n' roll," she parried, "as you know, I do a neat jive, and I'm totally in love with the wonderful Elvis, but I've no intention of trying drugs, and I won't have sex until I'm married. So that's that. End of conversation."

June gave her mysterious smile. "Time will tell. You wait until you meet someone you really fancy. Then you'll see what I mean."

★★★

June and Brian were married in the parish church a few months later. No point in hanging around when you've made up your mind, they said.

"I'm sure there are people who think I'm pregnant," said June. "But I'm not. I just want to get married, and there is no reason to hang about. I've never agreed with long engagements, look what happened to your Mike."

Despite the short notice, the Barkers arranged a lavish wedding. As if making up for all the mistakes they had made, Barbara and Dickie were determined their daughter's marriage was going to be Brighton's event of the year and no expense was spared.

June looked sensationally beautiful in a plain white satin gown with a matching pill-box hat securing her long lace train.

Juliet was chief bridesmaid and she, three of June's cousins, and Brian's sister, wore pale turquoise dresses in the same style as the bride's; Brian and his groomsmen were formally decked out in traditional morning dress, while one of his young cousins was a page boy in a tartan kilt complete with sporran. It was certainly a glittering society event that drew spectators from far and wide and to which *Tatler* devoted a full page of pictures.

Afterwards, the bride and bridegroom left for a motoring tour of France. As the girls said goodbye at the reception, June waved her wedding band under Juliet's nose.

"If you won't have sex without a ring on your finger, get Mike to pop the question," she said. "I can thoroughly recommend it – the sex I mean, I'll keep you posted about marriage."

Part Three
Juliet and Enzo

(1962)

Reflection

> *"Can't Help Falling in Love"*
> Elvis Presley, on the album 'Blue Hawaii',
> Original Soundtrack (1961)

I'VE ALWAYS been captivated by Italian men. Even now, in old age, my head is still easily turned by a charming Italian. While this obsession began in my early teens with the eye-opening and exciting discovery of the iconic Italian film actor Marcello Mastroianni, who at that time was my idea of the perfect lover, the seed of interest was probably sown a couple of years earlier when my mother told me *apropos of nothing*, that she once had an Italian boyfriend.

I was astonished; my mother went out with an Italian? I had loads of questions, but after sparking my interest she was characteristically very coy about it, refusing to give any interesting details beyond 'it was a long time ago.'

Once I had discovered Marcello and *La Dolce Vita*, I tried to imagine my mother, like Anita Ekberg, in the arms of a sex god, but the image was too embarrassing, and I parked it deep in my memory for future reference.

So, I guess I was about fourteen when I met my first Italian. It was the school holidays, and June was away visiting some of her numerous cousins. Fed up, I took long cycle rides in the countryside, as we could in those far-off days when nobody had heard of 'Stranger Danger,' and children were free to spend time wandering around climbing trees, making dens, swimming, and cycling, without being chaperoned by an adult.

I often used to go off for a whole day, alone or with friends, taking a packed lunch and whiling away long, hazy summer hours, knowing that my parents wouldn't have a moment's concern about my wellbeing unless I failed to arrive back home in time for supper.

On one of these trips out I had a slight accident. My voluminous circular skirt, which was *de rigueur* for teenage girls in the nineteen-fifties, supported by numerous net and paper nylon petticoats, caught in the bike's back wheel and I unceremoniously tumbled onto a grass verge.

I wasn't badly hurt, suffering just a grazed knee and dented pride. I was more concerned about a small tear to my favourite skirt and was inspecting the damage when a swarthy young man with laughing eyes and shiny black hair worn in an unfashionable ponytail rushed up and held out his hand. "Let me help you up." He had a very attractive accent and a sparkling smile.

I took the outstretched hand, very tanned with beautifully kept nails, feeling a tingle of excitement. As he pulled me to my feet, he gave a tiny formal bow and said: "Good afternoon. I am Mario."

"Thank you, I am Juliet," I replied, equally formal, and we walked slowly back to my home, Mario pushing my bicycle. He told me he was Italian, seventeen years old and had come to England with his parents when he was ten. He was a real gentleman with perfect manners and I was dazzled.

When Mario asked if he could take me to the cinema, I felt the thrill of anticipation. I knew I was breaking all parental rules by accepting the invitation, but that made the assignation even more exciting. I was determined to go, foolhardy or not.

I made sure we parted before we got to my house in case my mother was looking out for me. If she saw us, the questions that would doubtless ensue were too alarming to contemplate. Not only that, but she would also forbid any liaison with Mario.

I felt very grown up. Back in the fifties, before 'teenagers' had been invented, girls of fourteen were still considered children and consequently, I was wearing black Mary Jane shoes and white ankle socks with my colourful circular skirt and white blouse. But Mario didn't seem to mind and certainly didn't treat me like a child. We made plans to meet outside the Odeon in two days' time.

The trip to the pictures was followed by a couple of other clandestine meetings, all very innocent: the most we did was hold hands and exchange a few shy kisses. But keeping these rendezvous away from my mother's prying eyes and vivid imagination eventually proved too difficult to maintain, and the fledgling romance fizzled out after a few exhilarating weeks.

Chapter One

IT WAS Juliet's new boyfriend Mike who arranged for her to go to Italy. Their relationship was low-key without any real passion, and his interest in gardens and hers in flowers meant they jogged comfortably along as good friends, with occasional chaste kisses and cuddles in Mike's car.

"I've got something for you," he said one evening shortly after June and Brian had left on honeymoon. He produced a brochure showing a trip to Italy for botanists.

"It looks great," said Juliet, studying the details with interest. "But I'm not really a botanist; I just do flowers."

"Yes, but you love looking at them and finding out more, and you're always taking photographs. Look at that garden trip we went on last month. You were more interested in the herbaceous borders than I was!"

Juliet agreed. "True, I do love flowers, and I am always interested in learning about them."

"So, wouldn't you like to go and look at flowers in Italy, on Capri actually? It sounds just your sort of thing."

Juliet was tempted. She hadn't been abroad before and a trip to Italy… she still had a secret admiration for charming Italians, spiked by the memory of Marcello Mastroianni and a few dates with Mario.

"But what about you?" she asked Mike. "Don't you want to go?"

"Heavens, no," said Mike, "I can't think of anything worse.

It will be all maiden ladies doing watercolours and real botanists being terribly earnest. No, it wasn't me I was thinking about. I just thought it would be something you'd like to do."

"Well, yes, I would," said Juliet slowly. "But I don't know if I can go on my own."

"Nonsense," exclaimed Mike. "This is the nineteen-sixties, not the eighteen-sixties. There can be no possible reason why you can't go on your own."

"You don't know my mother," retorted Juliet. "She'll certainly have an opinion on it." Mike laughed. "Don't worry, I'll make all the arrangements and it can be an early birthday present if you like. All you'll have to do is turn up and enjoy; you'll love it."

★★★

As Juliet had anticipated, Mary was scandalised when she heard about the proposed trip. "Go alone to Italy? Abroad! I never heard such a thing. Whatever are you thinking of?"

"It's not that bad," snapped Juliet. "You make it sound like I'm going to an orgy. I won't be alone or in any danger but with about twenty other people – most of them married couples and ladies a great deal older than me. It's a perfectly respectable organised tour of gardens especially for botanists. We will be accompanied by two lecturers while on Capri and looking at the itinerary, it seems there will be little spare time, what with talks and visits and whatnot. I want to go and the knowledge I gain will help me progress in my floristry career. It was Mike's idea…"

"Oh well, Mike," Mary rolled her eyes and shook her head. She did not think much of Mike and certainly didn't approve of Juliet going around with someone who had the lowly job of the gardener and was almost twice her age. He was not the kind of man she had planned for her daughter. She did her best to change Juliet's mind, to no avail.

"Mike has made all the arrangements, and he is paying for it as a birthday present, which is very generous, so I'm going," said Juliet defiantly. The more her mother protested and interrogated: "Are you sure Mike's not going too? That would be most unsuitable," the more determinedly Juliet dug into her heels.

Mary appealed to Dennis for support, but he was on Juliet's side. "Let her go, it will do her good. You can't keep her wrapped in cotton wool forever. She's got to go out into the world and, let's face it, things are changing fast. Young girls nowadays are not the shrinking violets they were when we were young, m'dear. Times are indeed changing. She's determined to go, and we might as well let her do so with good grace. No point in having a family row over it."

Mary was not convinced. "Suppose she behaves like June? We don't know that she's not going to go running after all those foreign men and she might get herself into all sorts of trouble, and even if she doesn't, will she be able to cope? You know she is very shy. How will she get on with loads of strangers? Oh dear, I'm not at all happy about it."

The thought of a teenage girl going off abroad on her own was anathema to Mary. She tried to bring Dennis around to her way of thinking, but he was unmoved. During their long marriage, it wasn't often that he put his foot down, preferring to allow his volatile wife her own way as much as possible. On the rare occasions he felt it necessary, he would overrule her and that would be that.

It did fleetingly cross Dennis's mind that Mary's concern for Juliet's welfare was more likely to be anxiety about how her smart friends at the Country Club where she was a leading light, might view Mary's own role as a mother…she saw everything her children did as a reflection on herself…but he quickly squashed the thought as unworthy. Turning to his wife, he said firmly: "We must support her and let her go."

So, Juliet was going to Italy with her father's blessing. Once everything was settled and she had arranged a fortnight's holiday from the flower shop where she worked, Juliet was ecstatic. She hadn't been abroad before and the excitement of getting a passport, stocking up on notebooks and drawing pencils, and buying a new camera and film took up much of her spare time. She was particularly thrilled that she would be making her first air flight.

Having a drink with Mike the evening before she left, Juliet told him again how grateful she was for his generosity. "You have no idea how excited I am about this trip," she told him, "I don't know how I can thank you."

Mike patted her knee. "Oh, I'm sure you'll find a way," he said with a surprisingly wolfish smile. "I can wait. You can thank me properly when you get back."

A sexual innuendo was the last thing Juliet expected from Mike, so she didn't pick up on his euphemism.

★★★

Her parents went to London Airport to see her off. Mary was still very unhappy about the trip, anxious that Juliet would get lost, catch the wrong plane, or get abducted and forced into prostitution. Hugging her daughter with rare affection, she started issuing instructions in case of emergency. Waving her directives aside, Dennis was upbeat and said very firmly when they reached the departure terminal that he and Mary would be leaving Juliet there. "I'm sure you're quite old enough to cope alone and meet up with the rest of your group. You don't need us hanging around."

Turning to Mary, he said: "Our daughter is perfectly able to get herself to where she is supposed to be. She's nineteen, not nine, and she's smart enough to deal with all eventualities; that's the way we brought her up and she won't let us down. So just let her get on with it." Dennis gave Juliet a swift kiss on the cheek and patted her shoulder, steering Mary back towards the car before she could open her mouth to protest.

After a sudden prickle of fear, Juliet mentally shook herself and took control of her nerves. She carefully navigated the airport's numerous twists and turns, eventually tracking down the group leader, who was desperately trying to match up people with the names on his clipboard.

Eric, a lanky, grey-haired man of about fifty, wearing baggy navy-blue trousers and a colourful Hawaiian shirt, was hampered by all manner of random travellers, attracted by the clipboard, coming up to ask questions. As most of them had nothing at all to do with his group the poor man was at his wits' end.

"Welcome, Miss Campbell," he said as Juliet introduced herself. "Good, another name I can cross off the list. If you go over and join the group already here, I'll be with you shortly."

"Should have given the job to a female," grunted a string bean of a woman standing next to Juliet, regarding Eric with exasperation. "We'll be here all day at this rate."

She turned to look at Juliet and said: "I'm Edna Lowe, and this…" she pulled on the arm of a sturdy woman by her side, "This is my cousin Jane. I'm going to photograph flowers and plants, and Jane paints watercolours. We're planning to put on an exhibition later in the year."

"I'm Juliet Campbell, and I'm training to be a florist, but I'm really interested in all plants," said Juliet shyly. "I'm hoping to do photography too."

"Are you on your own, young lady?" Jane enquired, peering at Juliet through thick pebble glass spectacles. Without waiting for an answer, she said: "Well you stick by us, we'll make sure you're okay, won't we Edna?"

"What? Oh, absolutely, dear. Look, it seems as if something is happening at last."

More people had now joined the group and were standing

around making their own introductions as the harassed Eric joined them, the list on his clipboard now covered in red pen.

"Right people. Everyone's here, so shall we proceed? You've all got a passport I sincerely hope. Excellent. Excellent. Here goes, then. Here we go. Follow me, follow me."

"I can see it's going to be a case of follow, follow my leader all the way," said Jane with a sly smile at her cousin. They joined the queue as Eric, his brightly coloured shirt a beacon, led them to passport control and through security, proving to be far more efficient than anyone had imagined.

"There you are, dear," said Edna, tapping Jane on the shoulder. "He's not as green as he's cabbage-looking!"

"Yes, well," replied Jane. "Time will tell. I'll withhold judgement until we are safely in Italy."

Strapped into her aircraft seat beside a sober young man who looked as if he had fallen out the pages of *The Boys Own Paper* and seemed to be travelling with little more than a string bag full of books on flora and fauna, and with Edna and Jane ensconced across the aisle, Juliet had a moment of panic with an uncomfortable knot of fear settling in her stomach. What was she doing? It was madness. Much as she hated to admit it, her mother had been right; she should never have done this on her own.

As the plane taxied towards the runway, Juliet held tightly onto the arms of her seat, squeezing her eyes tightly closed, hardly daring to breathe, the deafening noise of the engines adding to her alarm. It was going to crash and they would all be killed. Once safely in the air, the thrill of flying and the joy of anticipation kicked her fears into submission and she began to enjoy herself.

Juliet was very much taken with the dinky airline lunch tray delivered from a trolley pushed by a svelte and attractive hostess. She happily investigated the various dishes and pots, enjoying her unusual meal with an appreciation eschewed by more seasoned travellers.

Glancing across the aisle, she noticed that Edna and Jane were merely picking at their lunch while the young man beside her, head deep in a book, had tetchily cast his aside without even tasting it.

Chapter Two

WHEN SHE emerged from the plane in Naples, Juliet was hit by the sweltering heat of an Italian mid-summer afternoon. The passengers walked across the hot tarmac into the coolness of the terminal building, recovering suitcases and queuing to pass through customs.

It was while she was queuing that Juliet had her first experience of the hot-blooded Latin, very different from the formal politeness of Mario. She had her bottom pinched. Hard. "Ow!" Juliet jumped in surprise and pain, quickly turning to see a pair of liquid brown eyes beaming at her. "*Scusa, signorina,* but you are very pretty. Where do you stay in *Napoli*? My uncle has a bar…"

Before Juliet could react, Eric was by her side, moving the man on. "*Andare via!*" said Eric firmly, giving an unexpectedly rude Italian gesture.

"*Andare via!* Go, go!" The bottom pincher shrugged good-humouredly and disappeared into the crowd.

"You'll have to be careful," Eric warned her. "Italian men seem to like young English ladies. They're always willing to try it on just in case they get lucky." He regarded her with concern. "Are you alright? He didn't hurt you?"

"I'm fine," Juliet assured him, rubbing her bottom. "He just took me by surprise."

"Well, it's something you need to be aware of in Italy," said Eric. "Italian men are flirts."

"They're all Don Juans," snorted Edna, who was just behind her. "Everywhere you go in Italy, it's the same; I'm constantly being badgered when I'm here. Absolute pain."

Regarding Edna with her Eton crop haircut, floral cotton princess-line frock and sturdy Clarks sandals, Eric looked as if he was going to comment but thought better of it. "Right," he said briskly. "Let's keep moving. Let's keep moving. Come on, Miss Campbell, it's your turn. Off you go. Off you go."

Juliet dragged her luggage onto the low bench where two customs men were standing. The older officer put a chalk cross on Juliet's suitcase and then turned his attention to the small vanity case she was carrying. "What do you have in there? I will just look."

Juliet was about to open the case when the younger man put a large hairy hand caressingly over hers and said: "That is all good, *signorina*. It is not considered polite to investigate a lady's handbag, am I right?" He smiled at her, showing a perfect set of very white teeth. "This your first visit to Italy? *No?* And do you go, perhaps, to *Roma* or do you stay in *Napoli?* Ah, Capri! The island of love. I hope you will have a very happy holiday. Maybe I will see you on your return."

Juliet gave a shy smile, and Edna's scoff of derision was clearly audible as she walked out of the customs shed and into the bright Italian sunshine.

Chapter Three

THEY SPENT the night at a hotel in Naples, being woken in the early hours by an enormous thunderstorm with torrential rain. Juliet stood by her open bedroom window watching the rain beating down on the rosy tiled roofs with lightning illuminating the sky, making it look as if nearby Mount Vesuvius was on fire. Recalling a school lesson about the eruption of the volcano in 79AD when the towns of Pompeii and Herculaneum, together with some sixteen thousand citizens. were buried under the lava, Juliet shivered, feeling as if she had stepped back into history.

She stood there for a while in silent contemplation before going back to bed and sleeping soundly until she was awoken at seven by her travelling alarm clock.

The morning had dawned warm and clear, and anticipating a hot, sunny day, Juliet decided to wear a pink sundress with a matching bolero. She shook out her long hair, which fell like a waterfall down her back; maybe she should put it up if it was going to be hot? She looked at her watch: no time to fiddle with it now; it would have to stay as it was.

Checking her appearance in the mirror, she suddenly recalled her mother telling her when she was a child that she couldn't wear anything pink because it didn't go with her red hair. When she was older and started buying her own clothes, Juliet discovered that pink suited her very well.

That was just one of Mary's many pronouncements trotted

out over the years, most as far as Juliet could see, without any foundation. Mary had also stopped her daughter from wearing a favourite pair of red shoes with a green dress because 'red and green must never be seen.' And fish was never served in the Campbell household between May and September. Mary firmly believed you couldn't eat fish unless there was an 'R' in the month.

"I think that was in the days before refrigeration," remarked Dennis mildly after being prevented from having his favourite fish supper while on a summer holiday in Norfolk. Mary was unwavering; that was what she had been taught as a girl, and that was the way it was; nothing could change her mind.

Smiling at the memory, Juliet scooped up her handbag from the bed and made her way down to the dining room, where Eric and the group were gathering for breakfast. After enjoying delicious warm rolls with apricot jam and steaming hot, fragrant coffee, Juliet was ready for whatever new adventures the day might bring.

A riveting diversion was provided by a delicate, fair-haired woman asking for tea. "I've never taken to coffee," she explained in response to enquiring looks from those gathered around the table.

Her request was met with blank stares from the hotel staff before the faithful Eric intervened, and eventually a cup of lukewarm milky water with a yellow-tagged Lipton's tea bag drooping in it was put down in front of her.

The woman sipped cautiously and shuddered. "It tastes disgusting," she complained. Eric shrugged, raising his shoulders in a tiny, helpless gesture. "Best they can do, I'm afraid." Gathering up her bags, the woman left the rejected beverage on the table.

"You'll never get a decent cuppa in Italy," vouchsafed Jane helpfully. "Edna and I always bring some PG Tips with us."

"We always drink coffee here," said another traveller. "Tea is usually horrible and very expensive. The Italians just can't make it;

I'm sure they don't use boiling water. Anyway, when in Rome…"

"You should copy young Ricky here, he only drinks bottled water and juice," said someone else, indicating the young man who had been sitting next to Juliet on the plane. Ricky looked pained at being the subject of discussion.

"I never drink hot beverages," he said stiffly, taking off his round wire-framed spectacles and polishing them with a grubby handkerchief. Picking up his bag of books, he added: "And I never eat flesh. I'm vegetarian."

Ricky's disclosure caused a stunned silence followed by much whispering and muted laughter as Eric flapped around, anxious to get everyone out of the dining room and onto the coach waiting to take them to Sorrento, where they would catch the ferry to the island of Capri.

Sitting on the long back seat of the coach beside Edna and Jane, Juliet was pushed to explain what had happened at breakfast when one of the waiters had obviously propositioned her. Edna's voice, possessing remarkable and unexpected carrying power, reverberated around the vehicle, which was suddenly plunged into a hushed silence as everyone tuned in to Juliet's response.

Unused to being the centre of attention, Juliet's face was crimson. "He, er, um, well, he just asked me out," she said weakly. "Nothing to tell, really. I said I was leaving immediately after breakfast, and that was that."

"I can see we are going to have to watch you!" chortled Edna, elbowing Juliet painfully in the ribs. "We've not been in Italy twenty-four hours, and you've already had to fight off three men!"

Highly embarrassed, Juliet stared out of the window and didn't reply. Much to her relief, everyone quickly returned to discussing outings on Capri while Eric started to explain the talks that had been organised and the opportunities for photography and painting.

Juliet made a mental note to try and steer clear of Edna and

Jane as much as possible. It wasn't fair that she should be ridiculed for something that wasn't her fault. She certainly wasn't giving the young Italians any encouragement; they just seemed to pick on her.

The journey to Sorrento along narrow, winding roads was unbelievably beautiful, the scenery breath-taking. There were pretty terraces and an endless succession of olive groves, lemon orchards, and ancient churches, while the high cliff roads offered views of sheer rocky drops down to the sparkling, impossibly turquoise sea. Every so often, the coach would come to a sudden shuddering halt as a lorry packed with vegetables or livestock pushed through in the opposite direction with much shouting, gesticulating and blaring of horns.

Eric, wearing another colourful Hawaiian shirt, was proving to be more than worthy of his title of group leader, offering endless snippets of information about the area. Juliet was particularly enthralled to hear about the Path of the Gods, an Amalfi coast trail along ancient mule routes, named after the Greek legends because it gave the godly experience of being suspended between heaven and earth. *If it's not possible to do the walk this time, I must come back*, she told herself. Maybe she could persuade Mike to come with her. She was sure it was the kind of thing he'd really enjoy.

Lying back in her seat and closing her eyes as Eric continued his talk, Juliet became conscious of the sweet scent of wayside flowers and the smell of lemons floating in through the open windows. She relaxed, feeling happy and drowsy; this was going to be a great holiday. She was thankful she had stood up to her mother and taken this amazing opportunity so generously offered by Mike.

Chapter Four

WHEN THEY arrived in the picturesque seaside town of Sorrento with its warren of narrow alleyways looking out over calm, azure water, Eric suggested they had coffee at an outside café situated on the rocky tip of the peninsula right next to the jetty to await the boat to Capri.

Trying to avoid Edna and Jane in case the embarrassing questioning started again, Juliet joined two middle-aged couples at a small table under the cheerful striped awning. Once again Juliet caused a stir among the Italian waiters.

One of them, the youngest of the trio, boldly asked her in halting English if she would go out with him if he met up with her in Capri. "Only a short journey by boat for me," he said, beaming at her. I can meet any time." The ever-vigilant Eric shooed the young man away. He didn't seem at all downhearted and went off to join his chuckling friends, who slapped him approvingly on the back before they all went off to serve more customers.

"Like I said before, they always try it on," said Eric. "Best to take no notice; sometimes they strike lucky and sometimes not. Don't worry about it. Don't worry about it."

"It's probably your hair, dear," said one of the women, whose name was Alice. "They go mad for red hair, them all being so dark, and girls with blonde hair get similar attention."

She turned to her husband. "Do you remember, Ken, when we were in Venice last year? There was a young girl, well, she was a married woman, who was constantly fighting off the local men. She was blonde; her husband wasn't at all impressed, I can tell you!"

Ken hooted with laughter. "Really, Alice, you are a case. It's because Juliet is young and pretty, nothing to do with her hair. Italian men like women. Full stop. All young women get the same treatment, some enjoy it and flirt back, and others are just uncomfortable."

The other couple laughed. "We cold English aren't used to the hot Latin blood," said Nancy, the disappointed tea drinker. "It's just the way they are; they don't mean any harm by it. Even some older ladies get the same amorous treatment!"

Her husband Ron agreed: "You just decide what you want to do," he advised Juliet. "If you want a little holiday romance, this is the place to be. If you don't, give them the cold shoulder, and they'll soon get the message and leave you alone. There are plenty of foreign girls willing to have a fling."

Juliet nodded. "I'm here to look at the flowers and take some photographs," she explained, "and I've got a boyfriend at home, so I'm not really looking for romance."

Despite, she thought with a guilty inward smile, that I seem to find Italian men so attractive, and they seem to quite like me, at least the waiters do, although as they are all so flirty I suppose I should take that with a pinch of salt.

"Well, there you are then," said Nancy briskly. "You'll be alright. You look as if you can take care of yourself." Juliet noticed that she had not attempted another cup of tea and was drinking orangeade instead; perhaps she had taken Ricky's advice.

Alice leant across the table to Juliet. "Talking of red hair, have you put some suncream on? You look as if you're starting to burn. Juliet looked down, noticing that the pale skin on her arms was beginning to look flushed.

"Here." Alice pulled a tube of cream out of her bag. "Use this for now." Thanking her, Juliet was about to say, "Better safe than sorry," but stopped herself, thinking that she would sound like her mother. She applied the ointment to her arms and face and handed the tube back to Alice. "I have some in my vanity case, but that's gone ahead with the luggage to the hotel."

Ron squinted up at the cloudless sky. "I'd say it's going to get pretty hot today. Best keep covered up, and maybe wear a sunhat. Better safe than sorry."

Juliet smiled. Now, *he* sounded like her mother; it was obviously a generational thing.

Edna and Jane, having finished their coffee, walked over to Juliet to point out that the ferry was on its way in. "Soon be on Capri," said Jane. "I feel as if we have been travelling forever."

As everyone was finishing up their drinks and preparing to make their way to the jetty, Edna lifted her sunglasses and peered in the direction of the waiters. "Were those men making a nuisance of themselves?" she queried. "Do you need someone to sort them out?"

"No, thank you. It's all right. I coped," said Juliet firmly. "Honestly, it's not a problem."

"Hmm. Well, I've never known anything like it. As I told you, these Italians can be a nuisance, and I've certainly had problems myself, but I've never known anyone to attract quite so much attention." She regarded Juliet with a critical eye. "Perhaps it's your clothes. Maybe a slightly longer skirt? Really, these modern fashions do have a lot to answer for."

Juliet glanced down at the hem of her pink sundress, which ended modestly, she thought, just above her knees. "Well, it's not really a mini skirt," she said defensively. "Some of my friends wear much shorter skirts than this."

"That's as maybe, but they are not in Italy; you must be a bit careful about what you wear here," retorted Edna.

"Mmm," murmured Juliet politely, wondering how she could get away from this annoying woman.

Overhearing Edna's remarks, Alice and Ken moved across to Juliet. "Come on, Juliet, ferry's here," said Ken, taking her arm. Get a move on or we won't get a good seat." Gratefully, Juliet went with the couple to join the horde of passengers making for the gangplank. Edna and Jane, caught up in the crowd, were left quite a long way behind. "Thank you for rescuing me," muttered Juliet.

"Well, I did feel you were being rather overwhelmed," replied Ken. "She's a forceful woman that Edna. You mustn't let her bully you." Alice put an arm around Juliet's shoulders. "What you wear has absolutely nothing to do with her; I think it's a very pretty dress."

Ken looked down at Juliet. "Thank God you weren't wearing a bikini. We would never hear the last of it," he said jokingly. Juliet giggled. "Actually, I do have a two-piece swimming costume in my suitcase."

Ken put a hand over his eyes in mock horror. "I should leave it there. I don't think I could stand the excitement."

★★★

The short journey across the Tyrrhenian Sea to Capri was magical, with turquoise water so clear you could see straight through it like glass. As they landed at the busy Marina Grande, Eric was there, clipboard in hand, gathering everyone together like a demented mother hen rounding up wayward chicks.

"Come along, come along, people," he cried, flapping his hands. "We need to go up a level on the funicular, and there should be a coach waiting to take us to our hotel. Not far to go now. Nearly there. Nearly there."

He held out an arm, waving everyone through the milling crowds, towards the entrance of the cable car. A couple of the older women looked at the almost perpendicular rock face and then back at the funicular with disbelief. "Are we really expected to go up in that? Is it safe, do you think?" they queried.

Eric impatiently waved their fears aside. "Of course, of course, perfectly safe. Been up and down myself loads of times. Wait until you want to go up to Monte Solaro, that's Capri's highest peak. Then it's a trip up from Anacapri by chair lift, and they are *not* enclosed, but the views are amazing. Just amazing…"

He broke off as he saw Ricky queuing at the ticket box. "No need for tickets, no need for tickets," he cried, "we have a group pass. Come on, come on, there's an empty car on the funicular, so if some of you go in that and wait for me at the top, I'll come up in the next free car with the rest of the party."

The two nervous women looked at each other. "Well, if that's the only way up, I suppose we must, but I think I'll give the highest peak a miss," muttered Eva.

Somehow, all twenty members of the group eventually got to Capri's Piazza Umberto and piled onto a rickety bus, which slowly climbed along steep, heart-stopping hairpin bends up to Anacapri, where hotel rooms, their luggage and hot baths awaited them.

Chapter Five

THE VILLA Florentina epitomised the spirit of southern Italy. Set back from a quiet road behind a high stone wall, the attractive building was washed in pale blue and covered with tumbling purple and pink bougainvillea, the beautiful flowers that abound along the Amalfi coast. Arched windows opened onto balconies decorated with pots of scarlet, white and hot pink geraniums, while surrounding it all were beautiful formal gardens with a glimpse of the sea beyond.

Juliet was equally enchanted when she was shown into her ground-floor room by a polite and efficient maid. Rough, white painted walls with a cool tiled floor strewn with blue and white cotton mats and French windows opening onto a tiny terrace filled with terracotta pots of highly perfumed flowers. The bed had a colourful patchwork quilt thrown over it, and there were several pieces of local pottery with a particularly imposing Capo di Monte wall plaque depicting the Virgin and child that rather took Juliet's fancy.

She was slowly unpacking her suitcase while contemplating whether she could buy a piece of Capo di Monte and get it home without breaking it, when there was a quiet tap on one of the long windows. Standing on the terrace was an old man with weather-beaten skin the colour of rich mahogany.

"Gardener," he said curtly by way of explanation and held out a crisp white envelope. Inside was a note from someone called

Enzo de Martins inviting her to one of the local bars where he would be singing.

"Who is he? How does he know my name, and how does he know I'm here?" a bewildered Juliet asked the old man. But he merely shrugged his shoulders, shook his head, and gave a toothless grin. "No English," he said simply and hobbled away through the garden. Juliet watched his departure thoughtfully before carefully re-reading the note, written in careful sloping script on thick, expensive paper.

It's a joke, she decided after a couple of minutes' deliberation. Anyway, she had no intention of going off to an unknown bar at the invitation of a man she had never met. Memories of her mother's worries about her being kidnapped and forced into prostitution flashed through her mind. Very unlikely, she thought tartly and, dropping the note into a wastepaper basket, departed cheerfully to have a refreshing bath.

Lying back in the scented water, Juliet pondered the unexpected invitation, recalling her mother's insistence that she carried a small pepper pot in her handbag whenever she went out alone in the evening just in case she should be accosted by a man. "Shake that in his face and run while he is sneezing," said Mary solemnly.

Juliet had groaned, amused and exasperated in equal measure. Her mother couldn't be serious, but it seemed Mary was, and to avoid yet another pointless row, Juliet had acquiesced, tucking the pot into the bottom of her bag 'just in case.'

Maybe I should have brought my pepper pot to Italy, she thought, but honestly, I don't think there will be anything I can't handle. Italian men, while rather flirty, came across as admiring and respectful rather than threatening. Apart from the bottom pincher at the airport, of course, that pinch had really hurt, leaving a faint purple bruise where the man's fingers had squeezed her flesh.

All thoughts of Signore de Martins' note were banished from her mind as she flicked through her clothes looking for a suitable dress to wear for dinner. After much deliberation, she plumped for a turquoise blue sleeveless shift, which complemented her red hair and green eyes; how pleased her mother would be if she could see her wearing that.

With a bit of time to spare, she decided to pile her hair up into a beehive, adding kirby grips and copious amounts of hairspray to keep it in place. After a lot of practise she had learnt how to do a beehive hairdo properly, and although it took ages and was very fiddly, she thought it looked quite good. I'll need to wash it again in the morning to get all the spray and back-combing out, she thought idly as she walked down to the lounge where everyone was gathering for drinks before dinner.

During the enjoyable evening that followed, getting to know other members of the group, choosing field trips, and discussing camera shots with a woman who took pictures for a gardening magazine, Juliet totally forgot the curious note; but the following morning, there was another message left for her at the hotel reception desk.

"Signore de Martins left this for you, Miss Campbell," said the *patron,* holding out an envelope as she walked into the lobby.

"Who on earth is he?" asked Juliet, perplexed, tearing open the envelope and frowning as she scanned its contents.

Signore Fabrizio laughed, looking at her over his half-moon spectacles. "Oh, Enzo de Martins is our local celebrity. He is a singer – a very good singer, he is becoming quite famous – and it is fortunate for us that he is here in Capri for the summer. Then he goes off to Naples, Rome, Paris, and Las Vegas. He travels all over the world singing with his guitar. I understand he wants you to go and hear him sing."

"But why?"

The *patron* raised his bushy eyebrows in obvious surprise.

"Why not? Most young ladies would jump at the chance to be invited by Enzo de Martins."

"Well, not me," said Juliet firmly. Putting the envelope down on the desk she ran quickly down the steps to join her group on a visit to some highly recommended private gardens.

Staring after her, Signore Fabrizio shook his head in bemusement. What an unusual girl…but then, she hadn't yet met the man in question. He wondered what Enzo would make of a girl who just wasn't interested in him.

Chapter Six

THE NEXT day the group's nine photographers were having a quiet morning. The artists had left early to capture some particularly ravishing views of the rocky Amalfi coastline while the serious botanists were enjoying a lecture with an expert on Capri flora.

Juliet joined those having coffees and ices on the piazza in Capri town, sitting down next to Eric, who was wearing yet another of his brightly coloured shirts. Did he have a suitcase full of them, she wondered.

It was still quite early, but the dazzling Italian sun was already climbing slowly in the sky and it was beginning to feel hot. Juliet, who was wearing her pink sundress without its bolero, noticed that her usually pale skin already had a slight tan. She felt quite pleased.

"I never usually get a suntan," she told Nancy and Ron, who were sitting opposite her. "I usually just go red and burn."

Nancy nodded. "I'm the same; I'm always very pale. She pointed to her large floppy sunhat. "That's why I'm wearing this; not prepared to take the chance. It would be nice to sit in the sun and not worry about the consequences," she said, looking over at a few members of the group who had darker complexions and were already happily lapping up the ultraviolet rays.

As they sat watching the world go by, Alice nudged husband Ken and whispered: "Look at that old gentleman over there."

"Good heavens," said Ken, and everyone swivelled round to watch the elderly man who was sitting at one of the café tables on the opposite side of the square. He was leaning on a stout stick with a small coffee and a brandy on the table in front of him while passing children curtseyed and bowed as they passed. Every so often he patted a child on the head as if giving a blessing.

"Do you think he is royalty?" asked Alice. "More likely the town mayor," suggested someone else.

Eric, who was demolishing a limoncello ice with great gusto, stopped in the middle of a mouthful and said: "Oh, no, you know who that is. It's Gracie Field's husband, Boris. Well, I suppose you could say Gracie and Boris *are* royalty in these parts! And do you know, his surname – Alperovici – is an anagram of I Love Capri."

Everyone then recalled that the Lancashire lass from Rochdale, who had made her name as an international singer, had bought a villa on Capri and made local resident Boris her third husband.

"They say he is the love of her life," said Eric. "The love of her life!"

"Well!" Alice was captivated. "I call that a real fairy tale."

Ken was less easily impressed. "Doesn't stop her charging a pound for members of the public to use her private beach, he blustered. "A pound, indeed. Daylight robbery."

"Yes, but when you consider how steep and rocky the coastline is around Capri, I suppose it might be worth paying a pound to go on a beach that gives you easy access to the water so you can swim," argued fellow photographer Thomas. "I've spoken to quite a few tourists who say it's a lovely beach and well worth a pound. I must say, I did think about it myself."

"Hmm," Ken was not convinced. "A fool and his money are soon parted!"

"Ken!" gasped Alice. "Really, that was rude!" Both men were smiling. "No offence meant," said Ken. "None taken," replied Thomas equitably.

"But our Gracie is a clever lady," pointed out Eva, one of the nervous cable car travellers. "There's no toilet on the beach, so you must go off and use the ones in the town and then pay another pound if you want to return to the beach. Sounds like a money-spinner to me!"

Everyone laughed and the general chatter started again with plans for the afternoon's activities, so Juliet was totally unaware of a tall Italian in an immaculate white suit and dark glasses walking across the piazza, accompanied by a couple of men with the physique of nightclub bouncers.

Stopping at Juliet's table, the man removed his sunglasses and gazing sternly down at her demanded without preamble: "Why do you ignore my notes?"

Juliet was astounded; so this was the famous singer…Enzo, someone or other, she thought vaguely. He was a lot younger than she had imagined, probably in his mid-twenties, but radiating self-confidence and speaking almost perfect English with the slight hint of an American twang.

The rest of the group watched open-mouthed as the man who looked like a film star, a corkscrew of dark hair falling artfully over one eye, stared intently at her as if nobody else was there. Even Eric seemed rooted to his chair.

"Please come to Bar Russe tonight," said Enzo de Martins. "You will enjoy it, and I have a song to sing just for you."

Juliet, scarlet with embarrassment at once again being the focus of attention – this is becoming a habit, she thought wildly – managed to blurt: "But why? Why are you so keen for me to go?"

"I saw you by the harbour in Sorrento the other day and then on the ferry to Capri. I thought, I still think, you are very beautiful, and I would like to get to know you better." He had very dark blue eyes and the deep, gravelly voice of someone who spent much of their time in smoky bars and nightclubs.

Juliet, who had never been considered beautiful in her life, was acutely aware that her fellow travellers were watching in utter amazement. She gave a feeble giggle born out of nerves and confusion.

"Why do you snigger?" demanded Enzo crossly. "Do you not believe me?"

"Of course, I…"

"Then come tonight."

Juliet took a deep breath and paused, weighing up the options, before agreeing. "Alright."

"Good. Thank you." There was a sudden gentleness in his manner as he nodded with satisfaction, pushing the curl of hair back from his eyes. Biting his lip thoughtfully, he continued to stare down at her in the most disconcerting way, his eyes never leaving her face.

He was incredibly attractive with black curly hair, perfect cheekbones, and faint violet shadows under the dark blue eyes. Juliet, beginning to squirm, not knowing quite where to look, had to fight the most astonishing urge to reach out and touch him. Appalled, she quickly clamped her hands firmly onto the arms of her chair.

As if suddenly recalling his manners, Enzo stepped back a couple of paces and said formally: "*Grazie.* Thank you. Signore Fabrizio at your hotel will have the directions." Giving her a disarming smile, he said: "I will wait for you at nine o'clock. *Arrivederci signorina.*"

Eric and the photographers collectively heaved an audible sigh of relief as the singer rejoined his companions and walked off towards the funicular.

"Will you go?" asked Eric curiously, breaking the ensuing silence. "Some would consider Enzo de Martins more famous than our Gracie. It's a bit of an honour to be singled out. Definitely. A bit of an honour."

All eyes turned to Juliet. "Absolutely not!" She was more

shaken by the episode than she cared to admit. She'd almost reached out and touched his hand, for heaven's sake, whatever was she thinking. Thank goodness she hadn't.

"I have no intention of going; I had to say I would, just to get rid of him. Anyway, I bet I'm not the only girl he asks to go and hear him sing."

A gleam of amusement lurked in Eric's eyes, but he said nothing.

"It's very romantic," sighed Alice. "And he's terribly handsome." She gave Juliet a conspiratorial wink: "Lucky girl, he's gorgeous. I would certainly go if he'd asked me. Despite what Ken says, I'm sure it's your long red hair he's fallen for."

"You women," said Ken, laughing. Looking fondly at his wife, he put an arm around her as everyone prepared to return to the hotel for lunch. "An attractive Italian and you all turn to jelly. Well, we can't say that Juliet doesn't provide more than her fair share of entertainment."

Juliet blushed faintly and gave a perfunctory smile, thanking her lucky stars that Edna and Jane had missed the exchange with Enzo de Martins, although they'd doubtless hear all about it from the others. It would furnish those two with ammunition for the rest of the holiday.

★★★

If Juliet assumed she had seen the last of Enzo de Martins, she was wrong. Later that afternoon, she was looking longingly at some bags in the window of the Gucci boutique, mentally calculating if she could afford to buy one. Turning round, she was startled to see Enzo standing behind her with a mischievous smile on his face.

"Well, *Giulietta,* we meet twice in one day." He looked deeply into her eyes before gently running a well-manicured thumbnail slowly down her cheek. "Tonight, it will be third time lucky."

Dismayed, Juliet stepped rapidly back out of his reach and, stuttering in embarrassment, said: "Signore de Martins, I'm…I'm terribly sorry, but I can't come tonight. There is…um…there is something else I must do."

"But you said you would come!" Enzo glowered at her, looking sulky, like a spoilt child, his dark brows knitted together in a frown. "And if I hadn't found you now, would you have told me? No! You would have left me to wait for you. That is unforgivable." His gravelly voice now sounded more like a growl.

Sticking out his lower lip – was that a pout wondered Juliet – his handsome face was uncompromising. Those dark blue eyes, narrowed now and almost black with irritation, were boring into her as if he could see into her soul.

It was obvious he was not used to being thwarted, particularly by a woman. Juliet guessed that women were usually only too eager to do whatever he wanted. Signor Fabrizio had assured her that most young ladies would be delighted to receive an invitation from Enzo.

She could feel herself starting to shake with nerves and suddenly felt surprisingly vulnerable; he was obviously very annoyed. Putting her hands to her flaming cheeks, she whispered: "I'm really sorry."

Abruptly changing tack, Enzo gave her a dazzling smile. "Then you will come? I will send an escort for you."

Juliet became aware that passers-by were beginning to stop and stare at what they thought was a lovers' quarrel, and no one likes a bit of *amore* more than a romantic Italian. There was added curiosity because many people knew exactly who Enzo was, and they had no intention of missing out on their favourite singer having a tiff with a girl.

With typical English self-consciousness and as someone who would do anything rather than draw attention to herself, Juliet found it impossible to let such an embarrassing situation continue.

"Right," she said quickly. "Yes, I will come. You don't have to send someone to pick me up. I'll find my way. I'll ask Signore Fabrizio for directions."

Enzo regarded her sardonically, his head on one side, his lips pursed: "Really? Are you sure?"

Juliet nodded. "Promise. Cross my heart and hope to die!" The childish expression seemed a bit incongruous, but Enzo appeared to accept it as a valid promise. His face softening, he beamed at her, and as the atmosphere lightened, the onlookers melted away: 'Nothing more to see here.'

Gently squeezing her arm, Enzo said quietly: "You have made me very happy. *Grazie mille*. I will see you at nine o'clock. *Ciao-Ciao*." And he was gone.

Juliet stood transfixed, watching him stride quickly across the piazza. What was happening? She felt like pinching herself to check she wasn't dreaming. Why was someone like Enzo de Martins chasing after her? He could surely get any woman he wanted to go and hear him sing.

Chewing her fingernail thoughtfully, she reasoned that he probably made passes at women all the time. Ken had pointed out in Sorrento that Italian men liked women, and Eric had warned her they were all flirts. Enzo doubtless saw her as just another conquest, particularly as she hadn't immediately succumbed to his charms.

She recalled June saying she would never appear too eager to go out with a boy, even if she really fancied him. "It makes them so much more grateful when you eventually say yes."

Juliet, always desperately seeking affection and longing to be liked, would immediately accept any invitation a boy offered, and so often, these meetings did not end well.

"You need to stay cool. Just say no a few times," advised June when yet another of Juliet's dates ended in disappointment. "The less keen you are, the more eager they get."

Maybe at long last, I have learned not to jump every time a man shows an interest, thought Juliet, even if he *is* an attractive Italian. Mind you, it did help knowing she had Mike waiting for her at home; as she had told Alice and Ken, she was not in Italy looking for romance.

Wandering slowly back to Villa Florentina in the bright afternoon sunlight, Juliet ran through the situation in her mind. She would keep her promise and go to Bar Russe that evening; how dangerous could it be? Admittedly, he was very charming and undeniably handsome, but she was determined that a one-off visit to hear him sing would be where it ended. She had no desire to become another notch on Enzo de Martins' bedpost.

Suddenly, she laughed aloud at her own foolishness. She was taking this far too seriously; what had happened to her sense of humour? Italian men liked women, and flirting was a part of life. It was merely a casual invitation to go to a bar and enjoy some music. He most likely needed to boost his audience and probably had invited other people as well. Notches on bedposts were a figment of her over-active imagination.

Feeling much happier, Juliet arrived back at the hotel and went off to have a luxurious bath and get ready for a pleasant evening. It would make a nice change from spending all her time with middle-aged botanists.

Chapter Seven

BAR RUSSE turned out to be a large candlelit room with a long counter sporting an enormous silver espresso coffee machine and cloth-covered tables, all occupied by young couples. Others had squeezed into the closely packed white-painted tables and chairs arranged outside the folded-back open doors, while those not lucky enough to have secured a seat were sprawled on the grass.

A chalkboard propped up against a gargantuan flowerpot overflowing with purple bougainvillea advertised Enzo's performance, and Juliet quickly realised that he was the reason most of them were there.

A couple of smartly dressed waiters weaved between tables serving Chianti in raffia-covered bottles together with large platters of antipasti for the expectant audience to enjoy while they waited for Enzo's appearance, and the chatter and laughter were deafening.

Startled by the unexpected crowd, Juliet had to admit that she had totally misunderstood the situation. She was expecting a quiet evening in a local bar, listening to Enzo sing a few songs. This, it appeared, was going to be a full-scale performance, a far bigger event than she had anticipated. He certainly wasn't short of an audience.

Beginning to regret her promise and feeling the creeping tendrils of anxiety, Juliet was contemplating returning to the hotel. As she hesitated, Enzo suddenly appeared at her side and, dropping a light kiss on top of her head, murmured: "I am so happy you have come, *Giulietta*." The angry man she had encountered that afternoon had completely disappeared.

Holding her at arms' length, he slowly looked her up and down, carefully scrutinising her short, full-skirted, dark green dress and the soft white cardigan she had thrown around her shoulders to guard against the balmy evening breezes; she had left her waterfall of hair hanging loosely down her back.

"You look beautiful," he said with approval and tucking a hand under her elbow, steered her inside to a small table beside the counter, beckoning to a waiter who swooped over with a glass of red wine and a plate of grissini, cheese, and olives. Smiling her thanks, she noticed a small '*reservato*' card on the table. Juliet's mind once again went into overdrive: he had kept a place for her. Why?

Slowly drinking her wine and gazing around the packed venue, Juliet recognised a few English people she'd seen at Villa Florentina. She wasn't surprised exactly, but it made her once again consider his popularity. How strange that she hadn't heard of him before.

After wandering around shaking hands and chatting with some of the audience, Enzo disappeared for a while before returning, slowly strumming his guitar, to be greeted by a storm of clapping, foot stamping, and wolf whistles.

He stood quietly, hands on hips for a few moments, smiling and nodding to acknowledge his welcome, before opening with one of Elvis Presley's rhythm and blues numbers, *Lawdy, Miss Clawdy,* followed by the popular Jimmy Reed chart hit *Baby What You Want Me to Do*.

The appreciative audience went wild. He really does have an amazing voice, thought Juliet as Enzo deftly took the tempo down and sang two Elvis ballads, *Love Me Tender* and *Can't Help Falling in Love*.

He paused to introduce his backing musicians: Marco, a young Italian guitarist with dreadlocks and a butterscotch tan, and an older drummer called Raf, who was American and sported a goatee beard and shoulder-length greying hair pulled back into a ponytail. They were, said Enzo, among the best in the business and had been working with him for a couple of years.

Most of the fans knew them well, and the duo received an enthusiastic reception, which Raf accepted with a wave of his hand and a loud drum roll while Marco strummed a few chords.

They then reprised *Baby What You Want Me to Do,* giving it a long instrumental introduction, allowing all three to showcase their musical expertise. The ecstatic crowd tapped their feet, clapping in time to the beat, while some of the couples outside danced on the grass.

As Enzo moved seamlessly from one popular song to another, Juliet was able to study him more closely. He had exchanged his white suit for an equally immaculate white shirt worn with black jeans, leather jacket and fashionable suede desert boots, looking much more American than Italian, although his high cheekbones, beautifully shaped brows and those unforgettable dark blue eyes were certainly Latin, as were his enviably long dark lashes, which any girl would be proud to own. He also had an endearing smile and very white and even teeth that were surely an advertisement for American dentistry. A devastating Italian American mix decided Juliet.

After singing several well-known Frank Sinatra ballads and more Presley numbers, interspersed with a few Buddy Holly songs and romantic Italian and Spanish medleys, Enzo asked for requests, which came thick and fast.

There's a touch of Elvis about him, thought Juliet as tumultuous applause erupted at the end of another set, not just because of his voice and the songs he sings but also the way he looks. Elvis with curly hair and without the famous sideburns.

Enzo was clearly tremendously popular with his Capri fans, some of whom had come over from Sorrento for the evening. He had a captivating singing style and was very assured and relaxed, as if among friends.

Casually shrugging off his leather jacket and letting it fall to the floor, he rolled back his shirt cuffs, handing his guitar to a girl at one of the tables while he went off to find a new plectrum. He stopped for a moment to exchange a few words with Raf and Marco, and as the drummer twirled one of his sticks in the air, drawling, "Hey man, it's true, I'm telling yer, she's a foxy lady, " Marco gave a loud barking guffaw and Enzo, shaking with silent laughter, moved on.

Coming back to pick up his guitar, Enzo put an arm around the delighted girl who was beside herself at being so close to him, saying, "Thank you, baby." Encouraged by enthusiastic wolf whistles, he put a hand on each side of her face, giving her a kiss before moving to sit casually on a bar stool. That stray curl of hair had once again fallen into his eyes, Juliet noticed, and he emanated spine-tingling waves of sexual magnetism.

More Presley, Holly and Sinatra numbers followed, with Enzo keeping up amusing repartee between sets, not only with the exuberant audience but also with his musicians. He was very spontaneous, and his wicked sense of humour, infectious laugh, and gentle teasing provoked howls of amusement as Enzo joked with the men and flirted outrageously with the women. He certainly appreciates his fans, thought Juliet. He seems a genuinely nice guy.

Enzo had the natural gift of making every woman in the room feel he was singing only for her, and looking at their entranced faces, Juliet realised the secret behind his success was not only his wonderful voice but also that he clearly liked women and they knew it.

She spotted the two bouncers who had accompanied Enzo

in the piazza that morning. Dressed in matching black t-shirts and trousers, they were obviously policing the venue, and Juliet wondered whether they were there at the behest of Bar Russe's *patron* or if they were on Enzo's payroll. And what about the musicians? Was he famous enough to have a retinue: he certainly didn't behave as if he was.

Eventually, there was a lull, and getting off his stool, Enzo wandered over to Juliet and asked: "And you, *signorina,* do you have a request?"

As everyone turned to look at her, she blushed, embarrassed by her sudden visibility. Realising her discomfort, Enzo said quietly, "I have the perfect song; I have saved it for you," and he broke into *Quando, Quando, Quando,* a smooth romantic ballad capturing the anticipation of love.

Enzo sang it first in Italian and then softly in English. As he sang, Juliet gazed down at the table, pleating the edge of the cloth between her fingers, reluctant to look up and meet his eyes. It was as if no one else was in the room; the electricity between them was palpable. She clung to the edge of the table, her heart hammering, her palms sticky. This is nonsense, she told herself firmly; she was behaving as if she were a silly young girl at an Elvis gig.

Taking long slow breaths to recover her composure, she reminded herself of Enzo's ability to make every woman think he was singing only for her and joined in the ecstatic applause as the song ended.

Enzo glanced across at her and smiled. There was an indecipherable expression in his eyes, and Juliet's heart turned a ludicrous somersault. It would be so easy to fall in love with him, she thought. You're going to have to be very careful, said a warning voice in her head. This is moving much too fast.

During a short interval, Juliet wondered if Enzo might come over to talk to her, but he was nowhere to be seen and she felt a slight flutter of disappointment. Don't be so stupid, chided the disapproving voice. You're not interested remember, notches on bedposts!

Enzo sauntered back after about fifteen minutes, looking refreshed and ready for the rest of the show, which he devoted to songs from Frank Sinatra films. These were particularly popular with his avid fans, and the endless requests for favourite numbers continued until the end when he finished with another rendering of *Quando, Quando, Quando*.

Is it my imagination or is he watching me? Juliet asked herself. It was difficult to be sure, but she certainly had a twitchy feeling that those intense blue eyes were fixed on her.

When all the clapping and cheering and encores had finished, and the happy, noisy throng was preparing to leave the bar and make its unsteady way back down to the piazza, Enzo came over to ask Juliet if she would stay while he spoke to a few people. "There are some things to check and a few hands to shake, then I'll take you back to your hotel."

As she waited, one of the bar staff brought her over a small glass of Limoncello. Taking leisurely sips, she watched Marco and Raf packing up their instruments and the waiters clearing up and collecting plates and glasses from the tables. Raf sketched a salute in her direction as he and Marco left.

Eventually, Enzo came to find her. "I've got something very unusual to show you," he said, and as his hand closed firmly over hers, she felt a shiver of excitement.

Leading her out of the bar, he took her down to Marina Piccolo, where an enormous silver moon had emerged from behind translucent evening clouds and was now hanging low in the sky just above the Faraglioni sea stacks. Juliet caught her breath in wonder; she'd never seen a moon like it. She felt it was almost close enough to touch. Taking a mental snapshot, Juliet knew she would remember this magical moment for the rest of her life.

"Do you like it?" asked Enzo, putting his arm around her.

"It's perfect," she said, her voice wavering, still staring at the impossibly huge sphere suspended so close to the water; she felt unexpectedly emotional. "It's difficult to believe it's real."

"It is very beautiful. Like you," said Enzo. She couldn't see his eyes in the dark, but she could feel he was smiling.

As they turned back towards Bar Russe, Enzo pulled her into his arms, feeling the tension in her body as he held her hard against his chest. "So, when will you be mine, *Giulietta*?" he whispered, lightly brushing his lips across hers.

It was a disturbingly intimate gesture, and Juliet felt a shudder of pleasure shoot through her as she waited for the follow-up kiss. It didn't come. Like June, Enzo was skilled in the art of arousing desire.

Releasing her from his arms, he held her hand, rotating his thumb on her palm as they returned to the bar in silence. Looking very serious, he appeared to be engrossed in his private thoughts. Juliet was confused; she was getting mixed messages. Why hadn't he kissed her? Didn't he want to? She certainly wanted to kiss him.

Juliet's plan for a one-off visit to Bar Russe went quickly awry when Enzo asked her to meet him there again the following evening. She didn't even hesitate before agreeing. *I'm already in too deep, he's absolutely the most gorgeous man I have ever met,* she admitted, deliberately ignoring that annoying inner voice once again warning her to be careful.

Slipping his jacket around her shoulders, Enzo walked Juliet back to Villa Florentina. The feel of his jacket, heavy and warm with an elusive suggestion of his aftershave, made her feel jittery and excited.

The dark velvet sky was studded with a million stars, and that incredible moon seemed to be following them. Really, thought Juliet amusedly, *this is just like being in a romantic film. All the components are here…star-lit sky, huge moon, the sound of waves* lapping against the shore, and an incredibly handsome man by my side: she almost expected a hidden choir to start singing.

Except amazingly, this was not make-believe. It was happening to her right now. Would he stop and kiss her? She was slightly scared at how much she wanted him to. His lips brushing hers and the thumb rubbing her palm had left her stirred up and wanting more.

Enzo interlaced his fingers with hers, and as they walked, she kept taking covert sideway glances at him, but he appeared preoccupied and somewhat subdued.

Once back at the hotel, he removed his jacket from her shoulders and, courteously kissing her hand, said: *"Buona notte, Giulietta,"* before opening the door and seeing her safely inside.

Juliet felt like screaming with frustration. He hadn't even kissed her properly. She felt agitated, her nerves as taut as the strings of Enzo's guitar. Emotionally exhausted, she went to bed, but her heightened state of desire left her running the events of the evening through her mind like a cine film and sleep deserted her. Without the invitation for tomorrow she would have assumed he just wasn't interested.

★★★

It was inevitable that Juliet would fall heavily for Enzo de Martins, even though she kept telling herself she wasn't in Italy looking for romance. Everything was right. The location was one of the most beautiful islands in the world; the man was an attractive and rich Italian who had learnt from birth how to make women feel special and, as a bonus, had a singing voice to die for. Add to that mix Juliet, who was ripe for a love affair after her tepid relationship with Mike, and the outcome was a foregone conclusion.

Chapter Eight

THE FOLLOWING afternoon, Juliet was making her way to Villa Florentina's well-appointed sitting room for a slide show and talk on the botanical gardens of Augustus before a visit the next day.

Because she was meeting Enzo that evening, she was slightly disconcerted to find him in the hotel lobby, leaning up against the reception desk, deep in conversation with Signor Fabrizio.

She felt her stomach lurch when he gave his engaging smile as he saw her and came over to kiss her cheek. "*Ciao, cara,* I am here to take you for an adventure."

"Adventure?" Juliet looked puzzled, and the *patron* laughed. "It is a surprise. Do not worry, Miss Campbell. I will inform your group that you will not be joining them."

Juliet was about to point out that altering arrangements on her behalf without consultation was a bit high-handed. Then, remembering Enzo's rapid mood change yesterday, she stayed silent. She didn't want to upset him again, especially if he had arranged a surprise for her, and she certainly didn't want a repeat of his angry frustration when she said she wasn't going to Bar Russe. Anyway, there was no way she was going to refuse a date with Enzo. If it was a choice between him and a talk on botanical gardens, Enzo won hands down.

The insistent voice in her head was once again on its high horse: he's unquestionably dictatorial, it warned. You're going to have to fall in with all his plans if you want to keep him happy.

I like having a man who knows what he wants and takes the lead, countered Juliet, thinking of all those depressing times when boyfriends had expected her to suggest what to do and where to go. I like having decisions made for me. It makes me feel cosseted and more…feminine. His self-assurance is exciting. I've never known anyone like him.

Seeing that Enzo was wearing a blue open-necked shirt tucked into denim jeans, with espadrilles on his bare feet, Juliet asked: "Do I need to change?"

She had no idea if her lemon-yellow linen shift dress and flat silver sandals would be suitable attire for whatever Enzo had arranged.

He considered her clothes seriously for a moment, and then kissing his thumb and blowing the kiss towards her, he said: "*Bellissima*, you are perfect as you are."

"Perfect," agreed Signore Fabrizio with a smile, hurrying off to find Eric to inform him that the group would be one participant short that afternoon.

Well, he thought with a chuckle of amusement, Enzo is certainly on good form. It didn't take him long to change that young lady's mind.

★★★

Enzo took Juliet down to the marina, where a small motor launch was moored in the tiny cove just below the waterfront restaurants.

"We go to one of the islands where there are no other people, and I will show you my wooden house," Enzo informed her nonchalantly, as if sailing off to a deserted island was an everyday occurrence.

"Wooden house?" queried Juliet, intrigued, but Enzo just

looked mysterious and refused to explain. "It will spoil the surprise; wait and see."

In contrast to the rocky Amalfi coastline, the island, just across the water from Capri, had a strip of sandy beach bordering the crystal-clear sea.

"It doesn't have a proper name; I just call it The Island," Enzo told her as he secured the launch to a small slipway and helped her out. He pointed upwards. "Now look, *cara,* what do you think?"

Perched above the sand on a small bluff was a beach hut that wouldn't have looked out of place on the Sussex coast. Juliet gasped with amazement. "Goodness, that's not what I was expecting. Where did you get it? Why is it here? Who…"

Enzo laughed, delighted at her confusion. "It reminds you of England, *no?*" he said, adding casually: "It was given to me, a gift from a fan in America."

Juliet quickly glanced at him to see if he was joking, but he was quite serious. Enzo was a handsome and desirable Italian with a stunning voice, and rich women fell over themselves to give him gifts. It was the way of the world as far as he was concerned, and he accepted it without question.

Filled with curiosity, Juliet slipped off her sandals and swinging them in her hand, padded after him across the sand and along a narrow grassy track leading up the steep slope to the hut, which was painted pale green, blending in perfectly with the surrounding terrain.

Halfway up the slope, Enzo turned and held out his hand. "Let me help you; it gets a bit difficult from here." His palm was warm and dry, and Juliet felt an unsettling tingle as she held it. That disturbing longing to kiss him was still there, making her feel breathless and flustered.

At the top, the ubiquitous pink and purple Bougainvillea was much in evidence, as were lemon trees abundant with the fruit found everywhere in southern Italy.

"They match your dress," Enzo pointed out, pulling off a low-hanging lemon and offering it to her, his eyes deliberately locked onto hers, his mouth curved in an enticing smile. "You've got beautiful eyes, *Giulietta*," he said softly. "I could spend all day just gazing into them."

Juliet felt involuntary shivers run down her spine. Heavens, she thought, are all Italian men like this? Judging by the number of passes she had rejected during the short time she had been in Italy, she supposed so yet surely, few could be quite as blatantly seductive as Enzo de Martins. Just the Italian pronunciation of her name gave her goosebumps, and he did it all the time.

The flutter of butterflies started in her stomach as Enzo pulled away a large wooden security bar and unlocked the beach hut door. Inside it was dark and cosy, rather like a nest, thought Juliet, and then felt the colour rush to her face as she realised the implication. I wonder how many women he's brought here.

Throat dry and heart pounding with a dull thud, she caught Enzo's eye and immediately knew what he was planning; he was going to make love to her. Words from the song *Can't Help Falling in Love*, which Enzo had sung at Bar Russe – was it only last night – suddenly drifted through her mind: '*Shall I stay? Would it be a sin? If I can't help falling in love with you.*'

As the butterflies started doing an agitated tap dance, Juliet knew the questions were irrelevant. Sin or not, she was going to stay. The thought of sex with Enzo was overpowering, too tempting to resist. There had to be a first time, and who better to be with than this stunning Italian, who constantly gave her palpitations and that curiously intense yearning to touch and kiss him. It was what she wanted more than anything and just the thought of it was exciting her. For the first time in her life, Juliet was experiencing pure lust.

The miracle was that he was interested enough to *want* to make love to her. It seemed impossible, almost as if she had moved outside her body and was watching all this happening to someone else.

Taking a deep breath in a futile attempt at composure, she stepped slowly into the hut's intimate interior. This is crazy, she thought in rising panic as Enzo closed the door behind her, but when he held out his arms, she rushed into them, pushing herself against him with desire.

His unhurried kiss was very tender, carrying the promise of passion to come. That kiss, which Juliet had been craving since he brushed his lips over hers at Marina Piccolo, was everything she dreamed it would be. She could feel herself melting inside, wishing the moment would go on forever. She was shaking as Enzo led her over to a cushion-covered divan.

He was very gentle with her, knowing instinctively that she was totally inexperienced. He didn't want to frighten this extraordinary girl who was so different from his usual lovers yet had managed, somehow, to completely mesmerise him. Feeling her tremble, he slowly kissed her fingertips one by one, whispering audacious suggestions and breathing softly into her ear until she was calm.

"Relax, *Giulietta*," he murmured. "Trust me, baby. There's no rush. We can take our time. Nothing will happen unless you want it to." She could smell the spicy tang of his cologne and feel the beat of his heart as he kissed her.

Dizzy with desire, Juliet's last thought before completely surrendering herself to intense passion was 'No one ever tells you it is going to be like this.'

★★★

After Enzo had slowly and carefully made love to her, they made love together and now, as he dozed, Juliet lay in his arms, marvelling at this thrilling new world that had opened.

She recalled June's elation when she told Juliet about making love with

Pedro in Spain: "You never forget the first time you have sex," *and her confident:* "You wait until you meet someone you really fancy, then you'll know what I mean."

Well, now she knew. She hadn't expected it to be so exhilarating or that she would enjoy it so much.

Juliet realised Enzo was watching her with a contented smile. Pressing his lips into the palm of her hand, he said softly: "You were wonderful. I had no idea that you were going to be a natural at making love."

Pulling her closer, he added: "Now you can understand why it was so important to me that you came to Bar Russe yesterday. I was sure there was something very special between us, and last night, I knew I was right. I brought you here today because I couldn't wait for you any longer."

Realising how close she had been to giving Bar Russe a miss, Juliet shivered. The future can turn on a sixpence, she thought. A casual decision to do or not do something can change your life.

Chapter Nine

AFTER VISITING The Island, Juliet's interest in flowers waned a little. She still went on group trips and took photographs, but her heart was with Enzo. She spent every evening listening to him singing at Bar Russe before late suppers in tiny restaurants well off the tourist track when they would drink Chianti and Limoncello while Enzo sang the Presley and Sinatra songs she loved.

Occasionally, the restaurant *patron* and other diners joined them to enjoy an impromptu performance, but the best evenings were when Marco, Enzo's backing guitarist, turned up for a jamming session. Juliet found it enthralling to hear two talented musicians bouncing off each other, both musically and verbally.

Juliet liked Marco, who looked like a pirate, his dirty-blond dreadlocks tied with a red bandana and a wicked smile revealing a gap between his front teeth. Enzo told her he was a brilliant guitarist but had never been organised enough to progress his musical career. "Which is my good luck because it means he is free to play for me."

Juliet suspected that the pungent cigarettes Marco was always rolling were spliffs and probably more weed than tobacco. He was rake-thin and restless, often with an untidy roll-up between his fingers or drooping from the corner of his mouth.

Speaking almost fluent English with an engaging Italian accent, he was an amusing raconteur, invariably arriving with stories of exciting escapades. Exactly what you would expect from a pirate, thought Juliet. He was very sweet to her, calling her 'Jew-let' and flirting shamelessly, much to her embarrassment and Enzo's amusement.

Juliet toyed with the idea that if she hadn't met Enzo, she might have been at risk of falling for Marco. Although he didn't have Enzo's good looks, he possessed the same uninhibited animal magnetism, and she found him curiously attractive despite his eccentricities. She knew he was totally unreliable and that he would quickly leave her and move on, nevertheless…

"It is so sad Jew-let that we will never make love together," he told her one evening, pulling a pouty face and gazing soulfully into her eyes.

"Enzo found you first, and I would never take *la ragazza* of a friend, but I am sure we could make beautiful music together, baby, like I do with my guitar."

He gave her a long, considering stare, his narrowed eyes fixed on her face. "You are very foxy, *signorina*. Maybe I will take you to bed anyway. There are rooms upstairs, so we can go right now. I can make you very happy, and with me, all your dreams will come true."

Roaring with laughter, Enzo put his arm around Juliet, who was looking distinctly alarmed. "And suddenly, he's not too worried about taking my girlfriend! Ignore him, *amore*. Not only is he a disgraceful flirt, but he is also stoned. He won't remember any of this tomorrow."

Marco's piratical credentials were endorsed by the fact that he usually arrived with a girl he had picked up on his travels. In another age, Marco would have been a romantic swashbuckler carrying off women without consent; living in the twentieth century, he flaunted a raw sexual energy that so many women found they were unable to resist.

The current acquisition was a French girl called Didi, who

Marco had 'found' in a café in Amalfi. She was petite, dark, and very soignée but spoke neither Italian nor English.

"I really don't know how they communicate," said Enzo, "but she seems to understand what he wants and whatever that is, I'm sure he's getting it."

Juliet tried some of her schoolgirl French on Didi, but their conversation was limited. She had no interest in talking to Juliet and after a few moments, would look sulky and toss her long dark hair, her large green-brown Bardot eyes constantly fixed on Marco.

Enzo found Didi entertaining. "Marco's met his match this time; he's going to have difficulty getting away from her," he said with a grin. "She hasn't yet discovered that he likes boys as well as girls, so that may be his way out. He's charming but promiscuous and sexually indiscriminate."

Other than wondering how Didi would cope with Marco's sexual peccadilloes, Enzo paid her very little attention apart from the mild flirting that all Italian men did so innately. Juliet heaved a sigh of relief, still unsure how she managed to hold his interest.

Most evenings after supper, they made love in the spacious apartment overlooking the sea that Enzo was renting for the season.

Juliet was finding sex with Enzo addictive, so enticing it was becoming like a drug. His confidence and expertise as a lover made her feel attractive and desirable, and she was learning how to reciprocate and keep him satisfied. He had also helped her to perfect the skill of intense and passionate French kissing. She was, Enzo told her with a suggestive smile, an excellent pupil.

Afterwards, he would sit propped against pillows on the bed and sing to her. *Can't Help Falling in Love* had become their special song, an evocative expression of their relationship.

Like most Italian men, Enzo had a very passionate nature and was inherently romantic. Juliet, used to English reserve, was besotted. Drowning in happiness, she continued to ignore the irritating voice that insisted she had stepped into a fantasy world that could not possibly last.

Enzo was always holding and kissing her, stroking her long red hair, telling her how beautiful her eyes were and how much he enjoyed making love to her – things she felt sure no Englishman would ever say, however devoted. Under the influence of his admiration, she could feel herself growing in confidence.

Juliet pushed to the back of her mind any thoughts of having to return home. How could she possibly go and leave all this behind? More to the point, how could she leave him?

★★★

Enzo liked women and delighted in every moment of intimacy, from the initial kick of desire to romantic after-sex cuddles.

He knew without any hint of arrogance that he was a skilful lover who enjoyed giving pleasure as much as he relished receiving it. Consequently, there were always women of all ages eager to go to bed with him.

He had been sleeping with girlfriends – and a few times, their mothers too – since his teens; occasionally just a one-night stand, more often a few weeks of gratification before he moved on. In all that time, he had never made a declaration of love.

Even at the height of passion he had refrained from saying 'ti amo' to a partner because he knew, with absolute certainty, that one day he would want to say it to someone and mean it. When a term of endearment was needed, he would murmur 'ti voglio bene,' which assured women of his affection for them but didn't commit him in any way.

Chapter Ten

ENZO DID indeed have an international following; he was particularly popular in the States, as well as on continental Europe, and he knew all the famous and influential people on Capri.

Within days, he had swept Juliet up from a rather mundane world and set her carefully down in the middle of his cosmopolitan lifestyle. He was an exhilarating companion, and as someone who had grown up totally lacking in confidence, Juliet found his complete self-assurance irresistible.

While Capri's glitterati had become used to seeing Enzo with a succession of different women, they appeared unfazed by the fact that Juliet had become a more permanent fixture, and she was accepted as belonging to him.

Meanwhile, members of the botany group watched with growing misgiving as Juliet changed from a chrysalis to a butterfly before their eyes.

A rather shy, quiet, and diffident girl was suddenly replaced by a confident young woman, obviously radiant with love. "And who knows what else?" demanded Edna Lowe bitterly to her cousin Jane.

"Hush, dear," said Jane. "You have no proof that the girl is involved in *that* way."

"Huh!" sniffed Edna. "Just look at her face. Only a man can make a girl glow like that. Anyway, I thought she had a boyfriend back in England. That's what she said."

Edna was miffed. She had tried to take Juliet under her wing and look after her, offering friendship and the benefit of her considerable botanical knowledge, all to no avail. Like most young girls these days, she had simply gone off with a man. Typical!

Alice, who had become very fond of Juliet, was about to challenge Edna and tell her that nothing Juliet did had anything to do with her, but a warning glance from Ken stopped her in her tracks.

"Better not to get involved, pet," he murmured. Alice bit her lip, determined to assure Juliet of her personal support as soon as the opportunity arose.

It was Eric who eventually took Juliet aside and asked her if she knew what she was doing.

"It's not my place to interfere in your private life, but I am responsible for you as a member of my group, and I am concerned, definitely concerned, that you have become so wrapped up with Enzo de Martins," he said, putting a frothy coffee in front of her as they sat in the hotel's elegant garden under a spreading acacia tree, its highly perfumed blossom wafting around them.

The gentle rhythmic chirruping of cicadas faded into the background as Juliet braced herself for what Eric had to say. She regarded the grey-haired man opposite her with mild affection. His colourful Hawaiian shirts were almost part of his personality, and he had been an attentive and informative group leader – almost a father figure. She would listen to his advice, but it wouldn't deflect her from the decision she had made.

"I've known Enzo for some time," Eric continued, wrinkling his brow, "not well, admittedly, but as you yourself said that day on the piazza, you're not the first pretty visitor he's taken an interest in."

Juliet regarded him steadily. "I know," she said, carefully scooping the foam off the top of her coffee and licking the spoon. "He told me, but I do believe him when he says I'm different from all the others."

She stared at Eric reflectively for a second or two and then added: "I think I may stay on here when our visit is up. Enzo has a room for me at a friend's hotel, and I have enough money to tide me over for a while."

★★★

Juliet failed to mention that Enzo had suggested she share his Capri apartment for the next few months.

"Matteo has a room for you, but it would be so much nicer if you moved in here with me, *Giulietta*," he said.

After a very satisfactory session of lovemaking, they were curled up together on his vast bed, discussing Juliet's plans to return home at the weekend. Under Enzo's expert guidance, Juliet had become much more adventurous in bed, his evident delight in her dissolving the final vestiges of shyness.

"Why must you go? Stay here with me, we will be very happy together." He let a tiny pause fall before adding with an impudent grin: "No need for me to take anyone else to the wooden house!"

Juliet had turned over and was lying on her side with her back to him, her long hair fanned out over the pillow when Enzo leaned across to kiss her and said softly: *"ti amo molto."*

Juliet caught her breath, feeling a bit off balance. It was the first time he had said he loved her in a romantic way. He was always very ardent but had previously only used the more casually affectionate *"ti voglio bene."*

She rolled over and tilting back her head to look up at him, saw he was unusually solemn.

"You've never said that before, are you sure?" she asked, thinking as she did so, silly question, what if he says no?

"I've always known I would never say it unless it was true. I do love you very much. It was almost *colpo di fulmine*. I knew it when

I sang *Quando* for you that first night at Bar Russe. I think you felt it, too; I saw it in your eyes. Our souls recognised each other."

Good heavens, what a man: love at first sight and the meeting of souls. Juliet felt helpless with desire. She had never heard anything so passionately romantic in her life.

"*Anch'io ti amo,*" she replied quietly. "I love you too." Gazing intently into her eyes, Enzo kissed her with increasing urgency.

Totally adrift with love and lust, Juliet ran her fingers through his unruly curls, blotting out the nagging voice in her head: Things like this don't happen to girls like me.

★★★

Eric's horrified exclamation broke into her reverie. "What, not return to London with the group?"

And when Juliet shook her head, he said: "Oh, Juliet. Do be careful. Do be careful. You only met him a couple of weeks ago. You hardly know him. I would hate to see you getting hurt; he has a reputation for being a bit of a charming playboy, you know. Why not go home as planned on Saturday and then come back out again if you are sure about what you are doing."

"I want to stay with him," Juliet said simply.

"And your parents?" asked Eric with a meaningful look.

"I'm phoning them tonight."

"Oh dear, oh dear," Eric responded sadly. "I do hope it will be all right, really I do."

"Sometimes," Juliet told him firmly, "you must be allowed to bend the rules a bit. We should all take more risks."

Eric grimaced, wondering what his head office would have to say about him returning to London with a member of his group missing. He didn't think bending the rules and taking risks would go down very well with his boss.

Despite strong waves of disapproval and some outright

criticism from a few of her fellow travellers, Juliet was adamant that she was staying on Capri.

When she said goodbye to Eric and the botanists as they left Villa Florentina, Alice gave her a hug and whispered, "Go for it, girl, he's not only a one-off, but he's also utterly gorgeous." Following Ken onto the bus, taking them down to the ferry at Marina Grande, Alice pushed a piece of paper into Juliet's hand. "My phone number," she said with a grin, "I'm expecting an invite to the wedding."

As Juliet signed out of the hotel, Signore Fabrizio gave her an approving smile, offering Villa Florentina's taxi as transport to Enzo's apartment.

"I'm sure we will meet again, Miss Campbell," he said, kissing her hand. "It has been a pleasure having you to stay with us."

★★★

Enzo's housekeeper, Lucia, showed no surprise at Juliet's arrival. She was a stout, phlegmatic woman in her early sixties with an aquiline nose and very shiny black hair scraped into a bun at the nape of her neck.

Lucia adored Enzo with dog-like devotion, and when informed that Juliet would be a permanent guest while Enzo was on Capri, she accepted her without question, immediately including Juliet in her motherly ministrations.

Like the glitterati, Lucia was used to Enzo entertaining a string of different women, but she approved of this polite young English girl and was happy that he seemed to have settled down, for the moment at least.

"I didn't know you had a housekeeper," said Juliet in surprise.

"Oh, Lucia's not here all the time," explained Enzo. "She lives with her husband in a house behind the piazza, but she comes here first thing every morning and stays until lunchtime. She does the cleaning and shopping and cooks when necessary; she's an excellent cook, you must try her fish stew. You haven't met her before because you're not usually here in the morning."

He gave Juliet an amused glance. "Are you afraid she might walk in on us in the bedroom? Don't worry, *amore*, she is very tactful and discreet and she's never here in the evenings or at night. Between you and Lucia, I now have twenty-four-hour care!"

★★★

Although she had inevitably picked up a smattering of Italian during her holiday, Juliet began trying to speak more fluently after moving in with Enzo.

His English was almost faultless, but because she was in love with him, she wanted to make him happy by learning his language.

When she was able to ask for everyday things in shops and bars and conduct a basic conversation with Lucia, Enzo started teaching her the passionate Italian words he used while making love. Gradually, these whispered words became their own private language, filling Juliet with life-enhancing self-esteem.

Chapter Eleven

MARY CAMPBELL was furious with her husband. She knew something like this would happen. But would Dennis listen to her? No! And now their daughter was in a real scrape.

She went over and over Juliet's phone call in her mind. What were they going to do? Well, there was nothing for it. Dennis was going to have to go to Capri and bring Juliet back.

"No," said Dennis firmly when she issued her order. "No, I'm not; well, not yet. There's no point over-reacting; this may well turn out to be a storm in a teacup, and she will come back of her own accord."

Mary turned a tear-stained face towards her husband. "Do you really care what happens to our daughter? Because from where I'm sitting, I get the feeling that you couldn't care less."

"Stop talking nonsense," snapped Dennis, worry shaking him out of his normal calm. "Of course, I care. I'm just not prepared to dash off to Italy without considering all the pros and cons."

After the first phone call to tell her parents that she was extending her holiday for a while, Juliet sent regular letters, photographs, and postcards to reassure them she was all right and having the time of her life.

Both Mary and Dennis had tried to encourage her to return home, but she flatly refused to listen. "I can't hear you," she had once lied before putting down the phone mid-conversation, hoping they would think they'd been cut off by a faulty connection.

She called them again a few weeks later to underline the fact that there was nothing to worry about and to introduce them to the idea that she had met someone of whom she was becoming increasingly fond.

"You'll love him," Juliet told her mother. "He's very attractive; tall, dark, handsome and rich."

Mary didn't appear to pick up the irony, nor, it seemed, did she understand that her daughter was saying she had an Italian boyfriend; she just continued to tell Juliet of her concern that she was alone among foreigners.

"I'm fine, Mum, really," said Juliet, beginning to lose patience and itching to end the call. "I'm not alone, I have friends here who make sure I'm okay. Anyway, everyone is a foreigner to someone who isn't the same nationality."

Mary seemed to have run out of steam, and Juliet took advantage of the sudden silence. "You'll be pleased to know I'm making good use of my time in Italy."

She paused, wondering how to phrase it. Thankful that her mother couldn't see the enormous grin on her face, she added: "I'm learning Italian. I have found a marvellous teacher, and I'm making excellent progress."

If Mary had known the truth, she would have been outraged.

Chapter Twelve

BECAUSE IT was the summer and Enzo had only evening commitments at Bar Russe, they spent long idle days together, swimming and sunbathing on a private beach belonging to one of the glitterati, eating in local restaurants and enjoying occasional parties with others who were on Capri for the season.

Juliet, supremely happy and content lost count of the days, wishing her life could stay like this forever, being in this beautiful place with Enzo fulfilling all her dreams.

Marco and Raf turned up at the beach to talk to Enzo about some new music they were adding to the show at Bar Russe. While Raf and Enzo were sorting out dates and times for a couple of morning rehearsals, Marco joined Juliet at the beachside bar where she was having coffee. With him was a German boy called Karl, who was wearing a T-shirt several sizes too big for his spare frame, with a pair of deplorable shorts, and plimsolls that had almost certainly seen better days.

"Didi has left me, baby," Marco told Juliet, not looking in the least upset, the ever-present roll-up stuck to his bottom lip. "Her mamma wanted her home. Now I have Karl, and at least he speaks some English and attempts Italian."

He touched the boy's thigh and Karl blushed a dusky pink under his tan. Marco, looking more piratical than ever, gave an amused chuckle and taking a long drag of his joint, blew smoke into Karl's face.

Contemplating Juliet speculatively, he said: "But Jew-let, I still think you could make amazing music with me, baby, you turn me on. You know we would be very good together."

Juliet laughed, more confident now she knew him better. "Stop flirting with me, Marco." He winked at her and said mockingly: "That would be difficult. You are so pretty, *signorina*."

Looking into Marco's intelligent brown eyes, Juliet wondered how much of the personality he presented to the world was an act. He was a lot brighter and more with it than he pretended; whatever he was smoking, it hadn't strung him out or addled his brain. She raised her eyebrows and gave him a knowing smile. Marco, recognising that Juliet had him sussed, grinned back defiantly, his arm provocatively around Karl's shoulders. The boy was heartbreakingly young, with just the hint of a straggly blond beard and pale blue eyes that looked myopic.

Juliet waited until Raf came over to check the rehearsal dates with Marco before speaking to Enzo about Karl.

"It's obviously illegal. How old is he? Juliet wondered in concern. Enzo pursed his lips and shook his head.

"I asked that question. Marco says he's twenty, but I think he's more likely about seventeen. Of course, what Marco does is forbidden, and he is taking a big risk."

Enzo shrugged. "It will only be a brief fling, this boy's not Marco's type; he will find another girl soon. Don't worry, *tesora;* it won't last long. Marco is sexually incontinent in the biblical sense and not only the law, but my Church, and I am sure the English Church too, would condemn him but," he smiled, "I have known him a long time, and he has an innocence about him which is almost childlike; he has a good heart."

Juliet considered. She was not convinced about Marco's innocence. When was a pirate ever innocent?

Marco strolled over, his arm still across Karl's shoulders. "Are we going to jam tonight?" he asked.

Enzo nodded: "*Si, se lo desideri.*" Giving Juliet a teasing look, he added: "But not too late, *Giulietta* and I have something we must do afterwards."

★★★

The next morning, Juliet rolled over and sat gingerly on the edge of the bed, carefully flexing her limbs. She was stiff and achy; the sex had been a bit rough last night. Looking over her shoulder, she saw Enzo watching her.

"Are you alright?" he asked.

"Mmm, I think so."

When Enzo had told Marco that he and Juliet had something to do after the jamming session, aggressive sex was not exactly what he'd had in mind. But by the time they arrived back at the apartment, they'd both been in a state of extreme excitement, and their usual passionate lovemaking had progressed into something else altogether.

"We got a bit carried away," said Enzo.

It was a huge understatement; he'd had sex like that only once before, a long time ago with a much older woman. Then, it had been emotionless – just a crude experience that he hadn't been too keen to repeat. With Giulietta it had happened naturally and had been wild and uncontrolled but very loving.

Juliet reached for his hand. "Did I bite you?" she asked tentatively.

He chuckled and showed her the graze her teeth had left at the top of his thigh. She grimaced. "Oh my God," she said dismayed. "I'm so sorry."

"Don't worry, cara, I don't think I'll get rabies!" He added teasingly: "Lucky it wasn't a few centimetres further across, though, then I might have been in trouble."

She blushed, and he pulled her across towards him until she was lying with her head on his chest. He ran his fingers over her neck, where there were two dark purple marks.

"So, I bit you too – well, sucked you pretty intensely anyway," he said, kissing the bruises. "I don't even remember doing that."

Love bites. Juliet recalled June had love bites after she had been with Pedro in Spain. She couldn't remember the boys at home ever doing that. Maybe it was a continental thing.

"But you're alright otherwise?" asked Enzo with concern. "It wasn't all too much for you?"

"Actually, I thought it was amazing," admitted Juliet. "I really enjoyed it, although it's not something I'd want to do too often, and I am sorry about the bite. It certainly takes making love to another level, but now I ache in places I didn't know I had."

Enzo kissed her gently. "Go and have a nice warm bath, and you'll feel better."

As she turned to return his kiss, he gave her a little push, saying: "Off you go; otherwise it will be another hour before you get that bath."

Laughing, Juliet went into the bathroom, and Enzo lay there, listening to her moving around as she ran the taps and organised her towels.

She was definitely a very unusual girl. He couldn't imagine many women accepting sex like that with such equanimity. He loved her, and he was gradually coming to terms with the astonishing realisation that he wanted to marry her.

"I'll share the bath with you," he called, hauling himself out of bed.

Juliet smiled as she wound her hair into a knot on the top of her head and turned on the taps to run extra water into the tub.

Chapter Thirteen

ONE EVENING Enzo announced that the next day, they were going to Rome for a meeting with his manager.

"Rome?" said Juliet excitedly, "Will we be able to see the Colosseum and the Vatican? Oh, and I really want to go to the Sistine Chapel and see the *Pieta*..."

Amused at her eagerness, Enzo put a finger on her lips. "Whoa, cool it, baby. It's only for one day, and it's a long way. You might have time to visit the Trevi Fountain, but that will be about it.

"This is a business trip to meet up with Lorenzo, not a sightseeing tour, *Giulietta*. I'll take you back to *Roma* another time if you want to do the tourist trail. "

Lorenzo Russo sent a car with a liveried driver to pick them up from Sorrento, and the comfortable three-hour journey in a luxury limousine, complete with breakfast hamper, gave Juliet a taste of Enzo's celebrity lifestyle.

They left early and arrived in the capital just before lunchtime. At Enzo's request, the driver gave them a brief tour of Rome's most famous sights before dropping them off at La Campana, the oldest restaurant in the city, where Lorenzo was waiting for them.

He was a bespectacled, prosperous-looking man in his late forties, smartly but casually dressed in a beige linen suit with a white open-necked shirt and brown suede loafers worn in continental style without socks. Juliet noticed that he was wearing a plain gold wedding ring.

Giving Juliet air kisses on both cheeks, he said: "This *ristorante* is five hundred years old; can you believe it? It is a simple place, but the food is excellent. I chose it especially for you *Giulietta* because I think you will like it."

Holding Juliet's hand, he ran his thumb caressingly up and down her index finger, giving her an enchanting smile while gazing deeply and unwaveringly into her eyes.

"You are very beautiful, *signorina;* I can see why Enzo is so captivated."

My goodness thought Juliet, it is true: Italian men of all ages flirt, even the married ones; they just can't help themselves.

Lorenzo ordered lunch for all three of them and they ate a delicious Carbonara, the pasta dish that is synonymous with Rome, accompanied by glasses of local red wine.

During the meal, the two men spoke in English so that Juliet could be included in the conversation. Gossiping about people they knew in the music business, Juliet was astounded to hear a couple of quite famous names being mentioned in rather unflattering terms.

"Enzo tells me you are learning Italian," said Lorenzo, turning to her and giving her the benefit of his laser beam smile, holding her gaze slightly longer than necessary.

Juliet blushed slightly, reflecting that the intimate words she and Enzo shared were hardly suitable for general conversation.

"Yes…" she said hesitantly, avoiding his eyes.

Enzo, quickly picking up her thoughts, gave the suggestion of an amused wink.

"She is doing very well," he told Lorenzo, trapping one of Juliet's feet between both of his under the table, quietly laughing at her momentary awkwardness and thinking of the words he'd like to say to her right now. She was so adorable, and he could tell Lorenzo was charmed.

After the meal, Juliet left Enzo and Lorenzo talking business over a bottle of Grappa while she visited the famous Trevi Fountain. Having seen the film *Three Coins in the Fountain,* Juliet, ever the romantic, was determined to throw in coins as tradition demanded. Lorenzo had told her that she had to stand with her back to the fountain and throw three coins, one at a time, with her right hand over her left shoulder.

"The first coin ensures you will return to *Roma*; the second means you will fall in love with an attractive Italian…" he paused, giving Enzo an inscrutable look: "Or maybe you already have? The third means you will marry the person you met."

Enzo demurred. "It's not really tradition," he said. "Tourists have only been doing it since the movie."

Both men stood up as she was leaving, and Enzo took her in his arms to give her a slow and sensuous kiss. Something else an Englishman wouldn't do in the middle of a crowded restaurant thought Juliet, you'd be lucky to get a peck on the cheek. To her surprise, she realised she didn't mind in the least that other diners were watching them.

"Be careful walking around *Roma,* don't get lost, and ignore anyone who tries to flirt with you," ordered Enzo. "I will see you back here in two hours. The car will arrive, and we must leave promptly if we are to be back on Capri for Bar Russe this evening."

As Juliet walked out of La Campana, Lorenzo looked at Enzo with a beaming smile and slowly nodded in a gesture of approval.

★★★

While she enjoyed the trip to Rome, Juliet's favourite days were when she and Enzo went off on their own, spending carefree hours in the sun exploring the Amalfi coast and his home city of Naples.

It was while they were in Naples that he took her to visit his grandmother, a tiny, wizened prune of a woman with small black eyes like currants that twinkled with delight when she opened the door and saw Enzo standing there.

She had brought him up, he told Juliet, after his parents were killed during the war; his father while fighting for *Il Duce* during the 1940 invasion of Egypt, and his mother during an Allied air attack on Naples in 1943 when Enzo was eight. "So *Nonna* took over and turned a difficult small boy into the man I am today. She is all the family I have. This is where I come back to when I am not working. I suppose it is home for me."

Although she was in her eighties, *Nonna* still lived alone in the house that Enzo had bought for her, sharing her home with a menagerie of farm and domestic animals and cultivating her small plot of land with the agility of someone half her age.

She sat her visitors down in the verdant garden under a canopy of lemon trees, serving them homemade Limoncello and slices of almond cake while asking Juliet about England and her parents.

"She only speaks Italian – and in a Neapolitan dialect," explained Enzo as he translated his grandmother's questions and Juliet's answers. "Even with your ever-improving Italian, you will never understand her."

Leaving Juliet to relax in the sunshine with a skinny ginger cat on her knee and a few desultory hens clucking around her feet, *Nonna* took Enzo's arm and led him around her small holding, pointing out the various changes she had made since his last visit.

"She is a beautiful girl, that one," said the old lady with a sly sideways glance at her grandson. "Is it significant that she is the first girl you've brought here for years?"

Looking down at her with deep affection, Enzo gave an amused chuckle. "You still don't miss much, do you," he said fondly, kissing her wrinkled cheek. "You will be the first to know when there is something to tell."

Nonna gave a satisfied smile. He was her beloved grandson;

more than anything else in the world, she wanted him to be happy.

★★★

One golden afternoon, after an indulgent lunch with an American couple Enzo had met in Las Vegas, he and Juliet were having a siesta before an evening at Bar Russe.

Their lovemaking had been glorious, and Juliet, contented and drowsy, was suspended in that delicious moment between sleep and wakefulness when Enzo scooped her up into his arms and murmured into her hair: "I really do love you, *Giulietta*, and I would very much like to marry you. *Mi vuoi sposare?* Will you marry me?"

Juliet was immediately wide awake, her whole body tingling as if a bucket of cold water had been thrown over her. She was filled with a wild happiness; this amazing man wanted to marry her. She was frightened by the intensity of the feelings pounding through her.

"*Si, per favore, ti amo,*" she whispered back to him thinking, any moment now I am going to wake up and find this has all been an incredible dream. They stared at each other, stunned into silence by the significance of the words they had just uttered.

Juliet knew in that moment that any feelings she had felt for previous boyfriends had been merely infatuation; she had never experienced anything like this. She curled her body around Enzo, delighting in the warmth and intimacy of the moment.

Overwhelmed with love for her, Enzo tenderly laid Juliet down on the bed and after slowly kissing her bare shoulders, the inside of her wrists and her fingers, he sat astride her, leaning down to kiss her passionately on the lips. Everything became charged with intensity and pleasure for Juliet as she slid her arms around his neck, pulling him down on top of her.

While she adored his lovemaking, Juliet enjoyed his kisses even more. There was something about the way his mouth perfectly fitted hers; it was intoxicating. She could happily spend hours lying there just kissing him, but she knew that like most virile and passionate men, Enzo regarded kissing, enjoyable though it was, as merely an overture, a stepping stone to complete fulfilment.

Now he was intent on making love again and closing her eyes, Juliet prepared to give herself up once more to total bliss.

★★★

Juliet tried but failed to picture herself married to Enzo. She had always expected that she would, eventually, settle down with a husband and family, but marriage to someone like Enzo de Martins was way beyond anything she could have possibly imagined; even after his proposal, it seemed scarcely credible.

He was a rising international singing star, and his jet-set lifestyle was not the way most people lived; how would she fit into that?

A wave of trepidation swept over her. They were living so happily together on Capri, but within a few months, they would have to leave all this behind and go to America – and then what?

Shaking off her anxiety, she thought about how much she loved him, how much she wanted to be with him, and how amazing it was that he wanted to marry her.

Juliet didn't doubt Enzo's sincerity; she knew he was very honest and would not have proposed if he wasn't sure of his feelings for her.

However, she did fear that a man like Enzo, who so innately enjoyed the company of women, would find it difficult to resist infatuated females trying to tempt him into sex, something she knew a lot of women did without compunction. There were those who thought any desirable man was fair game, and for some women, it was always open season.

My imagination is running riot, thought Juliet, giving herself a mental shake. Enzo had never done anything to suggest he would be unfaithful.

Being handsome, charming, and liking women didn't automatically mean he would cheat.

He hardly seemed to notice the exceptionally beautiful women among the glitterati, and he had appeared totally unaware of Didi's charms, which had captivated Marco. It took two to tango, as her mother often said. Enzo would just say a firm 'No' to temptation, and that would be that. She had to trust him.

Pushing all her doubts to the back of her mind but still desperately in need of reassurance, she threw herself into Enzo's arms and said fervently: "Ti amo molto."

As he kissed her, gently edging her towards the bedroom, she reminded herself that he loved her. Everything would be all right; She had no need to worry.

Chapter Fourteen

IT WAS the next call from Capri that galvanised Dennis into action. After almost four months in Italy, Juliet rang to say that she was probably going to marry Enzo de Martins. "What do you mean, probably?" demanded Dennis. "Are you going to marry him, or aren't you?"

"Well, yes, although we're not quite sure ourselves about where or when. We want to get married, but, of course, he's a Catholic, and there are other complications. He needs to be in America at the end of the year, so I might go with him, even if we're not married by then. We might get married over there." There was an undertone in his daughter's voice that rang warning bells with Dennis.

"Listen to me, young lady. Either you come home immediately, or I will come out to Capri to bring you back; it's your choice. Your mother and I have been more than patient, but the time has come to stop messing around. May I remind you that you are under twenty-one and thus still my responsibility?

"If you are going to marry this Mr de Martins, then I want you back home to tell us all about it, and you can bring him too, if he'll come. If you're not going to marry him, I want you home anyway. So, you decide. Either you come under your own steam, or I come out and bring you back."

Juliet knew her father well enough to realise he would not be talked around and that he meant what he said. The last thing she wanted was a parent turning up on Capri to take her off home like a naughty child.

"I'll come back at the weekend," she said grudgingly. "But I won't be stopping. I'll book a flight back to Italy as soon as I can."

"Hm, we'll see," said Dennis. "You just get yourself home. I'll pick you up at the airport, and we can talk more then."

Enzo was sad but very loving when she told him the news. "I do wish I could come with you to meet your family, *tesora*, especially now you have met *Nonna* and Lorenzo, but it is just not possible.

"As you know, I have a commitment to sing at Bar Russe for another six weeks and then I must go to *Roma* for two weeks, but you will come back to me quickly. I do love you, and I want to marry you. We will go travelling together, and I will show you the sights of Italy and America."

They spent their last day together on The Island. After swimming, sunbathing and enjoying a picnic courtesy of Enzo's friend Matteo, they made love in the beach hut.

"A memory to take home with you, baby," said Enzo, gently stroking her cheek, "so you don't forget me. I adore you; you make me very happy."

Engulfed by emotion, Juliet felt a dark cloak of melancholy descending on her. "I could never forget you," she sobbed, lying in his arms as he kissed her, running his hands over her body to quieten her.

Enzo had asked her to leave some of her things in the apartment so he could feel she was near him while she was in England, and she had deposited in a bedroom drawer one of the dresses he had bought her in a chic Capri boutique. The other she kept; it was too nice to leave behind, even with Enzo, anyway she wanted to show it to June. To the dress, she added a lacy bra, a pair of sexy knickers and a small bottle of the Chanel perfume he loved her to wear. "You can sprinkle it on your pillow," she told him.

Enzo was feeling strangely reluctant to let her go – an unusual sensation for someone who was accustomed to constantly moving on, leaving a scattering of broken hearts in his wake.

This time it was different. He had, for a fleeting moment, considered abandoning his contracts and going with Juliet to England. He loved her and they were going to be married, he didn't want to let her out of his sight. Returning to reason, he accepted he was compelled to fulfil his commitments for the sake of his flourishing singing career, if nothing else. There was no way he could imagine telling Lorenzo that he was ducking out. That would be him finished in the music business.

Enzo accompanied Juliet on the Sorrento ferry, ordering a taxi to take them to the airport in Naples, not wanting to leave her until the very last moment. Juliet cried when they reached the boarding gate. "I can't bear to go without you," she said, clinging to him. "But I promise I will be back very soon."

"I will wait for you, *amore,*" said Enzo, giving her a long, passionate kiss, much to the delight of fellow passengers waiting to board the flight to London.

"Remember, I love you. Please don't be too long. Our new life together is waiting for us."

Juliet didn't care who was watching as she embraced Enzo. There was nobody on her radar except him. She was in utter despair at the parting.

Chapter Fifteen

THE JOURNEY home was a miserable one, and Juliet could scarcely raise a smile when Dennis met her in a cold and grey London. "I hear there are plans to rename this airport Heathrow, after the hamlet that used to be here," said Dennis cheerfully as he negotiated the car out onto the main road south. He decided that light conversation was the way to keep the atmosphere non-confrontational. "Seems sensible, I suppose, but it's strange to think that back in the thirties, this was all market gardens and orchards."

Glancing at Juliet's blank expression as she stared unseeingly out of the car window, Dennis remarked: "I've been talking to you, but I don't think you've heard a word I've said."

When Juliet didn't reply, Dennis decided resignedly that silence might be preferable to a one-sided conversation.

Juliet said nothing until they were in Brighton. "I *am* going back, you know," she hissed fiercely, brushing past Mary on the doorstep.

Dennis rolled his eyes and shook his head at his wife, warning her not to ask questions as Juliet ran up the stairs and into her bedroom, slamming the door behind her.

"Let her be," said Dennis, putting a hand on Mary's arm as she turned to follow their daughter. "She'll be okay. She just needs a bit of time."

Mary snorted. "You've always spoilt her. Pity she's too old to smack!"

★★★

Dennis poured himself a large Scotch and sank gratefully into the comforting embrace of the sofa. Women! He considered his relationship with his only daughter. He loved her but they were not close, not in the way some fathers and daughters were.

In a rare moment of perception, Dennis realised that he and Juliet had never really bonded, maybe because he was away with the army when she was born, and when he did return home, two-year-old Juliet had no idea who he was; she had even rejected an army Ration D bar of chocolate he had saved especially for her.

Feeling slightly hurt but sensible enough to realise that he couldn't force a connection, he had left the childcare to Mary rather than attempting to forge a deeper paternal link with his daughter.

Opportunities missed, he thought sadly. Dennis stretched out his long legs and sighed. The bachelor life suddenly seemed enormously appealing.

★★★

Faced with her parents trying their best to be understanding, Juliet found it difficult to explain why she wanted to marry Enzo, apart from the fact that she was madly in love with him, of course, and he was just the most gorgeous and exciting man she had ever met.

Standing at her bedroom window looking up at the night sky, Juliet was hit by the realisation that the moon in Brighton was the same moon that was looking down on Enzo in Capri. She consulted her watch; he'd be singing at Bar Russe at this very moment. She was overtaken by a tide of misery; she should be there with him.

Desperate to hear his voice, Juliet made several attempts to telephone Capri, but each time, she was unable to get a connection, and, almost crying with frustration, she was forced to give up.

"Like being back in the Dark Ages," she muttered, crashing the phone down onto its cradle. Once she had calmed down, she gave a rueful smile. It was probably karma, she thought, casting her mind back to the call home from Capri when she had hung up on her parents. The Gods were giving her a taste of her own medicine.

Juliet had hoped that Enzo would telephone her, but all she got was a picture postcard of Capri with a message in Enzo's distinctive sloping writing: *'Come back soon, amore. I am longing for you as never before. Ciao E.'* He had added in brackets: (*'Mi manchi bella. Ti adoro.'*)

Clicking her tongue with annoyance, Mary held out the card and said: "He might at least have put it in an envelope. Goodness knows what the postman thought!"

"Let's just hope the postman doesn't read Italian," Juliet retorted acidly as she snatched the card out of her mother's hand. She took it up to her bedroom and slept with it under her pillow.

Because she really missed Enzo and longed to be with him, Juliet never really understood why she hadn't rushed back to Italy. She spent hours in her bedroom playing records of the love songs Enzo used to sing to her, trying to evoke the atmosphere of Bar Russe and yearning to be back there. *Can't Help Falling in Love* was constantly running through her head.

Days passed without Juliet booking a flight to Naples. Frightened by her inexplicable inertia, she constantly told herself that she had to go and buy her ticket, but she always seemed to find a random reason for not doing so.

Night after night she dreamed of Enzo and Capri, waking in total desolation when she found he was not there beside her.

Alone with her thoughts, Juliet remembered the times when she had woken early and spent long moments in the soft morning light just watching him sleep, greedily eating him with her eyes. Even in repose, when his face was totally relaxed, he was so breathtakingly beautiful that she could gaze at him forever.

Gradually becoming aware that she was staring at him, he would come out of his sleepy haze and pull her down on top of him, telling her why he loved her and exactly what he was going to do to her once he was properly awake.

Tears streaming down her face at the memory, Juliet wondered why she hadn't brought something of his home with her, something she could hold close. She had left those things at the apartment for him, but expecting a quick return to Capri, it didn't seem important to take a memento of him with her. All she had were the photographs she had taken on Capri.

Dennis and Mary watched and waited and said nothing. They tipped-toed around their daughter, treating her with great solicitude as if she was bereaved, hoping her inactivity was a sign she was staying at home.

★★★

Later, when it was safe to unpack her deepest thoughts and consider them in the harsh light of reality, Juliet was able to acknowledge what the infuriating voice in her head had always known: her affair with Enzo de Martins had been a wonderful dream, and she was not going back to him; it was over.

She loved him, of that there was no doubt. He said he loved her and had asked her to marry him. Their lovemaking had been incredible; they were perfectly suited emotionally and sexually, and they genuinely liked each other as friends. Even so, their relationship was like a piece of exquisite and delicate porcelain, not for everyday use. It wasn't only the Capo di Monti that didn't make it back to England.

Sexy, handsome Italian singing star marries an ordinary

English girl training to be a florist, and they live happily ever after? Unlikely. It would never have worked out; the shine would have rubbed off, and he would have grown tired of her.

She could see now that Capri had been a cocoon that shielded them from the real world. How would she have held his attention when they moved on, and she had to compete with all the glamorous and sexy women Enzo met on his international travels? Maybe she wouldn't always have been able to accompany him to concerts and would have had to wait in their hotel room wherever they happened to be in the world while he travelled alone to the performances Lorenzo had arranged for him. How would she have coped with that?

Enzo had once told her that fans had thrown their underwear onto the stage while he was singing in Las Vegas. She sighed wearily: he had thought it was amusing, "I was dodging knickers without missing a note," he chuckled. "I thought I might get cancelled. It was only a few years earlier that Elvis was in trouble for arousing the sexual passions of teenagers with his suggestive dance moves. Both Lorenzo and I were worried that underwear thrown onto the stage might cause a similar problem. But we seemed to get away with it, although we have no idea how to stop it happening again."

Juliet knew she would be utterly incapable of sharing him with other women, even if they were fans and he found it funny. She was sure it wasn't only beach huts that obsessed admirers offered him.

He could have any woman he wanted. The tears dripped down her face as she recalled how he flirted during his appearances at Bar Russe, kissing and cuddling girls in the audience. Enzo constantly reassured her that it was not real; it was all part of the act, in the same way that he joked with the men and teased Marco and Raf. It meant nothing. "You must accept that it is harmless, *amore mio.* "It's not important."

But Enzo was a red-blooded Italian man, and flirting with

women was in his genes; it was to him as natural as breathing, and Juliet knew he would never be able to stop. Most of the time, he didn't even realise he *was* flirting.

Look at Lorenzo Russo: he was almost fifty, and he was still an incorrigible flirt, although Enzo had told her that Lorenzo loved his wife and had never been unfaithful to her.

"Flirting never has serious intentions," he explained. "It's just something Italian men do. It brings pleasure. And when I'm working, it's part of the job. It's what's expected." Juliet knew that if she nagged Enzo about flirting, he would come to resent her, but she was convinced that it sometimes went further.

She shook her head sadly; it would have ended in heartbreak, and she would have been badly hurt. Difficult as it was, she had to give him up. Regret was a waste of time; she must move on. Before she could do that, Juliet needed to grieve.

Feeling overwhelmingly bereft, she was incessantly in tears. Lying on her bed wearing the dress he had bought for her, she pushed her face into the pillow with another over her head so that her mother wouldn't hear her choking desolation.

I'm deliberately inflicting this pain on myself, she thought in one of her more lucid moments; it's insane. Why would anyone voluntarily put themselves through so much misery and pain? Maybe she could just take a chance, go back to him on Capri, and see what happened. It might be alright.

What was it she had told Eric about everyone taking more risks? Perhaps she should take her own advice and just go for it. Deep down, though, Juliet knew that the anguish she was experiencing now was nothing compared to the torment she would suffer if she went back to Capri and he eventually left her for someone else. She couldn't even bear to imagine that.

Juliet agonised over the letter she eventually sent to Enzo, trying to put her deepest feelings into words, but he had not replied and to be honest, she never really thought he would.

For a while, she had allowed herself the luxury of imagining that he would come to find her and take her back to Italy with him. She eventually forced herself to accept that would never happen.

After all, she had left him, something he must have found totally beyond belief. She knew that not only would Enzo have been deeply hurt and seen it as a total betrayal of their love and trust, but also as an unforgivable attack on his pride and masculinity.

In his world, he was always the one who did the leaving.

Chapter Sixteen

AS SOON as she returned from Capri, Juliet contacted June. Juliet's four months in Italy and June's marriage had been only the merest blip in their long friendship, and they picked up where they left off.

Next Juliet made her peace with Mrs Bishop, the owner of the flower shop in The Lanes, to apologise for leaving her in the lurch by not returning from holiday as expected. She also asked if her job was still available. It was.

"We've missed you," said Mrs Bishop, smiling. "That must have been the longest fortnight's holiday ever!" Breathing in the heady fragrance of flowers with real pleasure, a relieved Juliet promised she wouldn't take off like that again and agreed to return to work the following day.

Juliet's last port of call was, to her, the most significant. She went to the hairdresser and had her long red hair cut short.

"Are you sure?" asked the stylist, looking doubtfully at her in the mirror and letting Juliet's abundant locks run through her fingers. "It's really beautiful hair."

Enzo had loved her hair. He used to nuzzle it while he was holding her in his arms and stroke it as it fanned out over the pillows in bed. In the same way, she found his curly black hair incredibly sexy. The hair of someone you love can be very erotic, a real turn-on, she mused.

The stylist was still looking at her. Here's a girl who has just come out of a love affair, she thought. Being a hairdresser was like being a therapist; she'd seen and heard it all. Wonder if she's had her heart broken or whether she has left someone grief-stricken? Pretty girl: despite her sad eyes, it was probably the latter.

Juliet suddenly realised the woman was still awaiting her answer.

"Time for it to go," she said firmly. The stylist shrugged and reached for her scissors. Juliet closed her eyes. The grief was over; the healing process had begun.

★★★

Many people who knew Juliet had just returned from a long holiday on the Isle of Capri wanted to hear all about it. Hoping to keep her busy and her mind off Enzo, Mary Campbell had arranged for her daughter to give short talks to some of the clubs and groups she helped to run.

"Now, the ladies of the Luncheon Club are really looking forward to hearing all about the flowers and things," she told Juliet. "They're only expecting a twenty-minute slot, no time at all, really, and if you could show some slides of the flowers and plants you saw, that would be wonderful."

"Mum, I'm sure they don't really want to hear about it," protested Juliet gloomily, but it seemed they did, and so did many others.

After doing the rounds of Mary's voluntary groups, including the Over Sixties, the Gardening Club and the Happy Circle, Juliet was exhausted.

"It's awful," she told Mike one evening when they were having a drink in the local pub. "Mum keeps coming up with all these clubs and things and everyone is so desperate to get speakers that they don't care who it is. I swear half of them aren't interested in flowers and plants anyway, and I really don't have enough slides or enough to say. Spinning it out for twenty minutes is a real problem."

"I'll come with you if you like," offered Mike. "Perhaps we could show them slides of some of the gardens I've worked on. That would pad it all out a bit."

Juliet had slipped easily back into a relationship with Mike, more from lethargy than anything else. She just couldn't be bothered to break it off. Apart from the occasional kiss and sometimes a cuddle in the car, their relationship was almost platonic, and that suited Juliet very well.

Mike was charming and funny, but after Enzo, the last thing she wanted was a sexual relationship with someone else. She and Mike were fond of each other and had mutual interests; that, for the moment, was enough.

Part Four
Juliet and Mike

(1962-1963)

Reflection

"What a daughter learns about love from her mother will inform how she loves herself."
Peg Streep, American author

THROUGHOUT MY childhood and into my teenage years, I suffered from very low self-esteem. In retrospect, I realise that this was a result of my mother's own lack of confidence, which resulted in her relentless pursuit of perfection and the constant worry about how she appeared to others. I also believe that much of my teenage angst resulted from the fact that I had never bonded with my father, who returned from World War Two when I was a toddler and thus had little to do with my upbringing.

So, I grew up with a mother for whom I was never good enough and the lack of an effective male role model. The upshot of this was that I grew from an exceedingly anxious child into a young woman who was lacking in self-confidence, pathetically eager to please and be liked. Subconsciously looking to find the affection I felt I did not receive from my parents, I was desperate to have a boyfriend – any boyfriend – who would be attentive and thus make me feel better about myself.

Naively, and because my mother and I rarely had a meaningful conversation about anything, especially if it involved any hint of sex, I had no idea that there were boys who would chat me up in the hope of sexual favours. Naturally, young men soon sussed out my enthusiasm to please and ultimately took advantage. Not that any of my teenage relationships ended in lovemaking, but we certainly pushed the barriers of what was permitted as far as we dared, the fear of unwanted pregnancy always looming over us.

Totally oblivious to the issues facing teenage girls in the modern world, my mother taught me the lessons valued during her comfortable Edwardian childhood, all culminating in how to secure a suitable husband and be a good wife. Girls (obviously virgins until they were wed) got married and had babies; that was their role in life. I grew up knowing that the only thing a woman needed in life was a husband.

Chapter One

ALTHOUGH MIKE obviously knew about Juliet's 'Italian Adventure' as the family insisted on calling it, he chose to ignore the details and spoke only of the flowers and plants of Capri and the photographs Juliet had taken, chuckling over anecdotes she shared with him about Edna, Jane, Eric, and the rest of the group.

She told him about the Path of the Gods along the Amalfi Coast, and he agreed it was something they could do together. "That would be a nice holiday next year."

Juliet didn't mention Enzo, but she did wonder whether Mike knew about him. If not, why wasn't he more curious to find out why she had stayed in Italy for so long? It seemed a bit odd, especially as he had organised and paid for the original trip, but Juliet was just grateful she didn't have to confront the issue.

Everything to do with Enzo was just too painful; she needed time to heal before she could talk about him.

Mike hadn't even asked her why she'd had her hair cut. The first time they met up after her return from Capri, he gave her a startled look and said: "Oh, you look different. When did you do that?"

Once he knew she'd had it cut in Brighton and not Italy, he seemed satisfied and never mentioned it again. Juliet was perplexed. I really don't know what goes on in his head, she thought.

★★★

Shortly after Juliet's return from Capri, Mike called round to take her for a drink and found her in floods of tears. Her parents were away for the night visiting an elderly aunt in Birmingham, and in the solitude of the empty house, memories of Enzo welled up, bringing feelings of complete hopelessness and despair.

"Sweetheart, what on earth's the matter?" Mike asked with concern as she opened the door looking ashen and exhausted, her eyes red from crying. Juliet, totally distraught, muttered: "I can't tell you, it's too private," and then burst into tears again.

Following her into the sitting room he stood awkwardly, not sure what to do. Juliet offered no explanation and remained standing in the middle of the room with tears streaming down her face.

When Mike went across to put an arm around her, she shook him off petulantly. "Please don't, there's no need. There's nothing you can do to help," she said peevishly.

He moved away from her and Juliet went to sit on the sofa, desperately fighting for composure, twisting a sodden handkerchief in her fingers. Mike was worried; he'd never seen Juliet like this before. Was she ill? Should he try to contact her parents?

Ignoring her irritability, he sat down beside her stroking her back and murmuring comforting words before taking her face in his hands and gently kissing the tip of her nose. She looked so fragile, and even with a tear-blotched face he found her very desirable. He had loved her long red hair, but strangely, her new short spiky cut seemed to emphasise her wonderful silvery green eyes and her heart-shaped face; she really was lovely.

Mike felt a faint quiver of lust. He fancied her like mad, she'd always had the ability to turn him on. What would making love to her be like…he'd held off, not wanting to initiate sex before she was ready.

"Goodness, I must look a mess," she said, making an ineffectual attempt to wipe her face. "You look adorable," said Mike, "even if you do have a nose that would rival Rudolph's."

She had stopped crying now and he stroked her cheek with the back of his hand. She had such soft skin...he'd never noticed before. Mike licked his lips, feeling waves of nervous excitement surging through his body. Maybe it was time; he'd waited patiently long enough and now there was the opportunity of an empty house.

Putting both his arms around her, he slowly drew her close to him. Wearily, she sank against him and put her head on his shoulder. It was good to feel the comfort of a man's body again, even if it was only Mike.

"There, there," he said, gently taking her hand, "nothing can be that bad. Will it help to tell me about it? A problem shared and all that."

Juliet hardly heard him, her mind overflowing with desire for Enzo: the feel of him, the smell of him, his skin touching hers. Leaning back into the sofa's cushiony depths she took a deep shuddering breath and closed her eyes, trying to conjure up his presence. Attempting to make her more comfortable, Mike lifted her legs onto the cushions so she was lying horizontally. Briefly opening her eyes at the movement, Juliet gave a watery smile before sliding back into her dream. She felt bone-tired and emotionally drained.

Watching her lasciviously, Mike leaned over and tentatively kissed her forehead, moving his lips across her wet eyes, her tear-streaked cheeks and finally, her mouth. When she didn't protest, he became bolder and started kissing her with more fervour, his hands roaming over her body.

Yearning for Enzo and desperate to feel him holding her, Juliet hardly registered that Mike had slipped his hands inside her jersey. They crept over her breasts before moving down to carefully unzip her skirt. He kissed her eagerly, his manoeuvres becoming more determined, continuing the slow progress downwards.

Totally lost in her fantasy, Juliet was trembling now, feeling

Enzo warm and heavy on top of her as he fitted his mouth over hers and they wrapped themselves around one another, lost in their eager urge for each other. She should never have left him...

With a startled jolt, Juliet was abruptly forced back into reality with the horrified realisation that Mike was making love to her. His technique had so little impact that, submerged in her dream of Enzo, she'd been completely oblivious of what he was doing. For a moment, Juliet was paralysed, totally unable to move. Numb with shock, she wondered if it was just heavy petting or whether he'd really had sex with her.

Pushing herself up from the depths of the sofa, all the evidence was there, and Mike was tidying himself up.

White and shaken, Juliet asked herself how on earth she could have let it happen. How stupid; she should have realised what he was doing. Had he used a condom? She wasn't sure. I just can't bring myself to ask the question, she thought, feeling totally drained.

Mike saw the disbelief and panic in her eyes as she looked up at him.

"Oh dear," she whispered without thinking. "That was a mistake."

He regarded her with dismay, his face a rictus of embarrassment and pain. "A mistake? That's an incredibly insulting thing to say to someone who has just made love to you."

Watching a deep red flush creep up her neck and across her face, he demanded: "You mean, you didn't want to make love, or you didn't enjoy it? You could have said no, and I would have stopped."

He was completely unaware that she had been so lost in dreams of Enzo that she hadn't realised he *was* making love to her.

"Anyway," he said as if in mitigation, "you kissed me with more passion than you've ever shown before, so I thought you were with me."

Had she? Juliet realised she had thought she was kissing Enzo.

Heavens, she'd really screwed up. Juliet bit her lip and didn't reply. She couldn't meet his eyes.

"For Christ's sake!" Mike was suddenly furious, letting out a string of expletives. He was shaking with anger.

"We've been going out together for months and months, and this is the first time we've had sex. I didn't want to rush you, Juliet, but I'm only human, and I've been wanting to make love to you for ages. What about *my* feelings?

Juliet was flabbergasted. "I had no idea you felt like that," she gasped. "You've never given any sign that you wanted that kind of relationship, we've hardly done more than kiss in all the time we've known each other."

Mike made a slightly apologetic gesture: "I just thought you weren't ready. I didn't want to force you into something you didn't want to do, but…"

He looked so distressed that Juliet felt totally guilt-ridden. He was a nice man. Although he was a lot older than her, she knew that thanks to Enzo, she was far more sexually experienced than he was. She should never have gone off into a fantasy about Enzo while she was with Mike. What an irresponsible thing to do. A wave of tiredness swept over her and she felt as old as the hills.

Making love with Enzo had always been intense and exhilarating, a passionate meeting of bodies and minds. Was there some kind of precedent for this situation with Mike? Sex when one person didn't realise it was happening was bizarre.

Surely Mike must have noticed she wasn't responding, apart from that kiss, of course. Crickey, if she had kissed Mike the way she kissed Enzo, no wonder he thought she was keen. Or maybe his previous girlfriends had just laid back and thought of England while he got on with it, so he didn't expect any participation.

"Mike…" she took his hands in hers and squeezed them, suddenly feeling very protective of him. "Mike, I'm so sorry. I'm just not myself right now."

He regarded her coldly. "Don't try to placate me." He wasn't yet ready to forgive her for his embarrassment and humiliation.

Juliet grimaced, realising that a degree of grovelling was required if he was going to be pacified.

"Mike, I *am* sorry, truly. It's just that I wasn't expecting it. I wasn't… wasn't prepared. It was really my fault, I'm so sorry if I have hurt your feelings. It wasn't deliberate."

Slightly mollified, he gave a wan smile.

"Well, I obviously took you by surprise. But being here with you, I just couldn't help myself. I got carried away. I really wanted you and I was a bit wound up. I lost control." His anger had completely dissipated. "I'm the one who should be sorry." He suddenly looked miserable and deflated.

"It'll be better next time," said Juliet soothingly, giving him a kiss on the cheek and thinking, there's no way there's going to be a next time. This has got to stop. For both their sakes, she couldn't risk a repeat performance.

Chapter Two

WHAT WITH Juliet's 'Capri talks' and June's matrimonial engagements, it was a week or so before the girls managed to get a whole evening to themselves. Juliet was impatient to hear about the honeymoon in France and the vagaries of married life, and June was obviously desperate to know every small detail of Juliet's affair with Enzo.

The Two Js were back in business.

Juliet's new hairstyle was the very first topic of conversation. June certainly had no qualms telling her it was not the best decision she had ever made.

"My God, you look like a hedgehog," she said, staring with undisguised horror at her short, spiky crop. "Why on earth did you do that? You had beautiful hair."

Juliet drew a deep breath. "I had to," she said. "I somehow felt that my long hair belonged to Enzo on Capri. Now that part of my life is over, I had to change the way I looked."

June frowned. "Very philosophical; well, doubtless, you'll explain *that* in detail later. But for now, tell me, "Did you have fun?"

They were sitting at June's kitchen table for an evening catch-up. Brian was away on one of his innumerable business trips and the girls were enjoying a casual supper of Chianti and lasagne as a nod to Juliet's love affair with Italy.

"Great dress, by the way," said June, looking admiringly at the black and white A-line mini that Juliet was wearing.

"Enzo bought it for me," said Juliet, standing up and doing a twirl. June nodded with approval.

"I must say Enzo sounds utterly gorgeous, and he obviously has a good eye for fashion, which is a definite bonus. Most men wouldn't know a classy dress from a sack."

Looking at Juliet intently, she insisted: "It *was* fun, wasn't it? Did you have an absolutely fab time? I trust you have some pictures to show; hopefully they're not all of flowers and plants and views of the Amalfi coastline."

Juliet laughed and pulled a sheaf of photographs out of her bag. "You're the only one I'm showing these to. My parents won't ask about Enzo and just pretend he doesn't exist, and I have no intention of showing them to Mike for obvious reasons. He's seen all the botanical ones, of course."

"While we're on the subject, what *is* going on with Mike? Are you still together?" enquired June, and before Juliet could answer, she said: "Oh, never mind, tell me later. To be honest, I'm far more interested in the Italian stallion. Now show me those pictures."

Juliet spread her photographs out on the scrubbed tabletop, and after a few minutes, June gave a huge sigh.

"Okay, Enzo is totally fabulous, very up-market for you if you don't mind me saying so. Sex on legs – I can absolutely see the attraction. But what *exactly* was he like? I want to know every little intimate detail. You know, boxers or Y-fronts, or did he go commando? I believe that many continental men like him often do. And what about the romantic bits? I can tell just from looking at him that he's a good kisser, and she glanced at Juliet from under her lashes, good in bed. When did you first fall for him? That sort of stuff. Now, please start from the beginning. You got a note…"

Juliet wriggled down in her chair and prepared to settle in for a girly gossip. It was so good to be with June again, the only person in the world she totally trusted and with whom she could be completely herself.

After they'd finished eating, they took their wine into June's plush sitting room to continue their gossip in comfort.

As June gradually ran out of questions, Juliet said: "Enzo was the most exciting man I'm ever likely to meet in my life; extremely good looking as you can see, wonderful company, incredibly sexy and brilliant in bed – he taught me a lot.

"I was so amazed when he proposed; it was totally out of the blue and I wasn't expecting it. I was really excited at the thought of marrying him. Eventually, though, I realised we were just living in a bubble on Capri. It wasn't real life, the bubble was always going to burst. It's strange, although Enzo could see a future ahead for us, I had never been able to imagine our lives together beyond Capri."

"Mmm," said June thoughtfully, "But hang loose, as the lovely Elvis would say, I need to backtrack. You slept with him. Quite often, if I'm not mistaken. What happened to the girl who wasn't going to have sex without a wedding ring? Not that I can talk, but you were always so adamant."

Juliet smiled ruefully: "The temptation was just too great," she admitted.

"No one tells you what it's going to be like, do they? You grow up learning that girls should save themselves for their husbands and that only scarlet women have sex outside marriage, but it's not that simple. And Enzo was just so…" she paused, and June gave her a quizzical look: "Just so?" she prompted. "…just so *totally* irresistible," continued Juliet. "I absolutely adored him. There was no way I was going to refuse to go to bed with him."

June regarded her friend's blushing face with amusement. "Nothing wrong with that," she said. "I've found so many men totally irresistible. As you will remember, the first totally irresistible bloke I slept with was Pedro in Spain. Sex is the best thing ever. I'm pleased you've seen sense at last!"

Juliet burst out laughing. "Well, you told me often enough!

But seriously, that first afternoon on The Island when I realised that Enzo was going to make love to me in the beach hut, I didn't for a moment think of the consequences."

"You mean you didn't hear your mother's voice in your head?"

"Didn't even give her a passing thought. I just knew that being made love to by Enzo was what I wanted more than anything else in the world. Nothing was going to stop me. Unfortunately, I was so brainwashed by convention that once I had got over the initial euphoria and the absolute amazingness of it all, I was constantly terrified of getting pregnant; you know, Italian women have loads of children."

June giggled. "That's a bit of a sweeping statement; remember, most of them are Catholic and don't use birth control. I hope you did!"

"Yes, of course. Luckily, Enzo is very much a man of the world, so he didn't have any of those religious hang-ups. Even so, I *was* worried about falling for a baby."

She leaned forward and grabbed June's hand. "It's all so unfair. You're brought up to believe that sex outside marriage is the greatest sin ever. What you're *not* told is that going to bed with a gorgeous man you really fancy is the only thing you want to do, and not doing it is virtually impossible. And then you have the constant worry of getting pregnant."

June looked thoughtful: "It's all a dastardly patriarchal plot to keep women in their place," she said, giving the deep throaty laugh that still had the power to captivate men of all ages.

"It's always the girl who takes the rap when things go wrong. Well, a woman can't get away from her mistake like a man can. It's there for nine months for all to see. It's not having sex before marriage that you get punished for; it's getting found out. You can sleep with a guy for ages without anyone knowing, but once you get pregnant, the whole world knows what you've been up to."

Settling herself on the chaise longue, June asked the question that had been on her mind all evening.

"But Jules, what you haven't explained is why, if you adored Enzo so much and you were going to marry him, didn't you go back to him on Capri?"

Juliet took a deep breath and sat looking down at her hands, gripped so tightly together in her lap that her knuckles were turning white. It was a while before she spoke. "Because frankly, I was terrified that marriage to Enzo would never have lasted. We live in totally different worlds, and I was seriously worried that he would eventually tire of me and leave me, and I would be injured beyond repair, in danger of never recovering.

"I loved him; I could have become very deeply in love with him. I was well on the way," she admitted quietly. "Running away was an act of self-preservation."

June jumped up and put her hands over Juliet's clenched ones. "Sorry to have asked," she said, "I didn't mean to upset you."

Juliet looked up at her. "That's all right. I've more or less come to terms with it now. Maybe men like Enzo aren't compatible with a monogamous marriage. Can a man who loves women ever be faithful to one woman? Especially when temptation is offered daily on a plate.

"I had to ask myself what I was willing to do for love; what was I willing to risk. And the answer was 'not my sanity.'

"I do fear, however, there is a chance that giving up Enzo may well be the one thing in my life I come to regret for ever, but I sincerely hope not."

She smiled. "Let's change the subject. It's your turn under the spotlight now. How is married life?"

June wrinkled her nose and moved back to the chaise longue. "Okay, I suppose; not all it's cracked up to be, though. I'm told you must take the rough with the smooth, and currently, there seems to be rather a lot of rough."

"Oh, June, no! And you've only been married a few months. Is Brian being difficult?"

"It's not Brian really. He's fine, and we get along surprisingly well together. No, it's just that I'm bored. Now I'm a married woman I can't go out and do all those things I used to do. I must be respectable, so my in-laws inform me now that Brian has qualified and is going places. His parents are very old-fashioned, and I'm finding it all a bit of a bind. After all, I'm only twenty, and I feel forty!"

June settled herself more comfortably on the daybed, putting a cushion behind her head for support.

"Honestly, Jules, they keep on and on about it being different when we've got a family, but I'm not that bothered about having children right now. There's plenty of time for all that. Of course, I have no proper job; oh yes, I know, I've got a house to run, as my mother-in-law keeps trenchantly telling me, but that's not difficult. I don't have that much to do except a bit of shopping and cooking.

"Brian's mother organised a cleaner for us, and all the washing goes to the laundry. I did try doing it – we got given a brilliant twin-tub washing machine as a wedding present – but Brian complained that I didn't iron his shirts properly, well, not to the standard he was used to at home, and the bed linen was just too much to cope with. So now it all gets collected on a Monday and returned in pristine order on a Friday, which lets me off the hook completely."

June jumped up and started wandering around the room. "I have joined a few things, you know, the Women's Institute and the Flower Guild at church – baulked at the Mothers' Union, though.

"I get invited to coffee and drinks at people's houses and things like that. Then I go to the hairdresser a lot and have my nails done. There are endless ways to fill my days.

"What I really want to do is to go out to work like I used to, but that's not allowed. Respectable married ladies don't work, apparently. Brian says it wouldn't look good, and people would think he couldn't afford to keep a wife. Have you ever heard such twaddle?"

"It all sounds very Jane Austen to me," said Juliet. "Like you're living in the nineteenth century."

"That's it exactly," agreed June. "It's totally ridiculous, but it is the price I must pay for marrying into this pretentious family."

"My mother would be overjoyed if I was in your position," said Juliet. "A prosperous husband, lovely house, foreign travel, not having to work…she would have no idea what you were complaining about!"

"I know, I know. I'm fortunate, and it's not as if Brian is fat, ugly, and horrible. He's not, and he says he loves me. I admit I went into this marriage with my eyes wide open, only…"

"Be careful what you wish for?" suggested Juliet with a sympathetic smile.

"Exactly, and that's not all." Juliet, who was making her way back to the kitchen to pick up another bottle of wine, turned round and sat down again. "Go on."

"What I also hate is not having my own money. I really am a kept woman, daft as that may sound. Brian gives me housekeeping money, of course, but I feel guilty about buying so much as a pair of stockings out of that. Anyway, I also get a dress fund that is supposed to cover all the bits and pieces of clothing I might need, and Brian is always bringing me back gorgeous stuff from his business trips to the States. Then Daddy still gives me an annual allowance, which is paid into the bank and which is meant for emergencies or anything special. And…"

"Like a new ball gown?" interjected Juliet, who had hardly been able to get a word in edgeways while June was on her tirade.

"I saw that rather delightful grey tulle number in your wardrobe. I'm sure that's new. Was it an emergency buy?"

June laughed. "Sorry, love. Didn't mean to rant on and on, but it does rile me, all this keeping up appearances, because that's all it is. Why shouldn't married women work, even if it's only for pin money? Why should men feel they are somehow losing face if their wife has a respectable job? After all, I only want a part-time office job; I'm not proposing to go out on the streets."

She sighed. "Oh well, no point in fretting and trying to break the rules, well, not if I want a quiet life. My in-laws already think I'm not a very satisfactory daughter-in-law, I dread to think what would happen if I said I was going out to work.

"Maybe things will improve now you're back home. I've really missed you. Now come and try on that ball gown. It's certainly your colour rather than mine."

"But is it my size?" asked Juliet with a mock sigh. "You're looking incredibly skinny these days. I bet I won't even get it over my hips."

Giggling, the friends linked arms and headed towards June's dressing room.

Juliet was guiltily aware that she hadn't mentioned the ludicrous situation with Mike having sex with her. Normally, she would have told June about it in graphic detail, but for some unfathomable reason, she just didn't want to discuss it. Maybe because she totally blamed herself for what had happened.

Chapter Three

ARE YOU alright?" Mary Campbell looked up from her knitting as Juliet jumped up and made a beeline for the downstairs cloakroom. "That's your third trip to the loo in less than an hour!"

Juliet had been back at home for a month and family life was difficult. With her brothers away – Alan working as a farrier in Stow-on-the-Wold and Bertie back-packing around Europe – it was just Juliet and her parents, and the air was heavy with unspoken questions.

Thank goodness I am working, thought Juliet. Mrs Bishop had encouraged her to go on an advanced floristry course at the local Tech, which took up two evenings a week; she met June for coffee and a chat every Friday, and then she went out with Mike whenever possible. That still left endless hours at home, and Mary seemed to be watching her like a hawk. Getting no reply from her daughter, Mary asked again: "Are you alright, Juliet? Is there a problem?"

"I didn't know you were counting the number of times I used the bathroom," snapped Juliet rudely, slamming the cloakroom door. She stood on the other side and leaned her hot forehead against the cool glass of the mirror. Wearily, she sat on the lavatory seat and inspected her pants. Still nothing. Her period was ten days overdue. What was she going to do? Vague memories of bottles of gin and hot baths floated through her mind or jumping off tables, that often brought it on.

Terror gripped her as she contemplated the unthinkable. *She might be pregnant.* That's just imagination fired by a guilty conscience, she told herself. Get a grip.

She was brought back to reality by a bang on the door and Mary demanding: "Juliet, are you ill?"

Juliet stared into the mirror. She certainly didn't look very well. "Heavens! Could her mother have guessed? That was impossible, there was nothing to know. She would just have to keep acting as if everything was normal. No point in getting into a panic just yet. She put her shoulders back, sucked in her stomach, took a deep breath, and opened the door.

"No, I'm fine, Mum, really," she said steadily. "Just a bit of a tummy bug, I think. Nothing to worry about."

"Well," Mary gave her a considering stare. "You do look a bit peaky. Best have an early night. Take a hot water bottle and go to bed."

"Yes," said Juliet, and escaped thankfully into the sanctuary of her bedroom.

★★★

A week later, Juliet was lounging lazily in a wicker steamer chair in June's beautifully manicured garden. She closed her eyes and lifted her face to the afternoon sun. There was no sound except the gentle buzz of bees around the lavender bushes, and Juliet was suddenly transported to the garden at Villa Florentina with its chirruping cicadas when she had informed a shocked Eric that she was remaining on Capri with Enzo. How happy she had been then.

Quickly shaking herself out of her dream of the past, Juliet confronted the alarming present. She was pregnant. There could be no mistake; that morning, she had been sick.

Luckily, Mary had gone out early to chivvy up the ladies running the Women's Institute stall at the market, and Dennis was at work. There was nobody but the family dog around to witness her depths of despair as she lay weeping on the bathroom floor, gradually accepting the inevitable truth.

She ought to go to the doctor to have it confirmed, but she couldn't go to their family doctor, who had known her since babyhood. That was unthinkable. Her family was so well known in Brighton that she couldn't realistically go to any local doctor at all. Perhaps she could go over to Hove, or even further away, to Worthing and see if she could get an appointment there. Above everything else, her condition could not become public knowledge or even private knowledge; her mind shied away from any thought of telling her parents.

The knot in her stomach, which had been there since the morning, tightened with ever-increasing misery.

That relentless voice in her head had popped up again: This is Enzo's baby. I did bring something of his home with me after all. Should I write and tell him?

It could be Mike's, the voice insisted, playing devil's advocate. He had sex with you, remember? Wondering unhappily if it counted when it was only once, Juliet thought it wasn't fair if you got pregnant when you'd been hardly aware it had happened, and you didn't enjoy it.

She'd had ecstatic sex with Enzo nearly every day for almost four months. How could Mike have made her pregnant in one miserable first go?

"Drink?" asked June, breaking into her thoughts. Pushing herself up out of a deck chair she said: "I can offer you almost anything from cider to orange juice."

Juliet forced herself to open her eyes. "Gin," she replied firmly, adding as an afterthought, "with just a splash of tonic, please. Ooh, and do you have any crisps? I'm starving."

June turned round and stared at her in astonishment.

"Gin? But you never drink gin. Red wine, of course; an

occasional glass of white, yes; sometimes a cider-shandy, but spirits of any kind, never. And you hate crisps. You said they were tasteless and unhealthy. So, what's up?"

She stared down at Juliet, shocked to see the sadness and worry in her eyes. Her skin was almost transparent and dark shadows made huge smudges under her eyes.

"My love, what's happened? June knelt by Juliet's chair, grabbing both her hands and squeezing them tightly. "Tell me."

Juliet drew a shuddering breath and said: "It's something I can't tell anyone but you. I'm pregnant."

"You're *what*!"

"You heard. Pregnant. What on earth am I going to do? There's no way I can be an unmarried mother."

June, completely lost for words, stared at Juliet, dumbfounded. "Does Enzo know?" she asked at last.

"I don't know if it's Enzo's baby. It could be Mike's," admitted Juliet miserably. June clutched her forehead. "Oh, my God, you late starters certainly don't do things by halves, do you? You were sleeping with *both* of them?"

"Well, not at the same time, obviously," replied Juliet with asperity. "I lived with Enzo for four months on Capri, and Mike made love to me almost immediately after I came home, so I suppose there is a possibility it's his baby."

As June gave her a startled questioning glance, Juliet explained: "Well, I was feeling low and really missing Enzo, and Mike made a move…and one thing led to another. It was a mistake; I didn't mean it to happen. It was only once, and I really regret it."

Tears started sliding down her cheeks: "Oh, June, quite apart from anything else, it was the worst sex ever. He was hopeless, and it happened before I realised what he was doing. I should never have got into that situation. I'm not even sure he used a condom. I can't bear to think he might have made me pregnant, and I didn't even enjoy it."

"It happens," said June bluntly. "Don't beat yourself up about how it happened. We just need to find a solution."

Tears were now coursing down Juliet's cheeks unchecked. "It's the end of my life. I can't go on." Putting her arms around her friend, June said soothingly: "Keep calm honey, there's always a way out of every dilemma. So just don't panic."

"Too late for that," said Juliet grimly. "I'm panicking already."

"Let's think," said June. "There must be something you can do; we just need to think of it. She sat back down in her deck chair and closed her eyes; ten seconds later she snapped them open again.

"Okay, you're having a baby and you don't want to be an unmarried mother, so you get yourself a husband. Simple. Problem solved."

"Oh, ha ha! Very funny. This is no time for frivolity. It's the rest of my life we're discussing here."

June grabbed hold of her arm. "Come on, Juliet, stop the headless chicken routine and use your brain. Tell Mike you are pregnant, and I bet he'll assume the baby is his and offer to marry you."

Sniffing back her tears, Juliet thought for a moment and then said: "Firstly, I don't think Mike is the father. I'm pretty sure it's Enzo; secondly, and perhaps more importantly, I don't love him, and I'm certain he doesn't love me. I should have stayed on Capri."

"Yes, well, if you were pregnant in Italy then at least you would know who the father is, but I'd gamble on the fact that you'd still be an unmarried mother. You wouldn't have seen Enzo for dust. From everything you've told me, I don't see the playboy of the Western world as a father."

"Even if he *is* the father? He did say he loved me and wanted to marry me."

June said nothing but just meaningfully raised her eyebrows.

Juliet's face crumpled and she started weeping again, fat tears sending rivers of mascara running down her cheeks.

"That's me finished then," she cried, her voice rising in panic. "What am I going to do? How will I cope? It's no good, I can't cope. I wish I was dead."

June gathered Juliet in her arms and shook her. "Come on, sweetheart, don't be so melodramatic. It will all come out in the wash. I know it seems awful now, but you'll get over this and life goes on. Look at me and the state I was in not so long ago."

"But June, this is a bit different. Getting pregnant when you're not married is just the worst thing that can happen to a girl. You know that."

"Socially, it's a huge *faux pas*, yes," admitted June. "But suddenly finding out on your eighteenth birthday that you are adopted is a whammy too, and I got over that, so you can get over this. Now stop crying and be sensible."

They talked around the problem for over an hour before Juliet reluctantly agreed to take June's advice and tell Mike she was pregnant.

"You don't want to be an unmarried mother, you don't want to tell your mother you're pregnant, and you're adamant you won't have an illegal abortion, so you must get married. It's the only answer. Mike made love to you, and whether you enjoyed it or not this baby could well be his, so tell him."

Juliet was still not convinced. Deep down, she was sure the baby was Enzo's; pretending to Mike that the child was his would be dishonest.

"I don't really want to tell anyone; I just don't want this to get out. I don't want anyone to know," she wailed, beginning to shake uncontrollably. June put out a steadying hand, pointing out quite reasonably that keeping it quiet forever was not an option.

"Everyone's going to know sooner or later. You can't keep this a secret, that's nonsense. Tell Mike. I bet he'll immediately assume it is his and offer to marry you. He may not be as exciting as Enzo, or as fantastic in bed, and no way near as gorgeous, but he is a decent guy and would be a good father. Issue resolved."

Juliet hesitated. "It just doesn't seem fair to Mike, especially as I don't think it's his baby. Quite apart from that, it will mean a lifetime of bad sex. After Enzo, I don't think I can face that."

"I don't think you're really in a position to call the shots," said June brusquely, refusing to back down. "Bad sex or not, it's the only practical solution available. You can always take a lover if you want exciting sex. Anyway, there's more to life than sex." She frowned, "I can't at the moment think quite what, but there is."

Despite her misery, Juliet had to smile. Typical of June, even back in the days when they used to discuss boys in their bedrooms, she had thought sex was the most important thing in the world.

"One person who will be thrilled with the news you're getting married is your mother," continued June. You'll get no argument there. She'll be delighted to get you safely wed. Mine was."

Juliet nodded miserably. "You're probably right. I'll talk to Mike. I won't say it's his; I'll just tell him I'm pregnant and see what he says."

"Go home, have a nice hot bath, put on your prettiest dress, and then go and talk to Mike. In a few hours, you'll be an engaged lady and your problems will be over just like magic." Juliet gave a watery smile. "You make it all sound so easy, but there is still the baby, remember. I can't magic that away."

"You won't need to. Everyone will just assume you fell pregnant immediately and that the baby was born a bit early; it's called a honeymoon baby. There is nothing remarkable about married women having babies. Go on, off you go, strike while the iron is hot and sort it out."

She pushed Juliet through the garden gate and shut it firmly behind her. As she was walking away, June called: "Wait a minute." She rummaged in her handbag and produced a small oblong bottle.

"Use this. It never fails to have the desired effect." Taking it from her, Juliet read the elegant blue and gold label, *Après l'Ondée*.

"Gosh, June, that's Guerlain, it's really expensive."

June shrugged. "Brian brought it back from France for me. Use it – it smells amazing – and then ring me later and tell me everything's sorted," she said.

"Enzo used to buy me Chanel," said Juliet, and she started crying again.

★★★

Mike was very shocked when Juliet told him she was pregnant. His normally ruddy complexion went chalky.

"Shit! That's impossible. I was very careful, and we only did it once."

Was this child really his? Oh Christ, what was he going to do? He couldn't just abandon her. He hadn't planned to get married, although he had to admit that the thought of sex legally on tap with Juliet was tempting. Even kissing her had the astonishing power to reduce him to a quivering wreck, and that one time he had made love to her...it had been sensational; but what happened afterwards was just too embarrassing to think about. He still didn't understand why she had reacted as she did.

Mike was quiet for a long time before taking her hand and, looking at her very seriously, said: "Of course, we will get married. That's if you will have me? Will you marry me, darling? I'm sure we would have got around to it eventually, this has just speeded things up a bit." He kissed her cheek –"Goodness, you smell wonderful."

"Yes, please." Juliet nodded, looking at him with wide, scared eyes.

"Don't worry, it will be fine, Mike assured her. "We'll go now and tell your parents we want to get married as soon as possible. No need to mention the baby, though. Once we are married, it will be no problem at all."

★★★

If Mary and Dennis Campbell were surprised by the couple's news, they hid it admirably. "Congratulations!" said Dennis, kissing Juliet and clapping Mike on the back. "Let me go and open a bottle of something with bubbles in honour of the occasion."

Mary was overcome with delight. She beamed and hugged both Juliet and Mike, totally forgetting that she had never considered him suitable husband material and had not even liked him.

"I can't tell you how pleased I am," she babbled. "I am so happy to see Juliet settled at last. A girl needs a husband and home…and family," she added coyly.

Mike, with an arm around a blushing Juliet, looked at her and raised a querying eyebrow. "Well, Sir," he said to Dennis. "If it's all right with you and Mrs Campbell, we'd like to get married quite soon. I'm thirty-two, as you know, and Juliet isn't keen on a long engagement, so there doesn't seem any point in hanging around."

"How soon is quite soon?" enquired Dennis.

"We thought…" Mike paused, wondering whether he was about to blow open their secret. "Daddy," Juliet jumped in quickly, "we want to get married immediately, in a month to be precise, and we want to get married in the register office. Mike doesn't belong to any church, and as you know, I never go, so we want a civil ceremony."

"Oh, no!" cried Mary, aghast. "I was sure you'd want a white wedding at St Peter's, and there's so much to do for a wedding. A month is far too soon."

"I don't want a big white wedding," said Juliet, and burst into tears. "Over-excited," murmured Mary happily, giving Mike a knowing look. "Oh well, pity about the church wedding, but if that's what you both want." Nothing, not even the ignominy of a register office – so common – could mar her joy.

June had astutely predicted Mary's reaction to the news: a daughter married young was a huge coup. Why, several of her friends had daughters well into their twenties without an engagement ring in sight and were fretting that they would be left on the shelf. Once a girl got to twenty-five, a mother worried about the chances of getting a daughter off her hands; no one wanted an embittered old maid in the family. And here was Juliet, barely out of her teens and about to tie the knot. Although Mary had to admit that Mike wasn't the husband she would have chosen for Juliet, he was better than nothing; a husband in the hand, and all that…

Even though the marriage ceremony was going to be at the register office…Mary gave a disapproving sniff and thought longingly of the beautiful and ancient interior of St Peter's decked out with white lilies, stephanotis, and gypsophila, maybe even a touch of orange blossom…there was no reason why they shouldn't book the big meeting room at the Country Club for the reception.

It had better be a buffet, decided Mary, scrabbling in her handbag for a notebook and pencil; time to make one of her famous lists. Now, if she called into Tuckers tomorrow, she could order the cake. Plenty of time to get that made in a month. Humming happily to herself, she went to phone the caterer. Iris, a friend who played at her bridge club, specialised in organising upmarket buffets and had excellent contacts with licensed victuallers who could supply champagne at very sensible prices.

The forthcoming marriage of her daughter certainly gave Mary bragging rights among like-minded friends and acquaintances.

Chapter Three

IT WAS the day that Juliet had picked up the registrar's form her parents had to sign, giving their consent to the marriage as she was still under the age of majority, that Mike suggested they went for an evening drive.

They travelled along the busy coast road to Peacehaven, where Mike pulled into an empty lay-by at the edge of the shingle beach. Apart from the sound of lapping waves and squawking sea birds, it was quiet and tranquil.

They sat in companionable silence for a while, enjoying the view and the fact that no one else was around.

Then Mike suddenly turned to face her and said: "I'm terribly sorry, sweetheart, but I just can't marry you." Juliet fell back in her seat, totally stunned.

"Why?" she whispered. "What am I going to do? Why have you changed your mind?"

Her shoulders shook as a huge wave of misery shuddered through her. He had to marry her; she was pregnant. Her mind skittered off at a tangent…is that why he hadn't yet given her an engagement ring because he intended all along to call it off?

Juliet recalled Mike telling her he had previously been engaged and his fiancée dumped him. What if it was Mike who had left her? Maybe he was a serial jilter. She narrowed her eyes and moved up against the car door, out of his reach. Her head felt like lead and her stomach full of stones. Tears began to trickle down her cheeks.

Unaware of Juliet's thoughts, Mike exhaled deeply. "Marriage is a lifetime's commitment," he said seriously. "It is hard enough for two people to live together all those years when they are deeply in love. I know you don't love me, and I am realistic enough to accept that if it wasn't for this child – which I must tell you, I am not at all confident is mine – you would never consider marrying me.

"What have we got? A mutual love of plants and flowers and a vague fondness for each other. That's just not enough, Juliet. It's not as if we can't keep our hands off each other." Juliet, her eyes downcast, felt extreme embarrassment as Mike ploughed relentlessly on, all his pent-up frustration spilling out.

"It's not a lack of desire on my part, for Christ's sake. I still really fancy you, but we haven't had sex since that first time at your parents' house, and that wasn't an unqualified success.

"We're supposed to be an engaged couple…you know, desperately wanting to fuck each other."

Juliet caught her breath, perturbed at the expletive. Although June often used the F-word as shock value, it somehow sounded much more brutal when Mike said it.

He gave her a resentful look. "Well, I still really want sex with you. I know you don't feel the same, although I had hoped it might be different after we decided to marry. Sadly not. You will still only let me go so far before you stop and pull away. Fuck…or rather no fuck… do you have *any* idea how frustrating that is for me? It drives me crazy."

As Juliet gave another appalled gasp Mike added sarcastically: "I didn't think you were saving yourself for our wedding night, Juliet, so were you proposing we had a platonic marriage?"

Juliet thought she had never felt so mortified. After that first disastrous mistake, and with memories of her time in Italy so intense, she'd invented endless excuses not to go to bed with Mike. There had been kisses and cuddles and a bit of tactile petting, but nothing more intimate. Even after Mike had agreed to marry her, Juliet was determined not to let things progress further until she absolutely had to. She felt no desire or passion for him: how could she – Enzo had made it impossible for her to want anyone else.

Stopping things from going too far with Mike had been difficult and had taken all her ingenuity. Since agreeing to marry her, he had become very amorous and incredibly insistent.

"I have been giving our situation a lot of serious thought, and it's just not enough to carry us through a lifetime," continued Mike impassively. "Forever is a long, long time, and I now realise that we would be fools to get married."

Juliet had to admit that she hadn't given any real thought to life beyond the wedding which was going to prevent her from becoming an unmarried mother. The idea of forever with Mike didn't give her feelings of unalloyed joy, but she needed to get married.

"So now you are not bothered that I will be ruined, my reputation in tatters?" she snapped bitterly. Mike pulled her towards him and put an arm round her shoulders. He spoke briskly: "Come on, it's not the end of the world."

"It's the end of my world," retorted Juliet, the tears beginning to flow again.

"No, it isn't. I'll still help you. I won't just dump you and disappear. I'll take responsibility for the baby and you can even put my name on the birth certificate if you want. We'll go together to tell your parents. I may not want to marry you, but I won't leave you to face the music alone. I'm the bad guy here; I'll do what I can to help."

"Why do you think you're not the father?" demanded Juliet tearfully.

Mike stared at her impassively, his eyes hard. "Gut feeling; I just know beyond doubt. I suppose it's that Italian you went with while you were in Capri. You obviously fucked him. I realised you weren't a virgin when I made love to you. You've got the wrong man, sweetheart."

Juliet felt totally ashamed. Did he think she had been trying to trick him into marriage? Mike gave a mirthless laugh, "and to think I was responsible for sending you on that holiday!"

He grunted. "If I thought for one minute that I was the father, I would marry you without question. But I'm not prepared to commit to a risky marriage when the child you are having is not mine. "

He turned on the car ignition, "Well, we'd better get you back home. No point sitting here. I'll come in with you to explain to your parents."

Flatly rejecting Mike's offer to tell Mary and Dennis that their daughter was about to become an unmarried mother and besmirch the family name, Juliet insisted: "I must do it myself. Despite what you say, I *am* on my own now, I must face up to this alone. No one else can help, not even you." She knew she was whining, but she couldn't stop herself.

"Spare me the heroics," muttered Mike under his breath as he drove grimly back to Brighton. Juliet looked at his hands on the steering wheel. Gardener's hands: rough with uneven, broken nails from planting and pruning, totally different from Enzo's beautifully manicured ones.

When they arrived at the Campbell's home, Mike leant across her to open the car door, saying: "Well, like I said, I'm here if you need me. It's not my fault you won't accept help."

Picking up the slight tone of hostility in his voice, Juliet gave him a stony stare. His face was blank, his eyes devoid of any expression. Why did she ever think that marriage to Mike would be a good idea? What had happened to the cheerful man who shared her love of gardens and who she had considered a friend?

Juliet got out of the car in a daze, her stomach in knots. How on earth was she going to confess this 'little problem' to her parents?

For a split second, she was tempted to do a bunk, just walk off into the sunset. But running away never sorted anything out, and Juliet knew she was in no way brave enough to just disappear. After all, what would she do, where would she go, how would she manage? They would come looking for her anyway. There was no escape.

She gave Mike an unenthusiastic smile as she slammed the car door.

"Just go! I don't want to talk to you anymore. I must do this alone." With a crash of gears, he sped away leaving her standing on the pavement staring after him.

★★★

Mike drove off quickly before Juliet could see he was crying. He was devastated. Breaking off their engagement had taken every ounce of courage and determination he had. He had probably said too much – he rather regretted the swearing – but his total frustration with the situation had got the better of him, and once the words had started pouring out, he couldn't stop.

The thought of someone else not only having sex with her but making her pregnant was too much to endure.

He had thought he loved her but now realised that his feelings for her were not deep enough to accept another man's child. It was just that he still really wanted her; she had got under his skin. It was obviously lust, not love, Mike decided. He'd get over it eventually.

★★★

Taking a deep breath, Juliet ignored the lump in her throat that was now threatening to choke her and let herself into the house. She had hoped she might be able to postpone telling her parents until some amazing and brilliant solution suggested itself to her, but Mary was hovering in the hallway, having heard the slam of the car door.

She took one look at Juliet's white face and red-rimmed eyes and gasped: "Bad news?"

"Loads of bad news," said Juliet and slid down on the hall carpet, hugging her knees.

Once the Campbells had taken in the fact that not only had their daughter been jilted but was also pregnant and claimed she wasn't sure who the father was, they packed her off to bed with a hot water bottle and, armed with large glasses of Scotch, held a council of war in the sitting room.

Chapter Four

MARY WAS adamant. Juliet could not be unmarried, pregnant, and stay at home.

"She'll have to go somewhere until she has the baby and then have it adopted. I can't have her here. What will people say? I really don't want anyone to know about this; it's just too much to bear. People will have to be told that she has gone travelling or maybe returned to Italy for a spell."

She was so upset that she couldn't bring herself to speak to Juliet. To think that just a few days ago, she had been bragging about the forthcoming wedding to her friends at the Country Club. She'd even ordered the food and the cake. How was she going to cancel all that without Iris finding out the dreadful truth?

Dennis was despatched to tell Juliet that she would have to find somewhere to live where she wouldn't be seen by anyone they knew. "There can be no suggestion that she can keep the child. It's got to be adopted, or she can't come back here – *ever*."

Mary grabbed Dennis's arm and shook it, her nails digging deep into the tweed of his jacket. "You really have got to make her understand that. I mean it. There's no way round a situation like this." Her face was blotched with endless tears, and she looked a million years old.

Mary had briefly flirted with the idea of abortion. It was illegal and she had absolutely no idea who to ask or where to go; but somewhere she was sure there were people who terminated pregnancies at a price. Old women who had once been midwives or doctors who had been struck off, thought Mary vaguely, probably in London or another big city. Even as the thought flittered through her mind, she accepted there was no point even contemplating it. She knew beyond doubt that Dennis would never support something that was illegal, that his religious and moral scruples would forbid it.

To kill an unborn baby was against the law of God and Man, even though that child-to-be might only be a foetus and the size of her thumb. Thou shalt not kill – the sixth Commandment.

It never occurred to Mary that Juliet might have a view on the matter or that the baby she was contemplating in such a cavalier manner was, in fact, her future grandchild. She just wanted the problem to go away before there was any scandal or loss of face.

Dennis felt dreadfully sorry for her. Heaven knows he felt sorry for himself, but there was absolutely nothing he could say or do to make it better. Their daughter was unmarried and pregnant, and they were all constrained by the moral code of decent people.

No one must know about the shame Juliet had brought on the family. She had to be hidden away until all danger was past. How it would affect her, affect them, only time would tell.

Dennis left Mary to her lamentations and went to speak to Juliet, impressing on her that there could be no compromise.

"But Daddy, I'm thinking that I can keep the baby. I'm sure Mike would help financially, and I think I would be able to manage. I'm sure I could continue at the flower shop and the baby could go to a nursery or something…" Her voice faltered as she saw the expression on her father's face.

"Juliet." Dennis's voice was grave. "It is just not possible. You must have the baby adopted, or you will never be able to come back home again. The family cannot be associated with this child, so adoption is the only answer. It's the best thing for you and quite definitely the best thing for the poor little baby. This is serious.

You are not stupid; you know the rules."

Dennis tried not to notice that Juliet was sobbing uncontrollably. He had to stand firm. "Maybe it is harsh and maybe even unfair," he continued, turning away from her to look out of the bedroom window, "but that's the way it is. Keeping the baby is totally out of the question. You knew the risks you were taking when you did what you did. Now, this is the reality.

"Your mother and I are quite willing to help you out with money, at least until the baby is born. Then you and you alone will have to make the decision that will affect not only your future but that of your child. And I really do hope for everyone's sake that you will do what is right. I am sorry, my dear, but that's the way it is."

Juliet sat very still on the edge of the bed, her arms wrapped tightly around her stomach, staring at him in silence, hardly daring to breathe. Her father had always been there for her; even though they were not particularly close, he was usually on her side. Desolation flooded through her. Mary could never be relied upon to back her up, but Dennis always had, whatever the cost; the withdrawal of his support left her totally forsaken.

Dennis, feeling a total monster, left a white and shaken Juliet quietly weeping. He longed to tell her he would make it all right for her, as he had done since she was a little girl. But this was the nineteen sixties, and middle-class morality demanded that girls who got themselves 'into trouble' were removed from the public eye until everything was back to normal. What happened between their departure and their return a year later would never be mentioned; it would be as if it had never happened.

No one considered the trauma caused to those caught up in the ensuing turmoil or the potential distress suffered by adopted children in the future.

★★★

Dennis had already had an extremely uncomfortable interview with Mike. They had met man-to-man in the neutral territory of a local pub, but the casual surroundings could not lessen the strain of the situation. Dennis had been hopeful that he would be able to persuade Mike that marriage was not out of the question.

"I'm really sorry," said Mike. "Juliet's a lovely girl, but we just don't love each other. That is no basis for a successful marriage."

"Oh, love!" said Dennis dismissively, taking a long pull of his pint. "Young people put such a store on being in love. But you wouldn't be the first to marry because you had to and in such cases, I believe, love often follows later." Mike gave a cynical laugh: "I suppose you are referring to a shotgun wedding, but then you must have someone to point the gun at and that's not me because I am not the father of this child."

Seeing the surprise on Dennis's face, Mike twisted the knife: "I must tell you that Juliet was not a virgin when we had sex, which, incidentally, was after her return from Italy. Ask her."

Dennis was profoundly shocked. Despite Juliet's protestation that she really wasn't sure who had fathered her child, he had clung to the belief that the baby was Mike's and had refused to accept that it could be otherwise.

They had been going to get married, for God's sake; how could it have gone wrong so quickly? Or was Mike going to marry her because of the baby? And if that was the case, what had made him change his mind?

As her father, Dennis was desperate to believe that Juliet hadn't slept around. But had she? Her claim that she didn't know who the father of her child was meant there must have been at least one other lover.

To his lasting shame, he was forced to admit that he didn't really know his daughter as he should. Of course, there *was* that Italian fellow that she had wanted to marry. Did Juliet get pregnant in Italy? So many unanswered questions.

Now Dennis was forced to reconsider. Mike was adamant that he wasn't the father and that he would not marry Juliet. There was little hope that the Italian, or anyone else, would suddenly materialise and offer to marry his daughter. So that was it, then. Juliet really would be an unmarried mother with all the heartache and misery that was sure to follow. What a mess.

Mike reiterated that he was quite willing for Juliet to name him as the father on the child's birth certificate and that he was also prepared to pay Juliet a small weekly sum to help tide her over while she was unable to work.

Dennis held up a forbidding hand. "No, no! Thank you. It's much appreciated, but we will look after Juliet financially. It would appear this is not strictly your problem. However, I do think Juliet…and the child…really would appreciate having your name on the birth certificate. That would be a great kindness, beyond the call, and will almost certainly make life easier for both in the future."

The two men shook hands and parted, with Dennis promising to keep Mike in touch with events as they unfolded.

"It will probably be best if you don't contact Juliet again. You have my business card. Give me a call if you need anything. It will be better to keep the women out of it. Juliet and her mother are both in a highly emotional state."

Part Five
Juliet and The Morrisons

(1963-1964)

Reflection

> *"Love conquers all difficulties, surmounts all obstacles, and effects what to any other power would be impossible."*
> William Godwin, English journalist,
> political philosopher, and novelist

WHEN I went to live with Morrisons at Western House, my life was at its lowest ebb. I joined their family as a stranger, but their unconditional support and love offered me the security I craved and the courage to finally understand and accept who I was.

Wrapped in the warmth of their affection, I was able to assess and challenge the patriarchal rules that had governed me since childhood. I became closer to Mr and Mrs M than I was to my own parents.

Mrs M was a Lady in her own right, her father having been an Earl. Not that she ever used the title, and I only found out about it by accident.

"It's of little consequence," she told me in her usual down-to-earth way. "I left that life behind me when I married."

Both she and Mr M had the charm and courtesy bestowed by old money and lived in comfortably faded splendour, something to which my mother and her ostentatious Country Club friends could only aspire. Despite their obvious wealth and aristocratic ancestry, the Morrisons were modest and unassuming.

Mrs M's mother, known by everyone as 'The Countess,' only visited once during my time with them. She was an autocratic old lady, gracious but distant, and travelled with her own entourage of chauffeur and lady's maid. She apparently never stayed for longer than a few hours, preferring her London apartment in Cadogan Square to the hurley burley of her daughter's abode.

"She dislikes sleeping in strange beds," said Mr M, chuckling to himself. Although Juliet knew he was fond of his imperious mother-in-law, she suspected that, like everyone else, Mr M was slightly in awe of her. If he was, his kindness and natural good manners ensured it was never apparent.

The Countess brought a breath of nobility, charm, and a certain excitement to the household. Everyone rushed around to tidy up the spacious entrance hall, returning discarded bridles, muddy boots and a Barbour to the tack room and picking up toys and dog bones from the sitting room floor. Meanwhile, Moira, the Morrison's cleaner, spent extra time making sure the main bathroom sparkled, putting out fresh towels and a new tablet of Pears soap. The family knew these were the only rooms into which The Countess would venture, so the rest of the house was left in its usual state of cheerful disorder.

On this visit, The Countess was accompanied by a tall, elegant young man, thin as a reed and probably about my age. Sallow-skinned and blue-chinned, he had a curious accent and was dressed completely in black couture. He looked like a malevolent stick insect, but nothing could be further from the truth. He was very friendly, with easy manners, taking my hand and giving a little bow and a click of his heels as I was introduced to him.

"Michael is spending a few weeks with me while his mother is in Switzerland. She didn't want him living in Paris on his own," said The Countess, quickly forestalling any questions about her companion. Like many of her ilk, she upheld the mantra 'Never complain, never explain.' The Morrisons knew this only too well, and if they were curious, they gave no indication.

The children, their newly washed faces looking like polished apples, immediately gravitated towards this exciting stranger and, after politely kissing The Countess on a proffered cheek, they took Michael with them into the garden where he happily entertained them all afternoon.

I later learned from Mrs M that Michael was the heir of a now deposed Eastern European monarchy, which doubtless accounted for his striking appearance, expensive clothes, and impeccable manners.

The Morrisons had hardly waved their visitors goodbye when there was a ring at the back door and Bob, the farm manager, came into the kitchen, gripping the arm of a young village boy he had caught stealing eggs from the hen coops.

"Says his mother and brothers have no food. No money," he explained shortly. "What you want me to do with him?"

"Sit down," Mrs M quietly commanded the frightened lad. He perched on the edge of a stool at the large, scrubbed kitchen table while she fed him buttered toast and cups of sugary tea, asking him gentle questions about his family as she did so.

She turned to Bob and said: "Thank you for bringing him up here, Bob. I'll deal with him now."

"Right, ma'am," said the farm manager, and as he moved towards the door, Mrs M called: "Oh Bob, when you're back at the farm, please will you send someone up with a box of eggs for me." He nodded: "Certainly. Will do."

Moira stopped on her way through the kitchen to the broom cupboard, making a little moue with her mouth and shrugging her shoulders. "Never turns no one away," she told me as she nodded towards the boy. "Don't matter who they are. Proper saint she is."

When the lad had eaten his fill, he was sent home with a basket of groceries from Western House's abundant larder, together with vegetables from the farm; I noticed there was a box of eggs among the bounty.

"Tell your mother I'll come and visit in a few days to see how you're doing," promised Mrs M seeing him out, before putting on an apron and returning to the kitchen to organise the family supper.

I mention this incident more as an aside and as a contrast between the regal visit of The Countess and that of the village boy, both ends of the social spectrum, all within the space of a few hours.

Everyone who came onto the Morrisons' radar, whatever their station in life, their shortcomings, or problems, were accepted and valued by this exceptional couple. I was just one of the many they helped, and I will always be grateful to them. Their example changed my life.

Chapter One

MARY RETURNED from the eight o'clock communion service at St Peter's with a leaflet, which she slapped down in front of Juliet, who was unenthusiastically contemplating a boiled egg with toast soldiers.

"I saw this on the church porch. Thought it might be useful," she said curtly, removing the pins from the navy velour hat she wore to church. It was from the Diocesan Committee for Moral Welfare and claimed to offer 'a lifeline to girls in trouble', urging them to contact the Moral Welfare Officer.

Juliet picked it up and then dropped it as if it was hot coals. "You have to be joking," she told her mother. "I'm certainly not having anything to do with people who have the ghastly name of Moral Welfare. It's not my morals which need welfare."

Mary regarded her coldly. "That is debatable. Some may say your morals are certainly suspect. However, if you won't take the help that is on offer, there is nothing I can do. All I will say, though, is that you had better hurry up and get things sorted. Another few weeks and you will be showing. And I can't have you here then." She turned on her heel and walked out of the room.

★★★

It was June who told Juliet about the Society for Unmarried Mothers. She'd seen an article about the charity in a woman's magazine and wrote down the telephone number.

"Give them a call," she said to Juliet. "It can't do any harm. From what I understand, they have several mother and baby homes in London where you can go. I know it all sounds horrid, sweetheart. But it is worth checking out."

June was feeling excessively remorseful about the way Juliet's relationship with Mike had ended. She was the one who had encouraged the expectation that Mike would marry her if he knew she was pregnant. It seemed a good idea at the time and the only solution to a difficult problem, but it just hadn't worked out as she had expected.

It hadn't occurred to June that Mike might have concerns about committing to a loveless marriage or that he would be adamant he wasn't the father. She knew he really fancied Juliet, and she had believed that sexual desire would overcome everything else. She had been proved wrong.

Of course, Juliet could have saved the situation if only she had let Mike make love to her now and again. Surely that wasn't too much to ask.

Although she had sympathised with Juliet's refusal to have sex with Mike while she was still grieving for Enzo, June had to admit she really didn't understand Juliet's reluctance after she had recovered, especially when he had agreed to marry her.

She had asked why she was so adamant that she wouldn't let Mike sleep with her, but Juliet had been uncharacteristically snappy, saying: "I just don't want to talk about it." June put it down to hormones. Pregnant women were well known for their unpredictability.

June sighed. Oh well, they'd always had very different attitudes towards sex, even when they were teenagers. All June could do now was to help Juliet cope with the difficult and painful months to come.

Chapter Two

IT TOOK Juliet several days to make the call to London. She wouldn't use the telephone at home in case she was overheard and walked up and down past the red kiosk in the town centre several times before going in and dialling the London number.

"It felt just like visiting the dentist," she told June afterwards. "I was terrified; I didn't want to give my name at first, goodness knows why, as they don't know me from Adam. I know it sounds pathetic; I just needed to be anonymous."

The woman who answered the phone had been bright and cheerful and made Juliet feel more relaxed. "Why don't you come and see us? Then, we can find out the best way to help you. Don't worry, my dear. I'm sure there is something we can do."

June went with Juliet to visit the Society's offices in Paddington. They were on the third floor of a dingy tower block and Juliet made June trudge up several flights of stairs because she refused to get into the dilapidated lift, which smelt of urine and vomit.

"I can't do this, it's horrible. Let's just go home," she whined. But June urged her on. "Come on. We might as well find out what it's all about now we're here. It might not be too bad." She grabbed Juliet's hand and hauled her up the last few steps.

Once they reached the charity's office, things were, indeed, much better. Although small, verging on the pokey, the office was bright and cheerful with modern art posters on the walls and a bunch of drooping pink carnations on the corner of a tiny desk. A woman who was, maybe, in her mid-forties stood up as they entered, gave them a beaming smile, and stretched out her hand. "Welcome. You must be Juliet. I'm Sandra Moran. And I'm sure you are June, yes? Now, you must both be gasping for a cup of something – tea, coffee? She looked at them enquiringly with her head on one side.

"Tea, please," said Juliet and June in unison. "No sugar," added Juliet. "Right, I'll get that sorted for you," said Sandra. "Meanwhile, take a seat and have a look at our brochures. They give you a better idea of what we are all about and the mother and baby homes on offer."

Feeling much happier, Juliet sat and read about the Society for Unmarried Mothers. It seemed there were a lot of girls who were pregnant and unmarried and needed the charity's help. This was confirmed a few moments later when Sandra Moran returned with three steaming mugs of tea and assured them that girls like Juliet were not at all unusual.

"We deal with girls in your situation all the time," said Sandra. "I know things are difficult at home. They usually are. Most parents do not understand at all. But you have no reason to get upset or worry. We'll soon sort you out." She explained that the usual way was to find a live-in job where Juliet could stay until six weeks before the baby was due. Then she would go into a mother and baby home; there were three to choose from in various price brackets, before going into the hospital to have her baby, then returning to the home with the child for another six weeks until it could go to its adoptive parents. It was all as easy as A B C. Nothing to worry about at all.

After hearing about the mother and baby homes, all in London, Juliet decided on the one in Clapham. "Why that one?" asked June. Juliet shrugged her shoulders. "I don't know, really. It looks all right. In fact, they all look much of a muchness, and as we can't go and look around before choosing, why not?"

Sandra Moran smiled. "You're right," she told Juliet. "There's not much to choose between them, really; it's just location and the price, of course. I'm afraid these facilities are not part of the NHS and so not free. You must pay for your bed and board, but it's very reasonable.

"However, if you go to Clapham, you'll have your baby at The Royal, which is very good, one of the best teaching hospitals in the country, you know. Hopefully, they will have a vacancy at the right time. Now you just sit there and drink your tea and I'll go and make a couple of phone calls. Won't be a tick."

Sandra returned about ten minutes later, a file of papers in her hand. "Well, you are a lucky girl. The mother and baby home can take you from the end of March, which is just right, and The Royal will have a maternity bed about the time you need to go in, so is that settled?" Juliet agreed and signed the various forms that Sandra put in front of her.

"Now," said Sandra. "All we must do is find you a live-in job somewhere away from Brighton. How are you with children? Most of the jobs are for nannies and mothers' helpers."

"That's fine," said Juliet. "I'm sure I'll be able to cope."

"Well, most of our employers are very special people, so I am sure we can find you somewhere you'll be happy. Sadly, it's not everyone who will take on an unmarried mum. Goodness knows what they are afraid of, although I do believe that some wives assume that unmarried mothers are floozies with loose morals who might lead their husbands astray." She looked at Juliet's horrified face and laughed. "Don't worry, pet, only joking!"

June chortled. "Can't imagine anyone thinking Juliet was going to lead a man astray with a figure like hers!" Sandra and June regarded Juliet's neat little bump, which was just about discernible under her loose blouse. Juliet gave a wan smile. "I already feel huge," she admitted. "Not at all glamorous, I'm afraid, and certainly not with any inclination to pull!"

Sandra smiled and, with the promise that she would contact Juliet with news of a live-in job as soon as possible, showed them out. "I know it's a bit grim around here," she said, "but as a charity we can't afford anything plush."

"Oh, that's all right, we understand," said Juliet. But she still refused to use the lift, and the two girls descended gingerly down the dirty stairs and out into a murky west London afternoon.

Less than a week later there was a letter from Sandra Moran to tell Juliet that a family in rural Hampshire would be happy to give her a job and a home.

'Mrs Morrison is herself pregnant and desperately in need of someone to help with four other children, all under the age of six.' wrote Sandra. 'Do give her a ring. I'm sure you'd fit in very well. They are a nice family.'

June was sceptical when Juliet showed her the letter. "Four children under six. Do you think you could cope?"

"Might be a case of having to," replied Juliet grimly. "I don't see a lot of alternatives."

She telephoned Mrs Morrison and immediately felt reassured. "How wonderful to hear from you," said a pleasant voice. "I was beginning to think I was going to have this baby with no help at all. It's all a bit manic here, I'm afraid. But you will be very welcome. Do you want to come over and see if you think you would be happy with us?"

Juliet was charmed. "I'm willing to take the risk if you are," she said. "When would you like me to start, Mrs Morrison?"

Mrs Morrison gave a chuckle. "Today? Well, as soon as you can, anyway. Oh, and by the way, everyone calls us Mr and Mrs M, so we hope you will, too. Morrison sounds far too formal."

★★★

Once Juliet had firm plans to move away from Brighton, Mary cheered up and was almost encouraging. "It's all for the best, and I daresay everything will work out well," she said, putting on the kettle to make Juliet a cup of tea while she was packing her case. Juliet said nothing. She felt tired and sick and scared.

Mary gave her a long glance and said: "You're sure to be a bit iffy about it. Everyone is of the unknown. But like you said, the Morrisons sound like a lovely family; I feel sure you have fallen on your feet and will soon settle in." Neither she nor Juliet mentioned the move to Clapham. Mary hadn't spoken about the baby for weeks, and it was almost as if it didn't exist.

A couple of days later, she drove Juliet to Brighton station. "Now you are sure you know how to get to Waterloo from Victoria. Get a taxi if you aren't keen on the tube, and then it's straight from Waterloo to Petersfield. No need to change trains." She looked down at Juliet's large suitcase. "Well, better get a cab anyway. You don't want to be dragging that case onto the underground. Now, have you got everything? Money, tickets…?"

"Mum!" said Juliet wearily. "You sound as if I can't look after myself."

"Hmm." Mary obviously decided it was better not to speak her mind. She gave a brief smile. "Ah, well. Just give us a ring and let us know you've arrived safely." She pecked her daughter on the cheek and left her standing on the London-bound platform, luggage at her feet, without a backward glance.

Chapter Three

SIX PEOPLE, including Juliet, got off the train at Petersfield, and from among the handful of country women and the gaggle of chattering schoolchildren waiting on the platform, it wasn't difficult to identify the middle-aged man with rosy cheeks as Mr Morrison. He looked like a farmer, but his expensive tweeds and well-polished brogues told a different story.

"Juliet, I presume?" he said with a big smile. "Welcome. We are all delighted to have you with us, particularly my wife. I hope you are prepared for the fray. I'm afraid our house is full of animals and children, all needing constant attention!"

He led her out to a battered grey pickup truck and slung her case in the back, where a bouncing black and white collie with a laughing face was jumping around. "Hoping for a w-a-l-k," said Mr Morrison, jerking his thumb towards the dog. "Not going to be lucky today, though, I'm afraid. He turned towards Juliet. "Come on, in you get. Can you manage the step?"

As Juliet settled herself into the passenger seat, Mr M said: "We're only about fifteen minutes from home, but I need to take a slight detour to pick up some hay bales that Bob, our farm manager, needs rather urgently. Is that okay?" He glanced at her anxiously. "You must be a bit tired after your journey. I know Mrs M has been really exhausted these past few months." Juliet smiled. What a lovely man. "No, it's fine," she said.

Mr M drove to the seed merchants, where a man was waiting

with the hay bales. "Bob phoned and asked if you would pick up some haylage, too," he said.

"Okay, thanks Dave. If Bob says we need it, then we must get it." Dave swung the bales onto the back of the truck, and Mr M gave him a wave of thanks as he returned to the driving seat. "Now off we go home," he said. "I bet you need a cup of tea."

The Morrisons lived in what could only be described as a small mansion. Juliet gasped as Mr M turned the pick-up through an ivy-clad wrought iron arch and down a sweeping drive, pulling up outside an ancient heavy oak door. "I'll just drop you off here and then take this hay round to the stables for Bob," said Mr M, heaving her case out from under the now slumbering collie.

As he spoke, the door was thrown open, and a heavily pregnant woman came tottering down the steps, surrounded by a trio of barking dogs.

"Careful cherub," said Mr M. "Juliet doesn't want to have to nurse you with a broken leg as well as everything else we're going to expect her to do. Down, you horrible mutts," he shouted at the dogs who, now joined by the black and white collie, were swarming around Juliet, wagging their tails, and yelping with pleasure.

"It's okay," she said, laughing and putting out a hand to stroke the smooth head of a beige greyhound with soulful brown eyes. I've got a dog at home."

"Well, just be firm," said Mr M, "and don't let them be a nuisance. Or the cats," he added, as a fat ginger tom with a loud purr began to wind itself around Juliet's legs.

Mrs M flung her arms round Juliet and kissed her cheek. "I am so relieved to see you. You've no idea," she said. "Welcome to Western House. I do hope you will be very happy with us. Now come and see the children; they are dying to meet you!"

With the warm waves of friendship and appreciation lapping around her, Juliet relaxed and felt happier than she had done for months.

The Morrison children ranged from Rupert, a serious five-year-old – "I'm really six because it's my birthday next week," he informed Juliet – to two-year-old identical twins Celia and Cora. In the middle was Adele, an angelic-looking three-year-old with flaxen curls. "They are all adopted," Mrs M explained as she and Juliet made beans on toast and poured glasses of milk for the children's tea.

"We were told we couldn't have babies of our own, and neither Mr M nor I could contemplate life without children. Then, out of the blue, I found I was pregnant. It was an absolute miracle, and the doctors are totally flummoxed."

She laughed, rubbing her swollen belly. "However, as you can see, I am quite definitely having a baby, and in the not-too-distant future. But deeply wanted though this baby is, it cannot be more wanted or more loved than the four we have already." Juliet glanced at the children, who were gently bickering around the tea table. No stranger walking in would have guessed that these four were not natural siblings.

"Each child came to us with a story," Mrs M continued. "Rupert's mother was an Australian, in London on a working holiday when she became pregnant. It seemed there was no way she could tell her family about the baby, so she put him up for adoption as soon as he was born. We've had him since he was six weeks old.

"Adele has a similar story, except her mum was a ballet dancer, not sure which company, but she was very successful, I understand. It was the baby or her career, and she chose ballet. So once again, we took Adele as a tiny baby."

Juliet, who had started washing up, sat down on the nearest chair, a wet plate clutched to her chest. "And the twins?"

Mrs M gazed into the distance. "Ah, well, they are a bit different. A rather sad story, really. Their mother was only fifteen, little more than a child herself, and didn't know she was pregnant until she became ill. She was very thin and malnourished; she came from an incredibly poor family somewhere in the Midlands, and for ages, she refused to say who the father was. Eventually the social workers discovered it was her twin brother.

"Yes, I know," she said, as Juliet gasped. "It is deeply shocking that things such as incest still go on. But the truly shocking thing is that because she didn't look after herself properly – well, I don't expect she knew how to, and maybe also because of the close relationship – the girls were affected and it was touch-and-go whether they would survive. They are much stronger now, but Celia is slightly brain-damaged and will always need care; she's never going to be able to live on her own. Cora's okay, although small for her age and she may eventually have some problems; we must just wait and see. But they are both very happy children."

"They are all very lucky children," said Juliet firmly, "to have such wonderful adoptive parents who are giving them a far better life than they could have hoped for otherwise."

Mrs M smiled and touched Juliet lightly on the shoulder. "And what are the plans for your baby?" she asked softly, taking the still-damp plate out of her hands.

"I have to have it adopted," said Juliet sadly. "I have no choice; my parents have made that very clear. Otherwise, I would have liked to have kept it."

Mrs M shook her head. "I know it must sound as if I am biased, but adoption really is the best solution all round. Can you imagine what it is like to be a single mum without support? Having to work full time to keep you both, sending the baby to a minder and then, after a busy day in the shop or office or wherever, picking up the baby, going home and having to cope with all the domestic things. Night feeds before being woken up at six in the morning to start again. It would mean a huge sacrifice on your part. There is still an awful lot of discrimination against unmarried mothers, I fear. You would doubtless meet with a lot of unpleasantness, and is that fair on the child? Will he or she thank you for it?"

Juliet looked stricken and Mrs M felt heartily sorry for her but decided to continue, hoping her words would strike home. "You are still very young and you will want to get married, eventually, you know. But it takes a very special sort of man to take on another man's child and love it as his own. And what if you had other children? Would this child be the odd one out? These are all things to consider, Juliet.

"Just remember, out there somewhere is a lovely couple who are desperately unhappy because they can't have a child of their own. The gift you are going to give them…your baby…is everything they have ever wanted. It will be cared for and loved as if it were their own flesh and blood."

Juliet nodded. "I know. My best friend is adopted and she had a wonderful childhood, although her parents didn't tell her about the adoption until she was eighteen, and it caused so much unhappiness and trouble."

"Goodness." It was Mrs M's turn to look shocked. "What a dreadful thing, and really against all modern thinking, you know. All our children were told from babyhood before they could really understand. Well, the twins still don't understand, but I think Adele has grasped it. She'll tell you her real mummy is a beautiful princess, and Rupert knows he is an Aussie and longs to go there when he is older. The highlight of his life so far has been seeing kangaroos and koala bears at the zoo. Knowing they came from Australia just like him!"

Chapter Four

JULIET VERY quickly settled into a happy routine at Western House. She felt more at home there with the Morrisons than she ever had at her parents' home in Brighton. Everyone from Moira, the cleaning lady, to farm manager Bob and his team, and the girls who looked after the horses, accepted her as part of the family. And more importantly, accepted her situation and didn't seem to treat her any differently because she was pregnant and not married.

Juliet became firm friends with Kathy, who worked in the Morrison's stables, and the two girls often went shopping on their days off and spent time gossiping and watching television together. Occasionally, they went to the cinema, and Juliet was pleased to discover that Kathy was also a devoted Elvis fan. She wasn't June, but it was good to have a friend.

There was only one blip when the grandmother of Rupert's young friend Christopher refused to let the child play at Western House because there was an unmarried mother living there. She was quite happy for Rupert to go to Christopher's home but didn't want her grandson to encounter an unmarried girl who was having a baby. Juliet felt totally humiliated when she heard, but both Mr and Mrs M refused to be browbeaten.

"Such ignorance shouldn't be acknowledged," said Mr M as his wife comforted Juliet. "Rupert has plenty of other friends to play with. It's poor little Chris I feel sorry for, growing up in such an unenlightened family."

★★★

Following the incident with Christopher's grandmother, Mrs M suggested Juliet wore a wedding ring. Juliet had resisted at first, thinking it was unnecessary, shying away from such a potent symbol of marriage.

Mrs M was adamant a ring would protect her from unkind gossip, and Mr M agreed, saying: "Really, Juliet, I think it would be a sensible thing to do. Life is still not easy for unmarried mothers, and it may prevent you from facing some unnecessary nastiness, especially when you go to London."

They were shopping for school shoes in Liphook when Mrs M urged Juliet into a second-hand shop where she found a suitable ring for a couple of pounds.

For reasons she couldn't articulate, Juliet refused to wear it immediately, but while out on a solitary walk she impulsively went into the village church. It was empty, and sitting quietly in a pew at the back of the nave, she took the thin circle of gold out of her purse and slipped it onto her finger.

My wedding ring finger, she reflected sadly; it wasn't meant to be like this. Breathing in the musty smell of centuries, with the sweet aroma of incense wafting down the aisle, Juliet looked down at her left hand, now with the gold band on the fourth finger.

She closed her eyes as memories of Enzo swirled around her mind; he was so often in her thoughts nowadays. She was sure the baby was his and wondered what would have happened if she had stayed with him in Italy. Would he really have left her as June had suggested? She would never know. Nor would he ever know that they had a child together.

Carefully manoeuvring her swollen body so she could kneel on a hassock, Juliet said a short prayer and began to feel peaceful and more positive than she had for weeks. Echoing the wise words of Mrs M, she told herself: "I will get over this and come out the other side."

★★★

A couple of weeks after Juliet's arrival, Mrs M gave birth to a daughter. "We are calling her Frances, and she will be known as Frankie," said Mr M happily. "Well, well, another girl; it's just wonderful."

He smiled at Juliet. "Your turn soon, young lady!" Juliet shivered. Despite her ballooning figure, she was trying to put giving birth, the mother-and-baby home, and the inevitable final step out of her mind.

It was Mrs M who noticed that Juliet was beginning to feel nervous about the future. Everyone else accepted her at face value, and because the girl was bright and cheerful, the bustling household assumed all was well. Mrs M knew otherwise. Her sharp eyes had seen the worry on Juliet's face and picked up on her new habit of going for long, solitary country walks, often accompanied only by the dogs and baby Frankie in her pram.

She caught up with her late one morning as Juliet was laying the table for lunch in the big dining room. "Put down those knives and forks, Juliet, and come a have a chat," said Mrs M, patting the seat of a chair invitingly. Juliet sat down and the fat ginger cat, which had become her shadow, immediately jumped up and, after padding around in the circle, settled down purring on her lap.

Mrs M came straight to the point. "So, what's on your mind, my love?" Juliet gave her a long look and sighed. "I am really scared about what's happening. For the first time, really, it is all beginning to sink in." She looked down at her swelling belly. "I've suddenly realised just what I have done."

"But it's not the end of the world, Juliet. No one has died. Yes, you are going to have to go through a difficult and horrible time. Nothing can be done to change that. But there is light at the end of the tunnel, and you *will* get back to normal."

"Mmm." Hugging the now sleeping cat and gently stroking its cushiony head, Juliet looked as if she was going to say something but stopped herself. "So, what else is bothering you?" asked Mrs

M. "I get the feeling that there's more to this worry than you're letting on."

"It's Moira…and Kathy."

"Moira and Kathy?" Mrs M was at a loss. She couldn't imagine how her cleaner and one of the grooms could possibly have anything to do with Juliet's state of mind.

"Oh, we've been talking," explained Juliet. "They know I am going to have my baby adopted, and they both have experience of adoption."

Mrs M suddenly understood the situation. She remembered hearing that Moira had been adopted as a baby and had endured a difficult life, but she had no idea that Kathy had been adopted – or maybe she had given a child for adoption?

"Ah, I see. They've been telling you what happened to them, and it's left you worried and confused."

"Yes, well, it's not their fault. I wanted to know, but now I wish I hadn't asked!" said Juliet and burst into tears. "Tell me their stories, if you think they won't mind," said Mrs M, handing over a box of tissues and settling down into her chair, and I'm sure I can put your mind at rest."

Chapter Five

MOIRA HAD been born in 1929 to a fourteen-year-old girl called Florry and was adopted at six weeks old, straight from a mother and baby home in Liverpool. Her adoptive mother, Olive, had lost a baby son and consequently had a nervous breakdown. So, Moira was adopted by Olive to 'replace' the baby who died at birth.

"A bit like my friend June, she was a replacement baby," said Juliet. "And my mother had a baby boy, who died before I was born." Mrs M nodded but didn't speak.

Olive's husband, Tommy, was in the army and the adoption was sorted without his knowledge, so when he returned home on leave, he discovered, to his surprise and slight displeasure, that he had gained a daughter. Unfortunately for Moira, her adoptive family was very poor and totally dysfunctional, but they appeared to scrape by with help from Olive's mother. Then, over the next few years, Olive and Tommy had a son and two more daughters.

Olive really didn't cope well with any of the children or life in general, but she was mollycoddled by her mother and Tommy, who, although still in the services, did what he could to help his slatternly wife. While Tommy was on a tour of duty abroad, Olive offloaded first Moira and then her two natural daughters onto her long-suffering mother. The boy she kept at home, maybe as a reminder of the child she had lost at birth.

"So, Moira was, in effect, given away twice – by her birth mother and then her adoptive mother – and was brought up by the woman she called Nan," Juliet told Mrs M.

Moira always knew she was treated differently from the other girls in the family, but never knew why. It was only when she was eleven and had to take her birth certificate to register for secondary school that she realised her certificate was different from all the others and discovered she was adopted.

She never really knew much about the circumstances. Nan would only tell her that her mother was very young and her father was much older. But the brother who stayed with Olive knew the story. He'd heard it from his mother and took great pleasure in telling Moira just how she had been conceived.

"The next bit is really not very nice," Juliet told Mrs M. "I really wished Moira hadn't told me this."

"Best get on with it and get it over with then," said Mrs M calmly.

A widower who lived along the road had asked if Florry would help him keep the house, doing bits of cleaning and washing in return for a small wage. The man was old enough to be her grandfather and had two married daughters. Nobody really found out exactly what happened, whether the old man forced himself upon the girl or whether it was more of a seduction, but Florry was only thirteen when she became pregnant, and he was sent to prison because of it.

"Although the way Moira was conceived was horrible, the bit that worries me most is Moira being given away twice," Juliet told Mrs M. "What if the people who adopt my baby pass it on to someone else? Suppose something awful happens to it."

Mrs M looked at her with real sympathy. What on earth was Moira thinking telling Juliet a story like that? She made a mental note to have a strong word with her.

"That was a one-off," she said gently. "Moira was just very unlucky, and it was a long, long time ago. Dysfunctional families aren't allowed to adopt nowadays. Everything is much stricter and there are so many hoops to jump through before you can even be considered for adoption. I think I can safely say that nothing like that will happen to your baby. It will be adopted by lovely people who will give it a good life, and it will grow up happy and content," said Mrs M, thankfully noticing that Juliet appeared a bit less strained.

"So, what about Kathy's story?"

"Oh, no way near as upsetting," said Juliet, sounding much more cheerful. She wriggled in the chair, trying to settle into a more comfortable position, and the cat, disturbed from sleep, jumped off her lap and stalked off, tail waving to signal his disapproval.

"Kathy was adopted too, by a nice couple who she loves very much. She has an older sister, who is also adopted and a younger sister, who is the natural daughter of her adoptive parents. She had a good childhood and although they didn't have pots of money, her parents paid for her to have riding lessons and do a stable management course because they knew how much she loved horses. That's how she got the job here."

Mrs M relaxed. Thank goodness, not another horror story. "So why has Kathy's story caused you problems?"

"Well, not problems, really," said Juliet, "except she said that she was absolutely nothing like her parents or her older sister, not in looks, colouring, personality, or anything.

"Kathy said she always felt the odd one out. Her big sister is a real bookworm and got a scholarship to Oxford and her parents are very clever too, so is her younger sister. But Kathy said that she was only ever interested in horses and left school at fifteen with no real qualifications."

"Oh, Juliet," said Mrs M, laughing. "I really do think you are reading too much into this. "Many children, adopted or not, are like that. Everyone in a family is an individual, everyone is different."

"But I thought the adoption agency was meant to ensure that a baby did at least resemble in some way the family that was taking it on," replied Juliet. "Kathy says her parents are both fair-haired and blue-eyed, while, as you know, Kathy has brown hair and brown eyes…"

"Enough," said Mrs M sternly. "You have just got to stop overthinking and leave the experts to do their work. The very best possible family will be found for your precious baby, and he or she will fit into it perfectly." Feeling much happier, Juliet continued with preparations for lunch, but deep down inside, there were still nagging doubts.

★★★

A few days later a telephone call from June underlined the precarious position of women who broke the strict rules of society. An unmarried typist in Brian's office was pregnant, and the father was one of the junior clerks. Although the man was also single, he had refused to marry the girl, claiming their affair was never 'serious' and that she had understood that from the outset.

"You cannot imagine the furore," said June. "Not just pregnant but made pregnant by a member of staff. It's an enormous scandal, but of course, in the eyes of the powers-that-be, it is all the wretched girl's fault. They are saying she must have led him on. That's patriarchy for you. Men come first every time. Isn't it strange that a woman's voice is never heard until something like this happens, and then it's obviously all her fault because she suddenly acquired the ability to make him do it.

"They were both summonsed into the presence of the senior partner, who read the riot act, and then – and Jules, I really can't believe this bit – he gave the girl the sack and sent the clerk back to his desk with a flea in his ear. So, she's lost her job with immediate effect, and he's kept his. How unfair is that? It takes two to make a baby.

"I ranted and raved to Brian about it, but he can't see there's anything wrong. It's what we were saying, Jules, about men walking away from their responsibilities and girls having their mistakes around for nine months for all to see.

"Brian doesn't know, but I've given the poor girl Sandra Moran's telephone number. Hopefully, she will be able to help her because it seems no one else is going to. Her father was killed in the war, and her mother can't be told. And that awful bloke won't even speak to her now and says he wants nothing more to do with her, the creep. So, she is quite alone. I only hope she may be able to get some money out of him. Really, it makes my blood boil!"

Juliet put down the phone, feeling slightly ashamed of the fuss she had been making to Mrs M about her fears and anxieties. At least she had friends and support – and even if she had been forced to leave home for a while, she still had people around to help her, unlike the girl in Brian's office. There's always someone worse off than you," murmured Juliet as she went off to help Mrs M with the nursery tea.

★★★

Time moved relentlessly on, and all too soon, the day came when Juliet had to leave the Morrisons and move to London.

"It's going to be a horrid time for you," agreed Mrs M as she drove Juliet to the station to catch the train to Waterloo, "but the baby is only seven weeks away, and that time will soon go. And then you will be in sight of getting your life back to normal. I am always on the end of a phone," she added as tears began to drip down Juliet's cheeks. "Bear up, my love. I'm sure all will be well."

She helped Juliet out of the car and thrust a piece of paper into her hand. "Now Mr M has written down the route for you, so you don't have to worry about getting lost. Make sure you take a cab from Waterloo. We don't want you travelling by tube in your condition. You're sure you have got enough change for the fare?"

Throwing her arms around Juliet and giving her a comforting hug, she said: "You'll be fine. Let us know when you have arrived safely, and keep in touch."

Part Six
Juliet and Blake House

(a brief interlude, 1963)

Reflection

> *"Does my sexiness upset you?*
> *"Does it come as a surprise,*
> *"That I dance like I've got diamonds,*
> *"At the meeting of my thighs?"*
> Maya Angelou, 'Still I Rise'
> in 'And I Still Rise: A Book of Poems' (1978)

I HAVE spent a lot of time recently recalling my sojourn at a London mother and baby home. I say sojourn, but it was more of a flying visit as I escaped its horrors after a couple of days instead of staying for the three months I intended. Nevertheless, the forty-eight hours or so I spent there made such an impact on me that I will remember that dismal house for the rest of my life. Even now, I have nightmares about Blake House, engulfed by feelings of helplessness, degradation, and complete worthlessness.

The women unlucky enough to find themselves there were treated with spiteful revenge simply because they had sex before marriage – and had been caught out by getting pregnant. The idea that a woman could enjoy sex as much as a man was something that offended society and must, therefore, be punished. But also punished without compassion were women who had been raped and had become pregnant through no fault of their own.

Even in the twentieth century, patriarchy – which began in Biblical times when Eve was blamed for Adam's fall from grace in the Garden of Eden – was still in evidence, with men being elevated over women, who were very much second-class citizens.

I recall with affection the girls I met at Blake House. Girls, who like me, had got themselves 'into trouble' and were paying the price for breaking the strict moral rules of society. Having a baby out of wedlock had been an unforgivable sin for generations, an outrage of epic proportions that had to be concealed at all costs. And if that was not traumatic enough, most unmarried mothers were then forced to give up their babies for adoption. Separation for life sanctioned by society and religion.

Abortion at that time was illegal.* Some women, particularly those who were married and were pregnant as the result of an affair or rape, did find backstreet abortionists. But this not only put the mother's life at risk but also faced the threat of severe punishment if caught.

Generations of women and children were left scarred for life by the cruel practice of parting mothers and babies forever. All this heartbreak on a mere whim of society or in the name of religion. That is what is truly unforgivable.

*Abortion became legal in the United Kingdom in 1967. Until then, the 1839 Act held sway, which allowed for a sentence of 'penal servitude for life.'

Chapter One

THE TAXI driver at Waterloo showed no sign of surprise when Juliet asked to be taken to Blake House in Clapham. He quickly registered her condition and the fact she had a large suitcase. She was wearing a gold ring on her wedding finger, but he wasn't fooled by that. Another unmarried mother, poor cow. "You hop in, dear, and I'll deal with the luggage," he said.

Juliet would have been horrified had she realised her situation had been summed up so quickly. But Len saw dozens of these young girls, and a few of them not so young, all wanting to be taken to Blake House or one of the other homes in Stratford East or Tooting. They didn't know what they were in for, he thought as he settled himself back into his driving seat. Blake House, indeed. Bleak House, more like!

As he pulled smoothly away from the taxi rank and into the afternoon traffic, he wondered what he would do if his daughter Deirdre got pregnant. Ha! He smiled to himself. She was too clever to get caught, that little madam. A smart piece if ever there was one and popular with the lads, but fussy with it; very particular Deirdre, always one to keep admirers guessing. But if she did get pregnant, he couldn't imagine him or the missus sending her off alone to an anonymous home to have the baby among strangers. They might not be well off, him and Maisie, but they knew right from wrong. And it was plain wrong to throw your daughter out because she was in trouble.

Len looked at Juliet's pinched, white face in the rear-view mirror. Hardly more than a child herself, twenty if she was a day, about the same age as Deirdre. Well-to-do, judging by her clothes, and she spoke nice, without an obvious accent; been to one of those posh schools, no doubt. All the same, what use was all that, Len wondered to himself, swerving to narrowly miss a cyclist who seemed hell-bent on suicide if your family didn't want you because you had a little problem?

That was the trouble with those posh nobs, he ruminated, all trying not to lose face with the neighbours and living their lives behind lace curtains. They were more worried about their social standing than about their children. They were the sort of parents who sent little boys of seven off to some awful boarding school, and he'd heard about the terrible things that went on in those places.

Len scratched his head. He had to admit it was not only the daughters of the well-off who ended up in those dreadful mother-and-baby homes. He knew a couple of people working on the market who had turned their backs on girls who were in the family way. Something to do with religion and living a clean life. He shook his head in bemusement; he just didn't understand it. There was no way he and Maisie would let one of theirs go and have a baby at Blake House.

Truth told, thought Len, Maisie would probably welcome a grandchild with open arms, in or out of wedlock. She loved kids; well, they had five of their own, and it might have been six if nature had been kinder. Sadly, she had been just thirty-five when the doctor told her that no matter how hard they tried, her time for children was at an end. "You may still be relatively young," he said, "but that's life. You'll have to wait for your grandchildren now." Maisie had cried piteously, and Len had been all for getting another opinion. But Maisie had quickly dried her eyes and said no, the doctor was right, 'the change' had come early, and there was nothing to be done. They had five healthy kids, which was a lot more than many people could claim. As the doctor said, they would have to wait for grandchildren, and hopefully, there would be dozens of 'em.

Looking again in his rear-view mirror, Len noticed that the girl in the back was quietly crying. "You alright, love?" he asked. "Want me to stop?"

"No, thank you," sniffed Juliet, grappling with a handkerchief. "Need to get there. The sooner, the better," Len grunted. "Nearly there," he said, carefully negotiating the traffic around Clapham Common. "Won't be two ticks."

He turned into a residential street and pulled up outside a large double-fronted Victorian villa that had obviously seen better days. It had a forlorn, uncared-for look about it and the front garden had been covered in tarmac and turned into a parking area. Len got out and manhandled Juliet's case off the luggage rack. "Want me to stay until you're inside safe and sound?" he asked, carefully helping Juliet out of the vehicle. "I'll be fine, thank you," said Juliet, handing over the fare. "Keep the change."

"Very kind of you, miss," said Len.

He deliberately walked slowly round the cab and fiddled with the door handle while Juliet rang the bell. The door was opened by a middle-aged woman dressed in white with a nurse's cap on her tightly permed bottle blonde hair. She opened it slightly wider to allow room for Juliet to drag her case inside.

Len sighed. Just as he thought that rat-faced bitch of a matron was still there, and she obviously wasn't going to give a helping hand. Fancy letting a girl in that condition carry her own suitcase inside, not much of a welcome for the poor lass.

Oh well, not his problem, as Maisie would say, but there had been something about that girl. She was a bit different from the usual type they got at Blake House. He just hoped she had the wherewithal to cope with the heart-breaking weeks to come.

Something to tell Maisie thought Len, and he might also find out her thoughts on unmarried mothers in general and what would happen if Deirdre got caught, in particular. No harm in being prepared, just in case.

He smiled jauntily, put up his For Hire flag and blew his horn at a hapless pedestrian who foolishly decided to walk across the road in front of his cab.

Chapter Two

LYING IN her narrow bed in a dormitory of six, Juliet was in a state of extreme anxiety. She didn't know what she had imagined a mother and baby home would be like – well, she hadn't imagined it at all – but what she had walked into had been a huge shock. She felt sick, helpless, and totally disorientated. Over and over, the words ran through her mind: "I'm in prison. This is my punishment for getting pregnant."

After that nice taxi driver had dropped her at Blake House and the door had been opened by Matron, who had a strong Irish brogue and was absolutely the coldest and most unsympathetic person she had ever met, Juliet's heart had sunk like a stone. She was shaking with trepidation as she lugged her suitcase into the tiled hall, which smelled of disinfectant, just like school. Matron led her into the dining room where a dozen or so girls in various stages of extreme pregnancy were having supper round a Formica-topped table that was looking a bit worse for wear.

"You'd better eat before taking your case up to the dorm," said Matron. "Cook doesn't like latecomers. When you've finished, come to my office and I'll explain our routine." She tapped a finger on the shoulder of a girl with short, dark hair. "Yvonne, this is Juliet. She's in your dorm. Look after her." Yvonne regarded Juliet unsmilingly. "Welcome to the madhouse. When are you due?"

"In seven weeks," replied Juliet in a whisper.

"Hard luck, that means you're going to be here even longer

than me. I've got five weeks to go now if this wretched child comes on time. And then you must add the six weeks afterwards. It's life sentence!"

"Why six weeks afterwards?" asked Juliet.

"Oh my God, someone else who hasn't been told the whole story," said Yvonne. She called across to a heavily pregnant woman, who had obviously been extremely overweight before she was pregnant and was now simply elephantine. "Hey, Sylv, this is Juliet, and she's another one who doesn't know about the six weeks afterwards!"

"So, what's new," said Sylv, making a vain effort to pull a well-washed cardigan around her distended body. "It's something they just forget to tell us." Juliet was bewildered. "What are these six weeks?"

"Well," said Yvonne, pushing Juliet down into a vacant chair and pulling an empty plate and dish of macaroni cheese towards her. "When you've had your baby at The Royal, you come back here and look after it for six weeks until it can go to its adoptive parents. It's the worst bit of all, really. Childbirth is nothing compared to having your baby taken away from you after you've had it with you for six weeks. You've bonded see, in that time. You should hear the racket that goes on sometimes when they come to take a baby away."

Somewhere in the depths of her brain, Juliet recalled Sandra Moran mentioning six weeks after the birth which would be spent at the mother and baby home, but she had totally forgotten about it until that moment. "I don't think I can do that," she said in panic. There was a ripple of laughter around the table. "Oh, we've all said *that*," said Sylv with a grin, picking bobbles of wool off her cardigan. "But it don't make a scrap of difference. Nobody's listening; they never do. What we think don't count."

"Eat up," said Yvonne, ladling spoons of glutinous macaroni onto Juliet's plate. "Matron's expecting you, and she doesn't like being kept waiting. Well, she doesn't really like much at all that one, as you will discover."

Matron made no bones about it. The girls at Blake House were sinners. They had broken the rules of respectability and decency and they now had to pay the price. She had no sympathy whatsoever. Trollops, the lot of them.

Sitting at her desk in a comfortably padded chair, with a huge crucifix on the wall behind her, she left Juliet standing. "You've met some of the other girls. They are the ones who are expectant mothers. The nursery for the new mothers and their babies is on the other side of the house, and that's where you'll go once your child is born."

Looking at Juliet over her *pince nez* she sniffed and said, "Everyone here has a job to do. There is a weekly rota pinned up in the dining room and you check on a Sunday evening to find out what jobs you are doing for the coming week."

"Wha…what sort of jobs?" stammered Juliet. Matron squinted at the nervous girl in front of her. "Everything here gets done by the girls," said Matron. "From clearing the table and washing up after meals to laying the fires and sweeping the corridors. It goes without saying that you all keep your own dormitories clean and tidy. They are inspected regularly, so no slacking. We do have a cleaner, but she has more than enough to do; it's a big house."

Matron's sharp eyes registered Juliet's well-made maternity smock and expensive jumper and skirt. Obviously, she was a spoilt little darling; it was really surprising that Daddy hadn't made better provisions for her. Staring intently at Juliet, she said: "Does having to work come as a surprise to you? I suppose you are one of those who have never lifted a finger at home. Well, things are different here. This is not a holiday camp."

Juliet was silent. Under normal circumstances, she would have attempted to defend herself, but the situation in which she found herself was anything but normal. She was completely out of her comfort zone, full of guilt and shame.

Matron gave a frosty smile that didn't reach her eyes. "Go and find Yvonne, and she'll show you your bed in the dorm and we'll see you at breakfast tomorrow. Eight o'clock sharp. Lateness will not be tolerated. There are penalties for those who break the rules."

Juliet walked out in a daze. This was madness. Had she really chosen to come here, and was she really paying good money to be in this awful place? With hindsight, she realised that after leaving Sandra Moran's office in Paddington, she had never given Blake House a moment's thought. She had been so happy to have something lined up, a solution to get her away from Brighton, that she had pushed the mother and baby home to the back of her mind as something she would deal with when it happened. Well, now it was happening, and she wished she had been wiser and asked a few more questions. It was a bit late now for remorse.

Yvonne was waiting for her at the bottom of the stairs. "I'll give you a hand with your luggage if you like; we should be able to manage it between us."

"I don't really think we should be carrying a heavy suitcase up these steep stairs in our condition," puffed Juliet, pressing a hand against a sharp pain in her side, worn out after only a few steps.

"Well, believe me, honey, no one else is going to help you. So, if you want your things safely in the dorm, then it's down to you, with me helping out of the goodness of my heart," replied Yvonne crisply. "Otherwise, your case will be staying down in the hall and within a couple of days, most of your things will go missing. I hate to say it, but there are some very light-fingered people in here."

Ignoring Juliet's gasp of horror, Yvonne gave the case a tug. "Now get a move on, or we'll still be on the stairs when the matron puts the lights out. And I must tell you that is promptly at ten o'clock every night."

Chapter Three

IN THE long, narrow dormitory, each of the six beds had a small wardrobe and a chair beside it. The room was clinically austere and despite its occupants' best efforts, it had a cold and unwelcoming air about it. The bathroom was at the end of the corridor.

"There's only one bath and lav on this floor, so you'd better look slippy in the mornings or you'll never get in, then you'll be late for breakfast and feel the sharp end of Matron's tongue," warned Yvonne as Juliet put her things away and stowed her suitcase under the bed.

Yvonne explained that in addition to herself, there were currently three other girls who slept in the room. The sixth bed was empty, but they were expecting someone else to come during the next few days.

"Girls come and go all the time. When someone goes into labour, they are taken to the hospital and then they come back and go to the other side of the house, so we don't usually see them again. They try to keep the expectant mums away from the new mothers, don't want them to spill the beans and tell us what it's really like."

Juliet bit her lip and nervously wrapped her arms around her now large bump. "No point attempting to make close friends in here," Yvonne continued. "We all try to get on, obviously, but hormones run riot and there are often clashes of personality. It all gets sorted out though, as it must when you are rubbing shoulders with the same people day in and day out."

Visions of prison once again floated through Juliet's mind. Looking at the cramped space between beds, she thought that solitary confinement might be preferable. At least she'd have a cell to herself.

Yvonne regarded her thoughtfully before saying: "If you want to survive here, you must remember that no one cares about you; everyone is out for themselves. Like I said, no point in trying to make friends. Just try and get on with people. We are all in the same boat, hoping to get this over as quickly as possible and get out.

Yvonne heard a sharp intake of breath and paused. When Juliet, staring at her with huge eyes, said nothing, she added: "Remember, we are literally at the mercy of the staff. Matron has a couple of helpers and they have no respect and are not bothered about what happens to us. Like her, they think we are here to be punished. There is no understanding. No care."

Realising that Juliet was looking totally shell-shocked, Yvonne gave her a quick pat on the back. "The important thing, I found, is to know what you're up against. Then there are no nasty surprises. You'll get used to it. It's pretty awful for the first couple of days, but you'll settle in, and the time goes fairly quickly."

Juliet swallowed hard, attempting to keep her ever-ready tears at bay. "If I were you, I'd have an early night," advised Yvonne. "I can see it's all come as a bit of a shock to you, but everything will look better in the morning," she said comfortingly. "I'll tell the others you are sleeping, and we'll try not to wake you up when we come to bed."

Emotionally strung out, sleep evaded her, and Juliet spent the next couple of hours tossing and turning, unable to settle in the uncomfortable and unfamiliar bed, her mind in turmoil.

She was so vulnerable now, and there was no one here to help her, so she had to get used to being on her own, looking after herself and protecting her child. A sudden irrational fear of solitude overtook her and big fat tears slid down her face. I can't cry now, she thought, sniffing, trying to take a firm grip on her emotions. I must just hang on and wait for whatever is going to happen and deal with it as it comes. When you fall this low, you have nothing to lose.

Once again she started to think about Enzo and how this journey had begun. Despite the terrible situation she now found herself in, she couldn't regret her time on Capri with Enzo. I wouldn't change a minute of it. If this is the price to pay for four months of absolute heaven, then it's worth it. Her only worry was having the baby adopted. Giving away forever the final link she had with him.

Juliet eventually fell into a heavy slumber but was woken in the early hours by a commotion in the room. A girl called Gillian had started to bleed and was screaming hysterically. Someone went for Matron, who was less than pleased to be woken up, and the terrified girl was sharply slapped and told to be quiet.

"Stop making such a fuss. You'll wake the whole house," said Matron. "You're not dying, and you're not going to have your baby within the next five minutes, so just be quiet. Now come along, put on your slippers and dressing gown and we'll get you to hospital."

Juliet watched in horror as the sobbing girl was pulled out of bed, pushed into her dressing gown, and marched out towards the stairs.

Matron briefly put her head back round the door and pointed to Gillian's recently vacated bed. "Make sure that bedding is stripped off first thing, and remember to soak it in cold water before putting it into the wash. We don't want stained bed sheets." Matron returned to Gillian, and Juliet could hear her haranguing the terrified girl all the way down the stairs.

★★★

The next morning at breakfast, Matron came in and said that six girls had appointments at The Royal. "You're expected at ten-thirty. Please don't be late."

"How's Gillian?" someone asked.

Matron frowned. "She'll live."

"Has she had the baby?"

"Not yet."

It was obvious no more information was going to be forthcoming and the girls knew there was no point in pushing. They would find out soon enough. Matron cleared her throat theatrically and looked around enquiringly. When there was silence, she returned to her list of names for the hospital appointment. To her surprise, Juliet was one of them.

"What's it for?" she asked.

"Blood tests and VD checks," clarified Matron in an uncompromising voice. She was not used to being questioned.

"What's VD?" Once again, there was a general gust of laughter around the table. The girls looked at each other meaningfully with raised eyebrows: Who is this girl? Doesn't she know anything?

"Venereal Disease, duckie," said Sylv. "We are all tested. The general opinion is that because we are pregnant and not married, then we must certainly have slept around or been on the game and picked up something nasty in the process. So, they test us. Treated worse than cattle, we are." Matron, irritated with this untoward exchange, tapped her pencil on her clipboard with such force that the lead broke.

Seeing Juliet's bewilderment, Yvonne added: You know, a sexually transmitted disease. They think that we are all tramps." Juliet was shocked. "But I haven't slept around, and I don't have this VD, so I don't need to be tested."

"How do you know," asked Sylv in an aggravating sing-song voice, "if you haven't been tested?"

"That's quite enough," snapped Matron sharply. Turning to

Juliet, she said: "You're having the test, and that's that. It's not up for discussion." And she swept out of the room.

★★★

For Juliet, the visit to the hospital was something she just wanted to forget. A steady stream of Blake House girls had appointments there most days and there was no question that they were considered of little importance. The overworked hospital staff, knowing that the unmarried mothers were unlikely to complain – and who would listen if they did – tended to leave them until all the regular patients had been dealt with. So, although the six of them reported at ten-thirty as instructed, it was after mid-day when the harassed doctor eventually called Juliet into the treatment room.

Afterwards, back in the dreary communal sitting room at Blake House, the whole experience was a complete blur in Juliet's mind. She remembered being pushed from pillar to post, being helped on and off treatment tables and handed over to a trainee nurse, who had little success at taking blood samples, leaving Juliet with huge blue-black bruises on both arms. She shied away from remembering the various tests that had been carried out but she felt battered and dirty, with her mind as bruised as her body.

Juliet longed for a long, hot, steamy bath but knew that only a quick dip in lukewarm water would be possible at Blake House, where Matron had drawn a black line around the inside of the bath with strict instructions not to fill the water above this mark. She was numb. There was nothing left to feel.

Janet, one of the girls from her dorm, had gathered Juliet up off a wooden hospital bench and dragged her back to Blake House. "I overheard the nurses saying she had fainted twice," Janet told Yvonne. "She looked dreadful. I thought she was going to pass out on the way back here." They glanced over at Juliet, who was sitting in a dilapidated armchair, head back, eyes closed.

"Do you think she'll be okay?"

"Have to be. What's the option?"

Sylv came waddling into the room, making a beeline for Juliet. "Leave her alone," said Yvonne. "She's really not well."

"We need her ring," said Sylv, a plump hand shaking Juliet's shoulder.

"What?"

"Her wedding ring. Alison next door, you know, the one all the fuss has been about, the one who has decided to keep her little boy, has found a nursery that will take him five days a week while she works. They obviously don't know she isn't married, and she has an appointment to go and see them, so she needs a wedding ring. Juliet is the only person I could think of who has one."

She looked down at Juliet, who had opened her eyes. "It's only a lend. You can have it back after teatime. You know how sniffy people are about unmarried mums. It's quite likely the nursery won't take Alison's baby if they think it's illegitimate. So she has to say she's married, see. And she needs to be wearing a ring." Juliet sat up and slid the ring off her finger. "Are some people allowed to keep their babies?" she asked eagerly, handing the gold band over to Sylv.

"Anyone can keep their baby," said Yvonne. "You can, I can, Sylv can… They can't force you to have it adopted. They don't *like* it, particularly Matron, who seems to think we don't deserve to be allowed to keep them, but they can't *make* you give it up if you really don't want to."

"What they do is make it as difficult as possible for you to keep your kid. And believe me, they use every trick in the book to make you have it adopted," added Sylv. "I've even known them to call in social workers who threaten to take the baby anyway if you don't go along with adoption. They say it's at risk because you can't look after it properly."

"I wonder if Matron gets paid for each baby that's handed

over," said Janet reflectively. "That would account for a lot!"

"Huh! Wouldn't surprise me," chuckled Yvonne.

Juliet thought for a moment and said: "What about Alison then? How is she managing to keep her baby?"

"*Well,*" said Sylv, lowering herself down heavily onto the settee, "she's a real fighter that one, had a bit of a tough life one way and another. Anyway, her boss at the fruit and veg shop where she worked before is happy for her to go back full time. They've also offered her a room over the shop, so all she needs is a nursery to put the boy in while she's working and she's sorted. Lucky cow! And frankly, her mum is not too bothered about her situation either. She can't go and live there because there's no room, what with all the other children, but her mum is happy to help out a bit, and that makes all the difference."

"What about you?" asked Juliet.

"Me?" Sylv gave a snorting laugh, her hands folded over her huge belly. "Oh, mine is going to be adopted, come what may. My parents don't give a fuck what happens to me or the kid, so I've got no one to give me a hand. No job and nowhere to live either, well, not at the moment. I'll get sorted once all this is over. Not that I care one way or the other," she added, tossing her head and hauling herself unsteadily to her feet. Juliet glanced at her podgy, defiant face and could see the hurt in her eyes.

She turned to Yvonne. "And you?"

"Same. No one to help and nowhere to go. Baby will be adopted. I worked in an office before, and when I fell pregnant, I gave in my notice, pretending I was getting married. They gave me a good luck card and present and everything. I felt dreadful, knowing I was lying to them. Of course, there was no way I could let anyone know what was really happening, so I went and stayed with a friend on the other side of London until I came here. She was brilliant, but I couldn't inflict myself on her any longer, her parents really weren't happy about me lodging with her, so here

I am. The baby will be adopted and I will then have to go job hunting and start life over again."

"Me too," said Janet. "Baby's going to be adopted. I'd give anything to keep it, but how? No home…me mam kicked me out when she found out I was up the duff…and I used to work on the family's market stall, so no job and absolutely no money."

"I think you'll find almost all the girls in here are having to go for adoption," said Linda, who had been sitting quietly listening to the conversation. "No one wants to, but it's just so difficult to keep your baby. Everything is against us. I'd love to keep mine, but how?" Linda had a Liverpudlian accent and was plainly from a different background to the London girls. Juliet would have liked to have asked her how she had ended up at Blake House, but she didn't want to appear inquisitive and fish for information that was not offered.

"Ann's the exception, said Yvonne. She can't wait to get rid of her kid; she would have had an abortion if she could."

Seeing Juliet's puzzled look, she added: "Don't think you've met her yet; she tends to keep herself to herself and doesn't mix much. She is older than most of us and quite posh. She was married, but she got raped, so the child is being adopted. She says she definitely doesn't want to see it when it's born."

Even Sylv seemed to feel sorry for Ann. "Her husband left her when he found out what had happened, and now she's not allowed to see her kids. Fucking men! I tell you, I'm not letting a bloke anywhere near me in future."

Yvonne laughed. "Oh, right. Don't believe that!"

"Please yourself," shrugged Sylv. "But I tell you, no man is worth what we're going through. I'd rather shack up with a woman. At least you'd get more understanding and respect.

"Look at Ann. She desperately tried to get an abortion, but by the time she found someone who could do it, it was too late. She was too far gone and no one was willing to touch her with a barge pole. Just too risky. So, she's here."

"Yes," said Yvonne, "and bloody Matron is vile to her, so Ann tends to keep out of the way most of the time. Poor bitch. I reckon she's worse off than any of us."

Juliet was horrified and filled with pity. What a dreadful thing to happen. She had never considered women becoming pregnant because they had been raped. How must Ann feel about the baby growing inside her? Love or hate. And being kept away from her children, how cruel was that? She shuddered. It was too awful to contemplate.

"So, what are you planning to do?" asked Linda.

"Oh God," sighed Juliet. "My baby must be adopted, too. My parents have made that quite clear. I can't go home again if I keep my baby."

"But can you go home eventually?" queried Yvonne. "Y-e-s, I suppose so," said Juliet doubtfully.

"And you have money," said Sylv. It was a statement rather than a question. "Mmm, a bit. But you know, in the end it makes very little difference whether you have money or not, the result is the same. Like you, I must give up my baby. It's not money that matters, it's the attitude of society that must change."

"Bloody hell," said Sylv, looking at the girls in open-mouthed amazement. "We've got a frigging Einstein 'ere!"

She waddled off, shaking her head and wondering if having money made you clever. Putting her head back around the door, she said: "S'pose you went to one of those posh schools. Bet you had a uniform and everything!"

Despite all the awfulness, Juliet was laughing. "You bet! And I wore a straw boater," she said teasingly.

Huh," said Sylv. "Might have guessed," and she disappeared, making her ponderous way to find the fortunate Alison and give her the ring.

Juliet was deep in thought. "So, if the new mums are kept separate from us, how is it you all know about Alison?

"Ah, well, said Janet, perching on the edge of the chair opposite Juliet, "they do try to keep us away from the mums on the other side of the house, but it never really works. Much to Matron's disgust, we manage to meet up for a bit of a chinwag every so often. That's how Sylv heard about Alison keeping her baby. I bet Matron is spitting feathers about that; someone has escaped her net."

"I often wonder why she is so keen for us to have our babies adopted," said Linda. "Maybe she does get paid, but somehow, I doubt it. I just think she's a vindictive old hag who gets pleasure out of seeing us suffer."

"That's it," said Yvonne, and because we are pregnant, we've obviously had sex, and heaven forbid, we may even have enjoyed it. You've only got to look at her face to know that no man has ever been allowed across her threshold."

Despite her unhappiness, Juliet joined in the hysterical laughter. "Yes, I see what you mean, but it doesn't make it any easier for us."

"Not a bit," agreed Janet.

"Oh well," said Yvonne, pulling Juliet's hand to help her up, "life goes on, and we must cope with it as best we can. Come on, shake a leg, I hear on the grapevine there are jam tarts for tea, and believe me, that's a rare thing in this dump."

★★★

After another sleepless night in the lumpy bed, Juliet had made up her mind. There was no way she could stay at Blake House. She had made the most dreadful mistake and had to get out. She had no idea where she would go or what she would do, but the mother and baby home was not for her; she'd never survive.

The realisation dawned that her soft middle-class upbringing had not prepared her for a place like Blake House. The girls from poor homes, the working-class girls like Yvonne, Janet and Sylv and the unmet Alison were the ones who could cope. It even sounded as if Ann, despite being what Yvonne described as 'posh,' was managing to get through it. They were tough, used to making do and coming to terms with hard times. Compared with their lives, hers had been one of comfort and privilege. Trouble was, she hadn't really appreciated it until now.

She thought guiltily of her parents and all the worry she had put them through. They might be strict and old-fashioned, but they had certainly given her comfort and security. Her remorse was, however, tempered by a feeling of betrayal. If they loved her, as they had assured her they did, where were they now? How could they have stood by and willingly let her go to a place like this?

Giving breakfast a miss, she went to the telephone in the hall (calls out only, no incoming calls allowed) and rang her mother. "I want to come home!" she said, tears beginning to course down her cheeks. "I can't cope here. It's horrible."

Mary Campbell listened in silence to her daughter sobbing down the phone before saying stiffly: "I'm sorry, Juliet. But you are well aware of the situation. I cannot have you here in your condition. Why not give it a bit longer? You've only been there forty-eight hours. It's sure to get better. I really think it's a case of what cannot be cured must be endured." With a few more platitudes and the promise of a visit in the very near future: "We could meet in one of the London parks. No one we know will be likely to see us there," Juliet listened to the click as Mary hung up. There's my answer, thought Juliet tartly. Her mother cared more about what other people would think of her and losing face socially than she did about her daughter's wellbeing.

Juliet put down the phone and, without really thinking, picked it up again and rang the Western House number.

When Mrs M heard Juliet's voice, she said: "What's happened, love?"

"Can I come back?" sobbed Juliet.

"Today? Of course. Just catch the train to Petersfield, and we'll meet you at the station. Can you make it the two o'clock? Yes? Great. Mr M will be waiting for you."

A huge feeling of relief swept through Juliet. Why on earth hadn't she thought of Western House before? If she'd given more thought to the situation, she could have stayed there until she had the baby and never come to this dreadful place.

She went to Matron's office. "I'm leaving," she announced. "I don't want to stay here. I'm going today."

"You can't do that," snapped Matron. "You're booked in. You signed up."

"Sorry," said Juliet firmly, amazed at her own bravery. "I am going."

"Not before you've seen the House Committee," retorted Matron, an angry red flush creeping up her neck. What on earth were things coming to? Girls making decisions and being defiant. Let's hope it didn't set a trend.

"Okay," said Juliet firmly. "But I need to leave before lunch." She went to the dormitory to pack her case and to tell a speechless Yvonne that she was escaping.

"Well, I never. How did you manage it? What will you do, where…"

Slow, heavy footsteps were heard coming up the stairs and Sylv flung the door open with so much force it bounced back in her face. "Well, well, well. So, you're leaving us. Matron asked me if there had been any unpleasantness; she wanted to know why you were going in such a hurry and asked if there had been any trouble." Glaring at Juliet with obvious dislike, she added: "I told her it was nothing to do with any of us."

"I'm just not prepared to put up with all this…this awfulness," said Juliet simply. "I'm going to stay with friends in Hampshire. I've had enough."

"So, money *does* matter," said Sylv shortly, narrowing her eyes. "If you haven't got any dough, you're stuck here, for fuck's sake, and if you have, you can leave just like that." And she waddled out without a backward glance. Yvonne looked at Juliet, shrugged her shoulders, and followed her.

Chapter Three

JULIET HAD just finished packing her case and was gathering up her belongings when she was summoned to appear before the House Committee. The three local worthies, a man in a dog collar, obviously the vicar from the church around the corner, flanked by two elderly, respectable-looking women, had been hastily called in to deal with this difficult girl. It was not at all what they expected; they told each other. Who on earth does she think she is, deciding to leave at a moment's notice?

All three sat squashed behind the polished mahogany desk in Matron's depressing office while Juliet stood in front of them, a firm grip on the back of a chair, desperately trying to keep her tears in check and hoping that no one would notice she was trembling uncontrollably.

With his eyes fixed on the wall behind Juliet's head, the reverend cleared his throat and looked embarrassed. His thin cheeks were flushed, and it was obvious that he would rather be anywhere than in this room with a heavily pregnant girl who, somehow or another, seemed to have got the upper hand. He harrumphed again. "So, young lady, you want to leave us?" Juliet nodded.

"May we ask why?" inquired one of the women, leaning forward earnestly. "I mean, this is a *very* respectable place offering a *much appreciated* and valuable service." She enunciated each word slowly and carefully.

"I... I'm just not happy here," stammered Juliet, her fingers tightly gripping the chair back. She had to hang on or she might fall over.

"Not happy? Not happy? What has happy got to do with it? In your situation, you are extremely lucky to be here. You aren't expected to be *happy*." The scrawnier of the women looked scandalised, while the other pursed her lips and shook her head in disbelief that any gel could be so ungrateful, especially in *that* condition.

The reverend cleared his throat again. "This is most irregular, most irregular indeed." He looked at his companions, obviously seeking either inspiration or support. Both ladies frowned and looked down at their hands carefully folded on top of the bags on their laps.

"Well, we've had a chat about you and decided..." he glanced again at the women, who looked up and nodded, "and decided that you may leave, but you must pay for an extra month's accommodation before you go, just in case we can't fill your bed for a while."

"Another month?" exclaimed Juliet. "But I've already paid for this month and another month in advance, and I've only been here two days."

"A month," he said firmly. "And," he added triumphantly, with the ghost of a smile on his thin lips, "you may not leave until you do." Juliet, despite her good intentions to remain calm and collected, burst into tears and rushed out of the room.

Back in the dormitory, she gave herself a mental shake and reviewed her options. A month's money on top of what she had already paid was outrageous. But what was the alternative, to stay at Blake House? Impossible. If that was the price of escape... It did occur to her that they probably thought she couldn't afford to pay the extra money and would, therefore, be forced to stay. She opened her case and scrabbled for her chequebook hidden among her knickers. Right. They could have their money, and she'd be free.

After bumping her luggage slowly down the stairs – there was no one around to give her a helping hand this time – Juliet went into the office and flung the cheque onto Matron's desk. Apart from a quick glance, Matron barely registered the fact that she was in the room, and Juliet walked out, childishly slamming the office door with some satisfaction.

As she made her way through the hall to the front door, she saw Yvonne halfway up the first flight of stairs, panting profusely as she lugged a large brass scuttle full of coal for the fire in Matron's private sitting room on the top floor.

"For heaven's sake, Yvonne, you shouldn't be doing that. You'll hurt yourself and damage the baby."

Yvonne rested her burden on the step and straightened up, a hand on the small of her back. "What's the choice? I have nowhere else to go, so I have to stick with the rules. Now fuck off while the going's good."

Juliet grimaced. "Bye then," she said, "and good luck."

Yvonne smiled. "Lucky bitch," she said without rancour. "Don't forget us when you're living it up in Sussex or Kent or wherever you're going. Now piss off!"

"Hampshire, actually," said Juliet. "And I think I can safely say that I will never forget. Ever!"

The journey to Waterloo was a nightmare. She didn't have enough cash for a taxi, and she knew the cab drivers wouldn't accept a cheque. Struggling with her heavy case – passers-by stared, but no one offered to help her – Juliet managed to get on and off crowded underground trains and up and down escalators and staircases. Thinking of Yvonne dragging matron's coal scuttle up the steep stairs at Blake House, she carried on. "I've got nothing to complain about, she told herself grimly, but she was crying nonetheless.

The tears started spilling out as soon as she got onto the tube and continued all the way to Hampshire. Much as she tried, she just couldn't stop crying. Whether it was the result of shock or relief, she just didn't know, but she felt cold and totally numb.

She did at one point vaguely wonder what her fellow travellers made of a young girl in the advanced stages of pregnancy, with a huge case, crying her heart out, but there was no controlling the shuddering sobs that wracked her body. She almost fell off the train at Petersfield and into Mr M's arms. "There, there," he said, picking up her case. "No more crying. You're back now. You're safe."

Part Seven
Juliet and Vittoria

(1964)

Reflection

> *"Choice, not chance, determines your destiny."*
> Aristotle, Greek philosopher and polymath

SO, THE big question was, who was the father of my child? Although I was convinced this was Enzo's baby, I couldn't prove it. Those were the days before DNA profiling, so there were no tests to prove or disprove paternity.

Lack of confidence and fear that Enzo would eventually lose interest and leave me, led to the difficult decision not to return to Capri. If it hadn't been for a stupid mistake I would have almost certainly gone back when I discovered I was pregnant. But a moment of carelessness with Mike changed the course of life for both me and my baby.

Without that complication I would have known beyond doubt that Enzo was the father and returned, hoping that he would accept both me and our child. But I stayed in England, not one hundred per cent sure who the father was. Consequently, I became an unmarried mother and my baby had to be adopted.

Knowing I would never see my child again or know what had happened to it, was a burden I would always carry with me. When I agreed to adoption, I knew it would be forever; I was under no illusions from the beginning. It was an impossible situation, but one to which I was resigned. So, I gave away not only my baby but also my only link with the man I loved.

As the Greek philosopher Aristotle so wisely said, "Choice,

not chance, determines your destiny." The original choice I made not to go straight back to Capri and Enzo was mine alone, and that decision determined my destiny and that of my child.

Chapter One

SIX WEEKS at Western House passed quickly and happily, and Juliet felt cosseted and loved. She tried to show her gratitude to Mr and Mrs M for taking her in by becoming an extra pair of hands, helping with the house and children.

She became particularly fond of baby Frankie and often cradled her in front of the long bedroom mirror, thinking to herself very soon, my baby will be here. Looking at her reflection, it was hard to believe that she would ever be a normal size again or that this baby would ever be born. She glanced at the smart, navy carrycot with the layette of baby clothes packed into it and found it impossible to imagine her baby existing, being a real little person.

Mrs M had taken charge of everything. Juliet would stay in the hospital for ten days after the birth, but the child would then go to a foster mother for six weeks before going to its adoptive parents. "Sheer cruelty, expecting anyone to look after their baby for six weeks before having to give it up," she cried. "I had no idea this kind of thing was going on. I feel a letter to *The Times* coming on, and maybe to *The Nursing Mirror*, too!"

She looked across the breakfast table at Mr M. "Perhaps you would mention it to Toby when you're up in Town this week? He has loads of good connections in Westminster, and one of his many committees is sure to be able to do something to help change things." Mr M nodded. "It's certainly something that needs looking into. I'll see what Toby says."

PERFECTLY IMPERFECT

One Thursday lunchtime as Juliet was serving the children with fish fingers and baked beans, a gush of water spilled out onto the floor at her feet. "U-oh," cried Mrs M. "That's it. Your waters have broken. Go and sit down and put your feet up and I will get Mr M to take you to the hospital. I'll phone and let them know you are coming."

The hospital was in the county town on the coast, some fifteen miles away, and once there, Mr M said goodbye and handed Juliet over to a waiting nurse. "Good luck," he said, kissing her cheek. "We'll be thinking of you. And Mrs M will ring later to see how things are going. See you soon."

Juliet was taken into a maternity ward and helped to bed. "Try to get some sleep," said a young nurse. "It's going to be some time before anything else happens, so you need to rest and gather strength." Juliet dozed and tried to ignore the little mouse that had started nibbling at the small of her back.

She was woken up by a different nurse who said: "Where is your husband, Mrs Campbell? Does he need to be called?"

"No," replied Juliet firmly. "He's working away."

"But surely he'll want to come and see the baby?"

"He can't," said Juliet, "he's abroad. With the Navy," she added for good measure and closed her eyes, hoping the woman would leave her alone. Keeping up the pretence of having a husband was going to be far more difficult here, but there was no way she could face the disgrace of having to admit to one and all that she was an unmarried mother. Mrs M had been right to suggest she wore a wedding ring.

Juliet was sleeping fitfully when the young nurse who had helped her into bed shook her shoulder and announced joyfully: "Your husband's here, Mrs Campbell."

"What?" exclaimed Juliet. "He can't be. He's working abroad."

"Surprise, then!" said the nurse. "Come on, up you get. I'm taking you to see him."

"It's really not him," protested Juliet as the nurse helped her into a dressing gown and brought a wheelchair to the side of the bed. "It's all a mistake."

"Come along, dear, don't make such a fuss. I thought you'd be pleased to see him." She pushed the wheelchair out of the ward and into a lift. Juliet sat quietly. It was fruitless to argue; the nurse had impatiently brushed away all her protests, and anyway, she just couldn't be bothered; the mouse that had been nibbling at her back had now moved round to her stomach and was beginning to hurt.

When the lift doors opened, a perfectly strange young man with a bunch of flowers and a hopeful grin stared blankly at Juliet and said accusingly to the nurse: "That's not my wife!"

"I tried to tell her," Juliet said feebly. With a huge intake of breath, the nurse turned the wheelchair sharply around and back into the lift. "He asked to see Janice Camberwell," she said as if Juliet had been passing herself off as someone else.

"I'm Juliet Campbell."

The nurse, now red in the face and obviously agitated, snapped: "Both begin with J and a C. She wheeled Juliet back to her bed. "It's an easy mistake to make." She looked down at Juliet in alarm. "I hope you're not going to tell Sister." Juliet gave her a forgiving smile: "I won't say anything," she promised.

Back in bed, Juliet slept, emotionally exhausted. When she woke up, the ward was in darkness except for a shaded light over a desk in the middle of the long room. A surge of pain gripped her body and made her cry out. Hearing the sound, a nurse came over and put her hand on Juliet's stomach. "Some time to go yet," she said. "Contractions need to be a lot stronger than that. Oh, and by the way, you've had two phone calls. One from your mother and the other from a Mrs Morrison; they're both going to call again in the morning. We should have some good news for them by then."

Chapter Two

JULIET'S BABY was born at five minutes to six on a bright May morning. Nothing had prepared her for the rush of pure love that spread through her as her newborn daughter was put into her arms. Looking down at the mass of black hair, perfect features, tiny limbs, and starfish hands, she was totally captivated.

As the baby looked back at her with Enzo's dark blue eyes, Juliet knew with certainty that she could never ever give her up. Never in a million years. She had decided to call her Vittoria, the Italian alternative to the classic Victoria, convinced that this was Enzo's child and that she was, therefore, half-Italian.

Back in the ward, the baby was put in a cot parked at the bottom of Juliet's bed. Watching her closely, Juliet looked for more signs of resemblances to Enzo, yearning to cuddle her to see if she could *feel* she was his.

This time with her infant daughter should have been a moment of rejoicing. Instead, Juliet was in panic mode, desperately trying to work out how she could keep her.

"Can I pick her up?" she asked a passing nurse.

"Best not, dear. We only really like mums to hold babies at feeding time. You let her sleep, and you need to get some rest yourself."

Juliet lay back on a pile of pillows and closed her eyes. What was she going to do? Now she had got Vittoria she had to keep her; there had to be a way. How on earth could she allow this child, who she was certain was Enzo's and had been conceived in a loving relationship, be adopted by strangers? It was totally out of the question. Anyway, the baby was all Juliet had left of him. The only thing of Enzo's she had brought back from Capri.

Hearing footsteps, she opened her eyes and saw her mother standing beside her. "Hello," said Mary. "So, it's all over. Not too bad, was it? The nurses said you had a fairly easy time of it. She went to the foot of the bed and peered into the cot. "You're calling her Vittoria? That seems to be an odd spelling, still just as well not to choose a family name, I suppose."

"Hello, Mum," said Juliet, peering past her to the end of the ward, "is Daddy with you?"

"I wouldn't let him come," said Mary. "I know what he's like. One look at the baby and he'd be impossible, and we must stay firm at a time like this."

"Mum." Juliet tugged repeatedly at a fold of the bedsheet with nervous fingers. "I really don't want Vittoria to be adopted. I want to keep her."

"There," said Mary in a vexed voice. "I knew this would happen. I told your father. I *knew* that once you'd had the child, you'd want to keep it. Well, it can't be done, Juliet. We've made our decision and we must stick with it. There is no way we can have you and the baby at home, and there is no way you can live by yourself and keep the baby. So adoption is the only way. I will not let you ruin the rest of your life on a whim, which you will almost certainly come to regret as time goes on, and then it will be too late."

Juliet lay back against the pillows as tears slid under her eyelids. "You're very emotional at the moment," said Mary. "Well, that's quite natural; it's your hormones at work. Given time, you'll see that the decision to go for adoption is the right one." Juliet was silent, without the strength to argue.

"Now," said Mary briskly, "anything you need?" She stared down at her daughter, her face a mask. If she felt any emotion at all, she was keeping it well hidden – but then, Mary was an expert at not showing her true feelings.

"Well, if you've got everything, that's fine. We'll see you in a few weeks when all this is behind you. Your father sends his love, and the Morrisons say they'll be here to see you today. We've spoken to them and they've agreed to make sure everything is properly sorted." She bent down, gave Juliet a quick peck on the forehead and walked out of the ward, her sensible shoes squeaking on the polished floor. My God, thought Juliet. Has that woman got a heart? How could anyone be that cool, no, not cool, hard-hearted?

Mary had no sooner left than a nurse swooped down on the cot, picked up Vittoria and thrust her into Juliet's arms. "Come on, Mrs Campbell, time to feed," she cried in a jolly voice. "Baby's feeling hungry. Now, we all breastfeed here, so if you need help getting started, just give a call and we'll be with you in a jiffy."

Juliet gulped. Mrs M had already arranged that the baby would be bottle-fed during the ten days she was in the hospital. "You really don't want to start with the breast and then suddenly stop," she advised. "Not good for you and not good for the baby. And, of course, the foster mother and the adoptive parents will be using the bottle, so best to start as we mean to go on."

"I'm not breastfeeding," Juliet told the nurse. "It's been agreed I can put her on the bottle."

"Bottle?" cried the nurse in horror. "My dear, do you know what you're doing? Think of all the antibodies and good things the baby will get from your milk. No, no, you must breastfeed. All our mums breastfeed. Breast is definitely best!"

"I can't," said Juliet stubbornly. "I mean, I don't want to. I……" By this time, Vittoria, obviously desperate for food, was crying with a long, thin wail. "Well," said the nurse. "I don't know. Wait a minute, I'll go and ask."

Mothers in nearby beds, with contented babies already sucking lustily at full breasts, stared at Juliet with distain. "Very modern thinking," said one. "I do know people who advocate the bottle, but I've breastfed all of mine, seems more natural, somehow." The others nodded in agreement. "A bit odd not to want to feed your baby yourself, don't you think?"

Juliet put her still-wailing daughter over her shoulder and patted her back. Was everything always going to be a battle? Could she phone Mrs M and ask her to talk to them? Eventually, the ward sister, dressed in a trim navy-blue dress and an enormous white cap with a waterfall of lace and frills, came rustling down the room. Vittoria's cries were becoming more urgent, and Juliet was beginning to panic.

"Oy-oy," said the woman in the bed opposite, "bringing in the big guns!" The others sniggered. Maybe they were in for a bit of argy-bargy. That would liven things up a bit.

"Now, Mrs Campbell, what is all this I hear about bottle feeding? Has the nurse explained to you that breastfeeding is so much better for babies? Now just give it a try…" Glancing down at the sheaf of notes in her hand, Sister Thomas suddenly broke off, looked at Juliet intently and motioned to the nurse to pull the curtains around the bed. When they were alone, she said: "I think we owe you an apology."

"Oh!" gasped Juliet.

"We obviously didn't read your notes properly and didn't realise your baby is going for adoption; that changes everything. Of course, you may bottle feed if you wish."

Juliet started crying, her tears falling on Vittoria's head. Sister touched her shoulder. "I'm sorry," she said gently. "Nurse will bring you a bottle of formula immediately and start you on tablets to dry up your milk. If you need someone to talk to, I'm always around. Just ask one of the nurses." Juliet nodded gratefully, unable to reply because the tears, which seemed to well up even more easily nowadays, were once again beginning to run down her cheeks.

Chapter Three

BOTH MR and Mrs M backed Mary on the question of adoption. "Your mother is absolutely right," said Mrs M, holding both of Juliet's hands in her own. "We've talked about this a lot, you and me. You've seen our lovely, adopted family. You know how happy the children are."

"I know," sobbed Juliet. "I know I agreed to adoption, but that was before I had her. Now, I can't go through with it. I must keep her; I can't give her away."

Mrs M looked at her husband and raised her eyebrows. He took his wife's place beside Juliet and asked: "But how will you manage? How can you possibly earn enough money to look after yourself and bring up a child? It's not some kind of fairy tale Juliet; this is real life. And it is for many, many years, not just while Vittoria's a baby, but when she's a toddler and a schoolgirl. It will get harder, not easier. And at the end of the day, it's not right, my love. It's not fair to either you or Vittoria."

This had been something Juliet had spent a long time deliberating, and she thought she had come up with a solution, a real answer to the problem. Agreement was so important she was almost too scared to ask the question.

"I was wondering," she said nervously, "if we could live with you, and I could work in the house and look after all the children together?" Mrs M sighed heavily. "Oh, Juliet," she said. "I was praying you wouldn't ask that. I'm afraid it is just not possible."

"Oh!" Juliet flinched, feeling as if she had been slapped in the face.

"The thing is," said Mr M, rushing to his wife's rescue, "we have promised your parents we wouldn't do that. Quite apart from respecting their wishes, we both honestly believe that adoption is the best thing for Vittoria and for you. This baby needs two loving parents, and you need to get your life back. You are so young, just starting out in life; you have everything to live for. I'm afraid, sweetheart, it must be adoption."

Juliet collapsed in floods of tears, and Mrs M called over a nurse. After a quickly whispered explanation, the Morrisons patted Juliet on the shoulder and said they would return tomorrow.

"Come on," said the nurse, hauling Juliet into a sitting position. "A warm cup of cocoa and a good night's sleep and everything will look brighter in the morning."

★★★

The next day, Juliet asked if she could speak to the ward sister. She was reluctant to talk to anyone by the name of Sister or Matron after her experience at Blake House, but this one was so obviously different from that harridan in Clapham that she decided to take the risk.

Sister Thomas felt exceedingly sorry for the young girl but knew there was nothing practical she could do to help. Mrs Morrison had visited her office the previous day and put her in the picture. Sister knew that all she could do was to listen to Juliet's worries and underline the fact that adoption was probably the best step to take, although it might be hard. She spent a quarter of an hour with her, and most of that time Juliet was in tears.

"I know it's sensible and the right thing to do, especially for Vittoria. But I'm not at all sure it's the right thing for me. I love her so much, and she's my only link to her father. I didn't think it would feel like this," she sobbed.

Pushing a box of tissues towards Juliet, Sister Thomas said: "I know it is hard. You are not the first young mother in here who has had to make this painful decision; and believe me, every one of them has felt the same as you.

"I ask myself if it is right that society demands mothers must be forced to make decisions that will separate them from their babies for the rest of their lives. Why can't it be easier for unmarried women to keep their babies? But before that can happen, we must take away the stigma attached to unmarried mothers and illegitimacy. Then, there must be a change in social conscience to allow the State to give some kind of weekly living allowance to women so they can look after their children without the support of a husband. There is a family allowance, of course, which single mothers can also claim, but that is hardly enough to live on."

Juliet had stopped crying and was listening intently. Sister sighed. "I'm afraid such thinking is ahead of its time, and I fear it will be many years before such a mindset comes about if it ever does. Meanwhile, you have this unbearable situation where you must give up your child for adoption. It's just not fair, is it? But it's life as we know it, and sadly, for you, there is no easy way out."

She stood up and pulled back the curtains around Juliet's bed. "I don't think I've been of much help to you, my dear. But be assured, I will be thinking of you in the days to come and praying that everything goes as smoothly as possible for you."

Chapter Four

THE WORST day of Juliet's life turned out to be another bright and sunny May morning. After giving Vittoria her morning bottle, Juliet took off the hospital baby gown and dressed her for the first time in clothes from the layette. Today, Vittoria was going to the foster mother, stage one of the permanent separation.

"Off today then, Mrs Campbell?" said a cheerful young nurse. "Be glad to get out of here, no doubt. Back home with your hubby, that will be lovely."

Juliet smiled. How little they knew. She would give anything to stay in the comfortable security of the maternity ward, feeding her baby four times a day and watching her sleep. If only the world would stop, and she and Vittoria could stay cocooned here forever.

She was pulled out of her daydream by the arrival of Mrs M with the carrycot. "All ready to go?" she enquired, kissing Juliet and stroking Vittoria's cheek. With the baby soundly asleep in her arms, Juliet was making the most of their final moments together. She nodded, unable to speak. Mrs M gently took Vittoria from Juliet and put her in the carrycot without waking her. "That's a trick that comes with practice," she said with forced jollity. "Let sleeping dogs and babies lie, that's my motto."

Juliet gave a watery smile, picked up the carrycot and followed Mrs M out of the ward. They put the carrycot with a still sleeping Vittoria on the back seat of Mrs M's car. "Not long to go now," she said, touching Juliet reassuringly on the arm. "I know the worst is to come, but once it is over, you can start to come out the other side." She glanced at Juliet, who was quietly sobbing. "You will get over this, Juliet. I promise."

It was about half an hour's drive to the foster mother's neat bungalow in the glorious Hampshire countryside, but Juliet, in a sea of misery, was totally unaware of the journey. If anyone had asked her where she was or how she got there, she would have looked completely blank. She felt ice-cold; her head was spinning, and her stomach was churning. Mrs M helped Juliet out of the car as solicitously as if she were an invalid before hauling the carrycot off the back seat. The front door of the bungalow was opened by a trim, motherly woman.

"Hello. "I'm Vera, and I'm going to be looking after your baby for the next few weeks." She ushered Juliet and Mrs M into her sitting room, where a neatly dressed middle-aged woman with glasses and a briefcase introduced herself as 'the county council social worker.' Vera bustled in with coffee cups and a plate of biscuits, and Mrs M gently pushed Juliet, who seemed rooted to the spot, into an armchair.

"Now," said the social worker, addressing Juliet. "I have some forms for you to read and sign. One says that you agree to Vittoria – does she have a second Christian name? No? Oh, and will you please check we have the spelling correct – being fostered and the other that you then wish her to go for adoption."

Mrs M gave Juliet a swift glance and looked as if she was about to speak, but Juliet nodded wearily.

"This is the first of three forms you will have to sign for the actual adoption," recited the woman in a dull monotone. "The second will be when the child goes from the fosterer to the adoptive parents, and the final one will be in three months, but that is the most important of all and must be signed in the presence of a Justice of the Peace. Once that form is signed, the adoption is complete, and there is no going back."

Juliet's coffee cup rattled against the saucer, and Mrs M leaned over and took it out of her hands. "Are you all right, dear," asked Vera in concern. "Mmm," replied Juliet, looking pale and strained. "I just want to get this over with."

"Yes, well," said the social worker dourly, marking Juliet down as one of 'those' girls who just wanted to put their mistake behind them as quickly as possible and move on; she had met plenty of them. "Let's get these forms signed then. Pen?"

Juliet signed with a shaking hand, handed back the forms and jumped up out of the chair. Vera held out a piece of paper. "Here, dear, my phone number. Do feel free to call me any time to find out how the baby is doing; you are welcome to come and visit her whenever you want; a phone call first is all I ask."

The social worker frowned. "All I would say is that visiting too often is not recommended; a bit unsettling, if you know what I mean."

Juliet made for the door. "Wait a minute," called the social worker. "You have to officially hand the baby over." Juliet stared at her. "But I've signed the forms."

"Hand her over physically. You must pick her up and hand her to me to show you are giving her up."

Mrs M moved forward and grabbed Juliet, who looked as if she was going to faint. "Oh dear, is that really necessary?"

"Requirement of the law," said the social worker shortly. "Must be done, I'm afraid."

Juliet went over to the carrycot where Vittoria was still sleeping peacefully, picked her up, thrust her into the social worker's arms and ran out of the bungalow, leaving Mrs M to thank Vera and say their farewells. She had given away Enzo's baby.

Five minutes later, Mrs M found Juliet in a sobbing heap on the pavement. In the distance was the sound of church bells as the village campanologists tolled away at their weekly rehearsal.

Part Eight
Juliet and Mary

(1977)

Reflection

"They fuck you up, your mum and dad,
"They may not mean to, but they do.
"They fill you with the faults they had,
"And add some extras just for you."
"This Be the Verse"
Philip Larkin, poet and novelist

ON MY mantlepiece, there is a silver framed photograph of my mother, aged five. The faded monochrome picture shows a small girl with long hair tied with a huge floppy bow, wearing a starched pinafore dress, long black socks, and shiny buckled shoes. Under one arm is a rather untidy bunch of silk flowers. Frozen in time, she is staring at the camera lens with a slightly perplexed expression that hints at a recent rebuke for swinging her legs, which now, crossed at the ankles, are some inches from the ground.

I often look at this picture and feel a creeping melancholy. What were the innocent hopes and dreams of that little girl? The clothes suggest an affluent family, but was she happy? I would never know; by the time I acquired the photograph, it was too late to find out.

My relationship with my mother had always been a difficult one. I knew, with that instinct possessed by all small children, that she resented the fact I was not a boy. She had, in fact, borne a son a year after her marriage to my father, but he was a sickly infant who took one look at the world around him and promptly died. My parents were devastated, particularly my father, who, like all men of his generation, longed for a son and heir.

I was conceived during my father's leave from the army during World War Two, and when he returned to his regiment in France, my mother, quickly realising she was pregnant, planned for the son they both wanted: a boy to replace the child who had died. She swiftly planned a blue-painted nursery, carefully assembled a blue and white layette, and chose the name Graham Peter. Her happiness was complete.

That idyll was shattered when she gave birth to a girl. For two weeks, I didn't have a name. Then, my mother, an avid fan of the works of Shakespeare, decided to call me Juliet after the bard's ill-fated heroine. Was this a sign of her feelings towards me? Even the arrival of twin sons just over a year later seemed to do little to soften her attitude, and her irritation that I was not a boy surfaced regularly throughout my childhood.

"I always dreamed of having a delicate, pretty daughter," my mother would sigh. "Why can't you be more like your friend June? Now, she really is a pretty little girl. Your father wanted to call you Primrose," my mother continued, blithely oblivious to the upset she was causing. "Just as well we didn't. Someone called Primrose should be tiny and dainty, flower-like." I knew then, beyond all doubt, that I was not attractive like other girls.

As if my self-esteem was not low enough, my mother relentlessly continued her wrecking spree. At a school open day, when I had a poem illustrated with a painting displayed on the classroom wall, she was dismissive. "Lovely," said my father, awkward in the unfamiliar school environment and conscious of trying to say the right thing. My mother stared silently at the picture and then pointed to the poem. "I'm surprised they put this on the wall when it has a spelling mistake."

My heart sank, and all the joy of success was sucked out of me. I was still not good enough. Not pretty and not clever. It was something I never forgot.

Chapter One

JULIET HAD been dreaming about Vittoria. She seemed to be thinking about her a lot recently. Despite her happy marriage to Ted, the two great gaps in her life – Vittoria and Enzo – remained, always just a whisper away. In her dream about Vittoria, Juliet could hear the church bells ringing as she was lying in a heap on the pavement after handing her baby over to the social worker. There were bells ringing all over the place. Struggling out of the depths of sleep, Juliet tried to make sense of it. No, it was one bell, and now it had stopped.

Juliet put her arm out towards Ted, but his side of the bed was empty, the duvet thrust aside. She was sitting on the edge of the bed struggling to find her slippers, when he rushed into the room, almost tripping over the long, trailing phone lead. "It's your father," he said breathlessly, handing over the receiver.

Juliet glanced at the clock. Five past seven. Before she could speak, her father said: "Juliet? Juliet, sweetheart, I'm sorry to say your mother died at three-thirty this morning."

★★★

Juliet was dry-eyed. "She needs to cry," June told Ted. "I know they didn't always get on that well, but everyone needs to cry when their mum dies." Ted nodded. He found it mildly concerning that his wife, who was well-known for her easy tears, had not shed even one for her mother. He'd called June as soon as he heard the news and she had dropped everything and driven over. Dropped everything, Ted smiled to himself; that probably meant getting out of bed and telling her housekeeper to sort out Brian's breakfast.

Brian and June had returned from the States several years ago and bought a large old house overlooking the sea in nearby Rottingdean. Although their circumstances were very different – Brian and June were, quite frankly, wealthy, while the Jacksons were comfortable but absolutely not in the same league – the Two Js' strong friendship endured, and Ted knew that June was the one person who would be able to comfort his wife.

Juliet was wandering around the bedroom throwing clothes into a suitcase, when June walked in. "I don't really know what to take," she said vaguely. "Where are you going?" asked June.

"Why to Cornwall, of course." Juliet looked at her with surprise. "I've got to go and be with Daddy. I don't know about Ted and the children, though. Do you think they will want to come with me?"

"Jules." June pulled her down onto the bed. "Sit still for a moment. You can't just take off; you've got to plan this. Have you asked your father what he wants you to do?"

Juliet frowned. "Oh, he'll want me to be with him, and there's so much to do. I know Alan and Bertie will be there sorting stuff out, but families need to be together at a time like this."

She looked at June with tears in her eyes. "Oh, I feel so guilty. I should have gone to see her ages ago, but I was so tied up with my own life and Ted and the kids; now she's dead, and it's too late. Too late to say thank you for everything she did for me. I know she could be difficult, well, so was I, of course, but she always did what she thought was right, and I didn't really appreciate that. I caused her a lot of pain and heartache, and I really regret that now." Despite the threat of tears, Juliet had still not cried.

"Everyone feels like that when someone close to them dies," said June, putting an arm round her friend. "Everyone has regrets, especially when it's your mum. All mothers are taken for granted; it's the way of the world."

"Well, anyway, I have to go to Cornwall," continued Juliet. June stared at Juliet, biting her lip while she considered the options. "Look, sweetheart, do you want to borrow the nanny to help with the children? Or maybe you and Ted should go down to Cornwall on your own, and you could leave the children with me? Then I'll drive them down for the funeral. I'm assuming you do want them to go to the funeral."

Although she had only one child, a delightful five-year-old son called Ned, June employed a Norland nanny to look after him. She hadn't really wanted children at all, but Brian said they had to have at least one, preferably a son and heir. Well, they had Ned, and as far as June was concerned, that was it.

"If I have to have this child, which I don't really want, then I'm having help to look after it," June had said when she knew she was pregnant.

"Oh, June, you sound so heartless," cried Juliet in horror. "You can't leave the poor little thing to be bought up by other people."

"Well then, Brian can look after it," said June, "because I'm not." Juliet had laughed. "You are so naughty! I'm sure you'll feel differently once you have the baby."

June was true to her word. When Ned was born she had a live-in monthly nurse to look after him, and as soon as she left, the nanny took over. His name was already down for Harrow. Brian's father and grandfather were Old Harrovians and although Brian had been a weekly border at a local school, the Turner family was paying for Ned to pick up the Harrow tradition. Ned was, of course, bottle-fed, and none the worse for that, thought Juliet wryly.

"Are you sure I can leave the children with you?" asked Juliet. "I must admit it would be a help not to have them around at the beginning."

"Of course," said June. "We'll go and spend some time with my parents. They adore your kids, and Rosie is old enough now to help with the boys. I know my mum wishes I'd had a quiver full of babies just like you!"

Chapter Two

TED GATHERED the children in the kitchen and told them over cereal and toast that their grandmother had died. Never having been in this situation before, Ted didn't know if he was doing the right thing, but they had to be told and as Juliet seemed to have gone off into a world of her own, it was down to him.

Nine-year-old Rosie stared at her father, her face white with shock. "Granny's died?" she whispered. "How? She was all right when I spoke to her on the phone last week. Did she have an accident?"

Ted took a deep breath. "No, sweetheart, she was ill and…" he stopped as Felix and Michael burst into tears. Rushing round the table to put arms around his sons, he continued: "She had been ill for some time, but she didn't want to worry us, so she didn't really say much about it. So now, although it's a big shock for all of us, and we are all very sad, we have got to be very grown-up and brave for Mummy."

The boys stopped crying and Ted wondered how much they understood. Aged seven and six, they were very young to grasp the meaning of death, although when their pet cat Lucky had been run over by a car, Juliet had spent a lot of time helping them to come to terms with what had happened.

Michael frowned and leaned against his father. "Was it like Lucky?" he asked. "Will Granny be buried in the garden?" Ted sighed. This was going to be more difficult than he envisaged.

"No. Not in the garden, but she will be buried in the churchyard in Cornwall."

"Will we go there?" asked Michael. "Will we see her? Will Grampy roll her up in a blanket like Lucky?" Oh dear, thought Ted. "Well, you can go to the church service for Granny if you would like to. But you won't be able to see her because she will be covered up and all snug and comfortable in her coffin." He really hoped the questions were coming to an end. For a six-year-old, Michael certainly hit the spot.

Ted glanced across at Rosie, who was very pale and had two bright red patches on her cheeks, making her look like a Dutch doll. She was staring down at her hands, tightly clasped in her lap. He knew she was trying not to cry in front of the boys. As their big sister, she would feel that she had to set an example. Evan at the tender age of nine, tried to do the right thing. She was much better behaved than he had been at her age. Felix, rolling a plastic tube backwards and forwards across the table, had said nothing since he heard the news.

"I'll just go and see Mummy," said Rosie, jumping up.

"Auntie June's with her," said Ted. "Don't forget to knock before you go into the bedroom; they may be having a private conversation." Rosie turned round at the kitchen door: "Are you *sure* Granny's dead? I really can't believe it."

"Well, it was very quick, darling," said Ted. "And because Granny didn't want to talk about being ill, none of us knew just how sick she was. It's been a huge shock for everyone. Just think how poor Grampy must be feeling." Rosie nodded and went off to find Juliet.

Felix stopped rolling his tube and looked up at his father. "I'm supposed to be playing at Dan's today," he said. "But I think I would rather stay at home with you and Mummy. You know, I feel so sad about Granny."

"Okay, old fellow," said Ted, ruffling his blond hair. "Whatever you want, I think we all feel a bit off-key at the moment." Felix put his arms around Ted's knees, clasping him tightly. "Hey, steady on," said Ted, grabbing hold of the table edge, "you nearly had me over."

"Daddy," said Felix, squeezing tighter, "You and Mummy aren't going to die, are you?" He stared up anxiously. "Everyone dies at some time," said Michael, "don't they?" he looked at Ted. "Well, yes, but hopefully none of us are going to die for a long, long time."

"But what happens when you die?" persisted Felix. "You go to heaven," said Michael knowingly. "Just like Lucky did. And you meet all your friends there and everyone is very happy." Felix gave him a withering look. "Oh yes, I know that. But Daddy, I meant, what happens *inside* you when you die? Ted began to feel that he was getting slightly out of his depth. "All the bits and pieces in your body get worn out, and your heart stops beating, and then you die," he said feebly, feeling that he was not dealing with the situation very well.

"Yes, but what......"

June put her head round the door. "Any chance of a coffee?" she asked. "There are two women gasping for a cup here." Saved, for the time being, thought Ted as he went gratefully to switch on the kettle.

Chapter Three

TED AND Juliet hardly spoke on the long journey to Cornwall. Ted drove and Juliet looked out of the window, her thoughts deep in the past. She knew she had been a sore trial to her mother and now, as a mother herself, she realised how much she must have hurt her over the years. Mary had been brought up in another era, a time when keeping up appearances and family honour meant everything. Juliet, a typical nineteen-sixties teenager in a have-it-now society, had failed to understand Mary's unshakable belief that personal disappointment was nothing compared with besmirching the family name.

When they arrived at the cottage, Juliet's brother Bertie was already there. "Arrived at the crack of dawn," he said. "Just jumped in the old jalopy and drove down."

Bertie, unmarried and unencumbered, worked as a freelance literary agent and was able to take off at the drop of a hat, unlike Alan, who was married with children and working for a busy rural veterinary practice. "Alan and family will be down as soon as possible," explained Bertie. "He had a book full of appointments this morning that he couldn't put off, and Emma wasn't able get the kids organised in time, or they could have come with me."

Juliet, Ted and Bertie sat down with Dennis and went through the various arrangements for Mary's funeral. It seemed that Mary had left strict instructions about what she did and did not want. "Although she said very little to us, she obviously knew how ill she was and she made many of the necessary arrangements," said Dennis sadly. "For instance, she left me a list of the hymns she would like sung, two Bible readings and the Bach fugue she wants played at the end of the service. Quite amazing, but so like Mary, totally in charge and not leaving anything to chance!"

They looked at each other, not knowing quite what to say as Dennis continued: "Oh yes, and she wants the Reverend David Lloyd, our vicar here, to take the service; she wants to be buried in the churchyard and not cremated, and only a single wreath from the family with everyone else giving donations to an animal charity." Despite their grief, they all smiled. "That's our Mum," said Bertie with a grin. "Hand firmly on the tiller until the bitter end."

Juliet got up and went over to Dennis. "What can I do Daddy, that will be really useful?" she asked, her arms around his neck. "There *is* something I would like you to do," replied Dennis. "There is a special suitcase that your mother kept on top of her wardrobe. She's had it forever and I've never seen her open it. I believe it's full of papers and stuff from before we were married. I would be so grateful if you could look through it and see if it needs to be kept intact or if I should get rid of it. It's something I just can't bring myself to do. She never showed it to me while she was alive, so I don't feel I can look at it now that she's dead."

"Of course I will," said Juliet, and Dennis kissed her on the forehead. "Then, while you do that, Bertie and Ted can come with me to the registrar, solicitor, bank and other boring places. You don't mind being left alone? The vicar is coming round at 4 pm, but we'll be back long before then."

Juliet waved them off and made her way to her parents' bedroom. There was the small blue suitcase still on top of the wardrobe. Juliet lifted it down; it was surprisingly light. Placing it carefully on the bed, she opened the lid with a little silver key attached to the handle.

The house was very quiet, almost as if it was standing on tiptoe, holding its breath. Juliet moved aside a swathe of yellowing tissue paper to reveal just five objects: a diary for 1934, a necklace of yellow and blue stones, three small envelopes tied with red ribbon, a dog-eared sepia photograph, and a small box.

She picked up the photograph first and saw a swarthy young man with dark curly hair and a beaming smile looking back at her. Turning it over, she read the words: "My Tom." Who was Tom? Juliet wondered. She'd never heard him mentioned. With a jerk of recollection, she recalled the Italian boy Mario she had met when she was a teenager and the even earlier mention her mother had made of an 'Italian boyfriend.' Both were long forgotten until now.

Next, she checked out the necklace, a pretty thing but obviously costume jewellery, or could that possibly be topaz and lapis lazuli? She opened the little box and found a gold ring with three sapphires surrounded by tiny diamonds. Gosh. What did it all mean?

Looking at the ribbon-tied letters, Juliet debated whether to open them or not. It seemed like prying, somehow. Mary had kept these things hidden away for over forty years. Would she want her daughter to read her private correspondence or her personal diary?

Nineteen-thirty-four, thought Juliet, her mother would have been what, twenty? The same age she was when she met Ted. Juliet tried on the ring, which wouldn't even fit her little finger. She had forgotten how small Mary's hands were. Dennis used to tease her about them: "Small hands, warm heart," he would joke. And Mary replied: "You mean cold hands." But she always smiled.

Juliet picked up the diary. Apart from a couple of birthday reminders, there was no entry until March. Then, on the 12th, in green ink, Mary had written: *"Met a wonderful boy called Tom Lazarino. He has asked me to go to the pictures with him on Friday."*

Intrigued, Mary turned the page to the following week and there on the Friday: *"Went to pictures with Tom. He walked me home and I am going to see him again on Wednesday. He is very handsome."*

Throughout the next few months, the diary was liberally sprinkled with *"Meeting Tom"* entries. Then suddenly, on July 3rd: *"Tom took me to have tea with his parents. The Lazarinos are a wonderful family"* (wonderful underlined).

Juliet leafed through the next few months; then, on October 17th, was an entry in capital letters written in black ink. *"TOM HAS ASKED ME TO MARRY HIM. I SAID YES!!!!"*

Oh my God, thought Juliet. Mary had been engaged to be married before she met Dennis. Did her father know about this? She continued leafing through the diary. No entries for a couple of weeks, and then: *"I want to die. My life is over"* on October 30th.

Why? What had happened? Had Mary been jilted? Or – heaven forbid – was she pregnant? Juliet dismissed that thought immediately. Remembering Mary's reaction to her own ill-fated pregnancy, she knew that would never have been a possibility for her fastidious mother. So why was Mary so distraught at the end of October when she had been so jubilant a couple of weeks previously?

There were no further diary entries to throw light on the situation. December 2nd simply noted: *"Tom's birthday – sent a card."* The last page, December 31st, merely stated: *"Tom, I will never, never forget you."*

Juliet closed the diary carefully and laid it back in the suitcase. She fingered the red ribbon tying up the clutch of letters. Did they contain the answer? She stared at the three envelopes, chewing thoughtfully on her thumbnail while she contemplated what to do. To open them, or not? Not, she decided. They were obviously very personal to Mary, and Juliet felt sure her mother wouldn't want her to read them. She obviously had not told Dennis about them. Juliet tucked the crumpled tissue paper back around the contents of the suitcase and closed the lid.

Time for a restorative cuppa, thought Juliet, feeling emotionally drained. Walking across the room, she stopped in her tracks and murmured "Blast" gently under her breath. She went back to the suitcase and took out the letters. Sitting on the bed and feeling extremely guilty, Juliet undid the ribbon.

Chapter Four

EACH OF the three letters started *"My beloved Mary"* and ended *"Your devoted Tom."* Written in a neatly sloping hand, they were dated between the beginning of November and the end of December 1934.

Halfway through the first one, Juliet was in tears. By the end of the third, she was sobbing uncontrollably. The three letters, six pages in all, together with the diary and peppered with the bits and pieces of family history Juliet had garnered from a reluctant Mary, who hated talking about the past, revealed a story of deep love and the cruel hand of fate which kept two young people apart. Juliet's grandfather had forbidden the marriage, and Mary had accepted his ruling. Why? If she and Tom loved each other so much, why didn't they elope? It just didn't make sense.

Juliet folded up the letters and re-tied them with the red ribbon. Why had her mother never told her about Tom and this huge sadness in her life? She would have understood so much better her mother's constant mantra of 'what cannot be cured must be endured' and the fact that she was able to accept disappointment and heartbreak with equanimity.

★★★

The sound of voices and general commotion in the hall told Juliet that the three men had returned from town and that Alan and his family had arrived earlier than expected. She went out to meet them.

"All right, darling?" asked her father once the children had been sent out into the garden with the dog, and Emma had gone into the kitchen with Alan and Bertie to make tea.

"Did you go through that suitcase?"

"Mmm. Juliet was in two minds whether to tell Dennis about the diary and letters. It might have been her mother's secret, but as her husband, surely he had the right to know.

Dennis took one look at his daughter's strained face and decided to put her out of her misery. "Juliet. I know about Tom Lazarino." At Juliet's look of utter surprise, he added: "Well, I do, and I don't. I know about Tom; your mother told me soon after we met, and I know why she didn't marry him. But I honestly don't know what is in the suitcase; she never told me, and I didn't ask. I'm assuming it's things relating to that relationship."

"That was why I wanted you to look. *She* would have wanted that. Mary would be happy that you knew. There were many times over the years when she was sorely tempted to tell you about it."

"So why didn't she? Especially as I also fell for an Italian?"

"Well," Dennis shrugged his shoulders. "You know your mother. She didn't find it easy to reveal her soul." Juliet nodded. "Well, now I've read her diary and some letters, but I need to know more. Why didn't they run away and get married in Gretna Green or somewhere like that? Why did she allow Grandfather William to ruin it all?"

Dennis wearily rubbed a hand across his eyes. "I can't help you there; I think you probably know more about that than I do if you've read a diary and letters. You must realise that all this is rather difficult for me, Juliet. I loved your mother very much, and even after so many decades, I still find it painful to talk about someone whom she loved more than me."

"Daddy!"

"Well, Juliet, let's be honest. I don't think she has ever loved anyone as much as she loved Tom. But we had a good life together and three wonderful children, so I certainly don't hold any grudges. He smiled at Juliet. "If I were you, I'd ask The Aunts. They are sure to know the whole story."

Part Nine
Juliet and The Aunts

(1977)

Reflection

"The Times They Are A-Changin'"
Bob Dylan, on the album 'The Essential Bob Dylan'
Revised Edition (1963)

HAVING SPENT a lifetime trying not to be like my mother, I came to the painful conclusion that I had, in fact, turned into her. Not only was I beginning to look like her but we'd both suffered similar heartbreak thirty years apart.

We both fell deeply in love with Italian men and while the circumstances were very different, the ensuing anguish and trauma were the same. And although we eventually married good men who loved us unconditionally, we were both left devastated by a loss that stayed with us for life.

I had always thought my mother was hard-hearted; maybe she was just broken-hearted. If only I had known what she had suffered when she was twenty, it would have made such a difference to our relationship. Why does the fickle hand of fate always mean we discover these things when it is too late to do anything about it?

The strangest thing of all was that she had never given even the slightest hint about Tom, the man she was forced to give up because of religious differences, even after she had found out about my love for Enzo. Having told me when I was a child that she had once had an Italian boyfriend, why didn't she tell me once she knew I, too, had fallen for a handsome Italian? It was a mystery that would never be solved.

Chapter One

OF COURSE, The Aunts. Juliet had momentarily forgotten about Mary's two surviving older sisters, who now lived together in splendid isolation in the Lake District. In their late seventies and widowed, Grace and Win had the menagerie of animals and pets that had been forbidden during their marriages to very conventional businessmen. They rarely travelled south and didn't welcome visitors. News was scribbled on Christmas and birthday cards, but that was about the extent of their communication with their youngest sister and her family, whom they hadn't seen for several years.

Juliet decided to telephone, feeling too impatient to wait for a letter to be answered. The phone seemed to ring forever, and Juliet was just about to hang up when a breathless Grace answered: "Sorry, I was out shutting up the chickens," and then gave a little shriek when she realised who the caller was. "Win, Win, it's Mary's gel!" she shouted. Then she said to Juliet: "I have to shout, she's deaf, you know."

Win had obviously replied because Grace said crisply: "Yes, yes, give me a minute, I was just about to say that!" Then she said to Juliet: "My dear, we were going to telephone your father and say how sorry we were to hear about poor Mary. What a shock. She's quite a few years younger than us, you know, so who would have thought she would go first."

Juliet could hear a shrill voice shouting in the background

again. "What? Yes, wait a minute, dear, I'm getting to that! And then, "Hush, Win. I can't talk to Juliet if you keep shouting at me."

Juliet smiled. The Aunts had always been like this. She imagined it was exactly as they were when they were girls. "Hold on a minute, dear," said Grace. "I've just got to sort out Win."

A minute later, she was back. "Juliet? Now, my dear, we are not going to be able to get to Cornwall for the funeral; such a long way for us, and who would look after the animals? But we will be sending some flowers if that's what your father would like. If no flowers, we know some people prefer donations in lieu, then we would like to give money to the RSPCA in memory of Mary, such a very *worthwhile* organisation. So just let us know what would be preferred. All right dear?"

For a moment, Juliet thought her aunt was going to put the phone down. "Aunt Grace, I have a question to ask you," she said quickly. "I'll get Daddy to talk to you about flowers, but there's something I need to know."

"Oh?"

Juliet told her about the suitcase and its contents. "What I really want to know is why did grandfather refuse to let Mum marry Tom and why did they obey him?"

"Oh dear," said Grace. "I feared this would all come out one day."

"So, you know?"

"Of course, I *know*. But I think you had better talk to Win. Along with Phyllis, she was the one who picked up the pieces."

Chapter Two

MARY ARNOTT had met Tom Lazarino in March of 1934. He played football with Mary's brother Charlie, and they had bumped into each other in the clubhouse when Mary and her best friend, Ella Nelson, were helping with after-match refreshments. Charlie introduced them and Tom immediately invited Mary to the cinema. She was very taken with this curly-headed, laughing boy and accepted the invitation. They both felt an instant attraction and after that first date they spent as much time as possible together.

Tom's family were Italian immigrants and owned a couple of fruit and vegetable shops in the East End of London. Mary's family had moved from Scotland in the 1920s when her father, William Arnott, took up the position of ships' chandler in the London Docks. His wife Jane had died in 1914, when Mary was only a few months old, and the eldest daughter Phyllis, who was just fifteen, had taken the family reins in her capable hands and became mother to her two older brothers and four younger sisters.

The Lazarinos were a large, noisy but very respectable family, well-thought-of in the neighbourhood, and Mary's father was happy enough for his youngest daughter to spend time in Tom's company if they were chaperoned by Ella, of whom he was very fond, or one of Mary's older sisters.

Of course, it was always Ella and a boyfriend who accompanied them, and once away from home turf, the two young couples usually went their separate ways, meeting up again to travel home. If Mary felt a slight stab of guilt about deceiving her father, she did not really let it trouble her. If she could be with Tom, she was happy.

What William Arnott had not envisaged was that the young couple would fall in love and want to marry. While he had no reason to dislike Tom and his family, there was one huge drawback to any liaison between them and his youngest daughter. Religion.

The Lazarinos were Roman Catholics, while the Arnotts were Scottish Presbyterians. Opposite ends of the religious scale. And, thought William grimly, never the twain shall meet. William was an austere, godly man who loved his family but ruled them with a rod of iron 'for their own good.'

William had no idea that Mary had already accepted Tom's proposal together with a sapphire and diamond engagement ring and a topaz and lapis lazuli necklace that had belonged to his maternal grandmother. Mary was ecstatic but said she couldn't wear either the ring or the necklace until Tom had spoken to her father. Although he was aware of the religious differences between the two families, Tom had no idea of William's hatred of Catholicism so he went quite happily to see the man he imagined would be his future father-in-law.

When Tom turned up full of excitement at the Arnott's home in West Ham to formally ask for Mary's hand in marriage, William simply answered his request with a forceful "No!" Shocked, Tom tried to argue his case, but William merely showed him the door, giving no reason for his refusal.

"Leave it to me," said Phyllis, now in her mid-thirties and considered an old maid unlikely to ever wed. The boy she had been walking out with had been killed at Ypres in 1917, and with so few young men returning home after the Great War, Phyllis had resigned herself to the fact that marriage and children were not for her. Her lot was to look after her father and her brothers and sisters for as long as she was needed, and then, she suspected, a lonely old age awaited her.

She looked with sympathy at the young couple desperately clinging to each other in the kitchen. They had been shattered by William's blunt refusal and the fact that he would brook no discussion. As far as he was concerned, the matter was closed.

"I'll talk to Dad and see what can be done," she promised. Mary was like a daughter to her, Phyllis thought, and if it was down to her, she would have given them her blessing, even though the marriage would mean Mary becoming a Roman Catholic. She understood her strict father's hatred of His Holiness the Pope and everything he stood for. William's religion was his life, and Sundays in the Arnott household were marked by two, and sometimes three, visits to the stark and simple Presbyterian chapel at the end of their street. Ruled over with absolute authority by an unbending and forbidding pastor, the chapel could not be more different from the ornate and richly decorated Catholic Church attended by the Lazarino family.

While the Lazarinos enjoyed a huge lunch with extended family after Sunday morning Mass, the Arnotts celebrated the Sabbath very quietly with a frugal and usually cold mid-day meal. No normal work was carried out on a Sunday and the children were not allowed out to play. The family spent the day reading, writing letters, or, in William's case, studying religious books and the Bible between visits to the chapel. Yes, Phyllis could understand how alien the Catholic religion was to that practised by the Arnotts, but when it came to other people's lives, did one person have the right to lay down the law?

She sought advice from her sister Win, who was already engaged to a dull but respectable young man who had recently qualified as an accountant. Although he was not a Presbyterian, George did attend the Methodist Church every Sunday and was an upstanding member of the community. Realising that he could not reasonably expect to find Presbyterian husbands for all his daughters, William had gladly given his permission for Win and George to be married. There was nothing wrong with a clean-living Methodist, and William had the greatest respect for Charles and John Wesley.

After the initial shock of hearing that their young sister wanted to marry an Italian Catholic, Win reluctantly agreed to try to think of a way of persuading William to change his mind. "It is unlikely he will," she told Phyllis. "You know, Dad, once he's made a decision, he sticks to it. And it is the Chapel we are talking about here. I honestly can't see a way of getting around it. Mary is going to have to give up Tom, I fear. It's plain as a pikestaff that she's never going to be allowed to marry a Roman Catholic, let alone become one."

"That's no help at all," cried Phyllis. "Can't you do better than that? But Win admitted she couldn't think of a solution. If truth were told, she was in complete awe of her strict father and saw her forthcoming marriage to George as a welcome lifeline. She couldn't wait to have her own home and to be away from William's rules and regulations.

Eventually, the sisters agreed that Phyllis should intervene on Mary's behalf and see if anything could be done to soften William's decision. "Although if you can change his 'No' to 'Yes,' it will certainly be a miracle and the Pope should be told," joked Win.

Phyllis frowned. "It's not a joking matter," she said severely. "I promised Mary and Tom I would talk to him, so I must try." As time went on, she was feeling less and less sure of her breezy "Leave it to me" promise to the young couple.

If anyone could change William's mind, it was Phyllis. Mary assured a bewildered Tom, who really didn't understand William's objection to the marriage. Phyllis had run her father's life and his household for twenty years, and he relied upon her absolutely.

The fact that she supported their engagement and was going to plead with William on their behalf gave Mary a flicker of hope.

But William was having none of it. Phyllis might have been able to persuade her father to change direction on a few minor family matters over the years, but this time, he was adamant. No daughter of his was going to marry a Catholic, and that was that.

"Blasted Papists are getting everywhere," he growled. "Well, Mary is certainly not getting mixed up with them, selling her soul to the Devil. And just imagine Catholic grandchildren, and she'd be having a baby every year. No. It's not going to happen and that's an end to it."

Phyllis was concerned to see that her father's face was bright red with a vein throbbing violently at his temple. He was obviously far more upset by the situation than she had thought. He really did believe that the Roman Catholic religion was not only foreign but wicked and that all Catholics would burn in hell for eternity.

Sad though she was for Mary and Tom, Phyllis knew that her father was not being deliberately cruel. He honestly believed he was doing the right thing in the sight of God by protecting his beloved daughter from a fate worse than death.

"Of course, I blame myself," said William. "I knew she was seeing young Lazarino, and I said nothing; I knew they were a Papist family, and I said nothing; but then, I didn't ever imagine she would want to marry him!" He looked directly at Phyllis for the first time. "Did you know about this? He regarded her severely. "Well, no matter, she's not marrying him. You can tell her it's over. I don't want to see him here again." He stomped off to talk to the pastor and gain comfort and refreshment by reading the scriptures.

So, Mary and Tom parted. Mary was distraught, but William ignored her plight. "She'll get over it," he told Phyllis. "She'll thank me in the end."

She did get over it eventually, but it took many months of care from Phyllis and Win to get her on an even keel again. However, thought Phyllis with some asperity, I doubt she'll ever thank him for it.

A couple of years later, Mary met Dennis Campbell at a friend's house. There were no emotional fireworks for Mary, but Dennis was a nice man and, as it turned out, a prosperous one with a job in a government Ministry. Mary never really understood what he did for a living and never really wanted to know. Nor did she ever know what he earned – something that scandalised their children in later years. But they got on well. Dennis was an easy-going fellow and was happy to let Mary lead the way, a situation that suited Mary admirably.

After going out together for a year, Dennis proposed, and this time William raised no objection, even though the Campbell family were pillars of the Church of England. "Good Scottish name, anyway," said William, "obviously got origins on the right side of the border."

Phyllis was secretly of the opinion that her father had been so upset by Mary's distress at his refusal to let her marry Tom Lazarino that as long as Dennis was not a Catholic, he would not stand in her way. And what objection could he possibly have? Dennis was a God-fearing man who was more than able to provide for a wife and family and was in line to eventually inherit substantial property and money from his parents. More to the point, Mary, if not exactly euphoric, was certainly very happy and wanted to be his wife.

Phyllis knew that her father still firmly believed he had done the right thing by refusing to allow the marriage with Tom Lazarino and, more to the point, that he had the power of the Almighty and the authority of the scriptures behind him, and thus Right on his side.

Juliet listened to the story in silence. As Win finished, she said: "What I really don't understand is why Mum accepted without question Grandfather William's ruling? If she and Tom loved each other so much, why didn't they run away together?"

"Oh, my dear," said Win. "How can you possibly understand how things were back then? In those days in families like ours, the husband and father was the absolute head of the household and his word was law. It would never have entered Mary's head to disobey him.

"That was the way we were brought up. I can see it is hard for you to understand, but different days, different ways. You can't judge the past by the standards of today."

Chapter Three

WHEN JULIET related this conversation to Ted and her brothers, Dennis, looking more distressed than Juliet had ever seen him, didn't want to hear the full story. Alan pointed out that Juliet, of all people, should understand how things were.

"Different days, different ways, indeed, Smudge," he said. "Now think of your situation and being forced to have your baby adopted back in the sixties. And now, not that many years later, unmarried mothers are blatantly wheeling their illegitimate offspring along the street."

"In Oxford," added Bertie, "there is now a house where unmarried mums can rent a room, *and* they get financial support from the government, I understand. That caused a bit of a stink among a few of the solid citizens on the city council, I can tell you. "In the words of Bob Dylan, *The Times They Are A-Changin.'*"

Juliet grimaced, and Ted shot her a worried glance. He knew it hadn't passed Juliet's notice that it was no longer a disgrace to be an unmarried mother. In just ten years, everything seemed to have gone topsy-turvy. Ted had only recently spent an evening trying to console his wife while she ranted about the unfairness of it all.

There was no doubt that Juliet did feel more than slightly bitter that girls nowadays were able to keep their babies without any recrimination. Indeed, they were being encouraged to do so. But then, she reasoned, had she kept Vittoria, her life would have been completely different. She would not have met and married

Ted, nor had her wonderful children. No, she had done the right thing at the time. There was no point in harking back to what might have been.

Juliet was also aware that two years previously, there had been a change in the law that allowed adopted children to find their birth mothers. The Children's Act of 1975 gave adopted people aged eighteen and over the right to apply for a copy of their original birth certificate and to find out which agency had arranged their adoption. It would be a few years yet before Vittoria was eighteen, but would she try to find her? Or would she be so happy with her adoptive family that she would not think of bothering?

Part Ten
Juliet and Clarissa

(1991)

Reflection

"Doubt thou that the stars are fire
"Doubt the sun doth move
"Doubt the truth to be a liar
"But never doubt I love."
William Shakespeare, 'Hamlet' (Act 2 Scene ii)

KNOWING MY daughter was out there somewhere in the world and that I would never see her again or know what had happened to her was a pain I had learned to live with. When Vittoria was given up for adoption, I knew it would be forever. So why should it be any different now that the law had changed? The problem was I had suddenly allowed myself to hope. Hope that she would want to find me.

It's a fool's paradise, I told myself sternly. Hope has no place in this scenario. It was unlikely that Vittoria would try to find me, and if birth mothers were eventually permitted to trace their children, would she want to hear from the woman who had given her away?

My daughter was long gone; it was as if she had died. I only had a memory, that mental snapshot of a tiny baby girl in a white shawl being handed over to a stranger. I wished I'd taken a photograph before I gave her up, but my distress at the time had been so great that I could think of nothing but my crushing loss.

All I knew was that I loved her. She would always be my daughter. My firstborn. Enzo's child.

Chapter One

PARTLY BECAUSE she hated secrets and partly because she always felt honesty was the best policy, Juliet had told Ted before they married about the daughter she had given for adoption. And because Vittoria was always in her thoughts, she told the children as soon as they were old enough to understand.

"I always think about June and the fact that her birth mother had not told her husband and children that she'd had an illegitimate child," said Juliet to Ted. "Just imagine someone turning up on your doorstep, as June did, and the shock that would be to a family. No, it's best to be upfront and honest. Secrets like that have a nasty habit of coming back and biting you on the bum."

Consequently, Rosie, Michael and Felix grew up knowing that they had a big sister whom they would never see.

Although as they got older, they each asked "how?" and "why?" being children they generally accepted the situation for what it was. Vittoria was one of the family, rather like a distant cousin they knew about but had never met.

"Don't you think they are a bit young for all this?" Ted had asked anxiously as the children blew out candles on a cake made to mark Vittoria's eighth birthday. "Not really," replied Juliet. "Remember what Mrs M said about telling her kids they were adopted from an early age? Now, they can't remember a time when they didn't know. Well, this is the same thing in reverse, if you see what I mean."

"Oh, well." Ted ruffled her hair. "No doubt it is for the best. At least we will all be prepared when Vittoria comes and knocks on the door."

"Oh, right. I should be so lucky," said Juliet, giving him a quick kiss, but a slight quiver of hope lifted her heart.

While Juliet noted changes in the law, allowing adopted children to look for their birth mothers, she didn't really think about it until Vittoria's eighteenth birthday, when she allowed herself to wonder whether her daughter would try to find her. After a couple of months 'on alert,' she put it to the back of her mind, and life continued as before.

Three years later, when Vittoria was twenty-one, Juliet's hopes rose again. Twenty-one was a real milestone birthday. If you were thinking of searching for your birth mother, surely your coming of age would be the catalyst? Juliet almost allowed herself to get excited. Nothing happened. No letter or telephone call, no knock on the door. Just silence. This time, Juliet allowed herself to hope for several months. Eventually, she accepted the chances of Vittoria now contacting her were extremely slim. Maybe she was completely happy with her adopted family and had no need to contact her birth mother (totally understandable), or maybe she had died of a childhood illness or accident (unthinkable). Maybe…Juliet gave herself a shake and firmly put behind her all thoughts of her daughter turning up on the doorstep. What on earth was she thinking? She had no right to expect to see or hear from the child she had given away.

She had grieved for Vittoria back in the sixties and had no intention of mourning all over again. She had been incredibly fortunate. She had a loving husband, a great marriage and three wonderful children. No doubt about it: Juliet Campbell-Jackson had been blessed and had no reason to feel upset. But secretly, in her inner depths, Juliet still felt she had been short-changed.

Chapter Two

THERE WAS no indication that this day was going to be different from any other. Nothing to suggest, when Juliet got up that morning and went downstairs to make her first delicious cup of tea that this was going to be a red-letter day. In fact, it started badly with Juliet tripping over dirty laundry left strewn on the stairs by one of the boys. "Ouch," she cried, hopping over the last two steps and bending down to rub her ankle. "Wretched boys!" She turned round and yelled, hoping to get some reply from her sons, who were presumably still asleep. "Michael! Felix! How many times have I told you about putting dirty clothes in the laundry basket? Get down here and pick this lot up. Now!"

Michael's tousled head appeared over the banister. "What?" he grunted, rubbing his eyes. "Why are you shouting? I was asleep." Juliet stared at him in exasperation. "You are a teenager, not a child. And it's half-past-eight on a sunny Saturday morning. Time you were up and about. Is Felix still in bed?" Going up a couple of stairs, she called: "I want both of you up and at the breakfast table in five minutes and all this washing put into the utility room. For heaven's sake, I was not much older than you when I was married, *and* I had Rosie as a baby and your father to look after, not to mention a house to run." Goodness, thought Juliet, I *have* turned into my mother. Just listen to me.

Half an hour later, Ted and the boys were eating breakfast in the civilised way Juliet demanded at weekends. Rosie had left at the crack of dawn for the local stables, where she and her boyfriend regularly mucked out in return for a couple of hours on horseback, and Juliet had a hair appointment in town followed by coffee and a catch-up chat with June. Just as she was leaving the house, the post arrived.

"Bills, bills, Band of Brothers' newsletter, I imagine from the envelope," she said, handing them over to Ted and kissing the top of his head at the same time.

"You know," she said, tousling his now greying hair, "You are starting to get a bit of a bald patch, sweetheart!"

"Getting old, Dad," laughed Felix, looking up from his mobile phone, his most precious acquisition. It had only just come onto the market and he was very proud of it, guarding it fiercely from his brother. Ted sighed, giving his wife and son a pained look, and Juliet handed over a couple more envelopes. "This looks like a charity asking for money, another bill, dammit… oh, and a letter from Maria Morrison; I'll read that when I get back."

She left Ted immersed in the Saturday supplements with the boys trawling the sports pages they had snaffled from under their father's nose, tucking Mrs M's letter into her handbag. "See you later, guys." She didn't really expect a response, so she wasn't disappointed when she didn't get one.

Back from the hairdressers and a pleasant, gossipy coffee break with June, Juliet suddenly remembered Mrs M's letter. Let's catch up with the news from Western House; she thought as she idly slit open the envelope. Inside, there were two letters. She opened the first and gasped.

'*London W8, November 2nd, 1991*

'*Dear Mr and Mrs Morrison*

'*I am writing to you on behalf of Ms Clarissa Phillips (Vittoria Campbell), who is searching for her birth mother, Juliet Campbell. Clarissa, who is now twenty-seven, was adopted at the age of six weeks, and the address on her birth certificate was given as Western House. If you have any knowledge of the whereabouts of Juliet Campbell, I would be most grateful for any information you could provide.*

'Yours sincerely, Liz Morgan (Accredited Psychotherapist and Councillor).'

Her head swimming and feeling decidedly sick, Juliet scrabbled for the second letter. Her fingers felt like lead and would only work in slow motion; she had difficulty opening the single sheet of writing paper.

She read:

'Western House, Hampshire, November 6th, 1991

'Dearest Juliet

'The enclosed letter arrived here this morning. I was not sure what to do. I was going to telephone you, but Mr M thought it would be better to send the letter to you by post. I do hope it is not too much of a shock and that I have done the right thing.

'Much love from us all. Please phone when you feel able.

'Maria'

Juliet gave a loud scream and burst into tears. As Ted rushed in to find out what had happened, she flung herself at him and clung to him as if she were drowning.

"Oh my God," said Ted in horror. "What on earth has happened? Juliet, talk to me."

But Juliet, totally choked with tears, couldn't speak. Eventually, she thrust the two letters at Ted and sobbed: "I'm okay. It's just the shock. I'll be all right in a minute. I opened the wrong letter first!"

Ted took the sheets of paper from Juliet's shaking fingers and read the letter that Juliet had been waiting nearly three decades to receive.

Chapter Three

IMPATIENT TO find out more about her daughter, Juliet made a call to Liz Morgan first thing on Monday morning. Liz, who had had several meetings with Clarissa, filled in a few of the gaps and suggested Juliet should write to Clarissa to clarify her situation and how she felt about them meeting.

That evening, Juliet wrote:

'Brighton, West Sussex, November 10th, 1991

'My dear Clarissa

'This is the letter I have often dreamed of writing – but feared I never would!

'First of all, I have to say how delighted I am you have tracked me down. I guess you are feeling pretty pole-axed at the moment, so I will try not to ramble on too much.

'I am sure you have lots of questions you want answered. But I must tell you first of all that you were a very much wanted and loved baby. Giving you up for adoption was the most difficult thing I have ever done in my life.

'When I became pregnant with you, I went to work as a nanny for Maria and Bill Morrison at Western House, which is why their address is on your birth certificate.

'As I expect Liz Morgan has told you, I am married to Ted, and we have three children: Rosie (25), Felix (19) and Michael (17). As you can see, you are all fairly close in age.

'I am enclosing a few photographs, and I would be interested to know if you can see any family resemblance. I look forward to hearing from you and maybe meeting up sometime.

'Lots of love, Juliet (Campbell-Jackson)

★★★

'London SW10, November 17th, 1991

'Dear Juliet

'Thank you for your wonderful letter. I never thought about how it would feel writing to you, but now I am, it feels very natural and exciting. 'I always knew I would look for you at some stage in my life and suddenly, something deep inside me told me now is the right time.

'I have always known I was adopted. My mother would talk to me about it long before I understood the words she was saying. We have a very close and happy family. Three years after I arrived in the Phillips household, my sister Bea was born. She is the natural child of my parents.

'I talked to Bea, Daddy, and Mummy together before I started this seriously and am very aware of their feelings during all of this as much as your family's too. I am keen to meet you, and to be honest, I would like it to be soon. Of course, I do have some questions, but I would rather talk about 1991 than 1964!

'Lots of love, Clarissa.'

★★★

Birth mother and daughter met the following weekend at Liz Morgan's office in London. After the astonishing recognition that they looked alike and Juliet had recovered from the initial shock of seeing Enzo's dark blue eyes looking back at her, Liz left them alone with cups of coffee, giving them the chance to catch up on almost three decades of history.

"We really gelled," a jubilant Juliet told Ted when she eventually arrived back in Brighton. "We 'recognised' each other immediately. Of course, we knew who each other was, but it was a much deeper recognition; we had a connection…I can't really explain. We spent almost four hours chatting, and the time flew by. It was just amazing."

Once again, those easy tears welled up in her eyes. "It's sheer relief," she gulped as Ted pulled her towards him in an enormous bear hug. "The thing I've longed for has happened. I've met the daughter I thought I had lost forever."

★★★

'London SW10, November 21st, 1991

'Dearest Juliet

'It is only just sinking in that we have really met. I can't quite believe how much we both learnt about each other over the last twenty-seven years in three hours and forty-five minutes!

'Keep in touch,

Lots of love Clarissa.'

★★★

'Brighton, November 22nd, 1991

'My dear Clarissa

'Having chatted for such a long time on Saturday, I got onto the train at Victoria and thought of all the things I hadn't told you! I am enclosing a card from Rosie and the boys. They are really looking forward to meeting you.

'Take care, and I hope to see you again soon.

Lots of love, Juliet.'

Chapter Three

"WELL, WHO would have thought it would all have ended so happily." June and Juliet were sitting in the garden room at Rottingdean, enjoying the thin winter sunshine while their menfolk were indoors reading the Sunday papers and watching football on the television.

"All that emotion and weeping, and here we are, talking about Vittoria – sorry, Clarissa – as if she had been a member of the family forever." June regarded her friend with a steady stare.

"But she has been," retorted Juliet. "I made sure that she was never forgotten and that Ted and the children knew all about her." June leaned across and squeezed her hand. "And what a lot of heartache you avoided. I only wish my parents were still around to see how it should be done. And Annie Brent, too. It would have been an excellent object lesson for her." There was a slight edge to June's voice, but Juliet saw she was smiling.

"I wish my mother was still alive and could meet Clarissa. I am sure they would have liked each other," Juliet added. "Dad absolutely adores her. He's a real fan. And Rosie and the boys are thrilled that she's turned up at long last."

"Ah, your mother! said June. "I really don't know how she would have coped with the world as it is today. What a lot has changed in the past fifteen years."

Juliet looked thoughtful. "Yes, but changed for the better, I think. An awful lot of hypocrisy has gone, and people are much freer to live their lives the way they want to. That *must* be a good thing."

"Well, certainly no one talks about 'unmarried mothers' nowadays," said June. "I think they are now referred to as 'single parents.' So, what would you do if you were pregnant and unmarried now?"

Juliet contemplated the question. "I suppose I would keep my baby," she said slowly, "because that's what everyone does today, and there's no shame or blame attached. In fact, it now seems a disgrace to offer your child for adoption. But having had three children *and* a husband to help bring them up, I know how hard it must be to cope alone, even these days. I would never ever give a baby away again, whatever the circumstances, but with the benefit of experience, I really do believe children do better with two parents."

"Or one parent and a nanny," said June briskly. "I can assure you that having a nanny is almost as good, if not better, than having a husband – without the benefits, of course!"

"Well, you had both, but how many mums on their own can afford a nanny?" June smiled. "That's true. I admit I was fortunate."

Giving Juliet a deep look, she said: "Veering slightly off the subject, I have been meaning to ask you for ages. Does Clarissa want to know about her father?"

"Hmm, well, it seems not."

"Has she said anything?"

Juliet looked anxiously at her friend. "Only that as he left us both in the lurch, she'd rather not know him. It does worry me a bit, June. I mean, Mike agreed to have his name put on her birth certificate, even though he was adamant he was not her father. It seems rather hard on him, you know, if Clarissa has bad thoughts about him. I also feel it's dishonest to let her think Mike is her father when I'm so sure it was Enzo. She ought to know she has

Italian blood and that it was my fault she didn't grow up with him.

"What do you think? I was going to talk to Ted about it, but I don't really feel I can. I think he has suffered enough of the Enzo-Mike scenario over the years."

June laughed. "You're still the great worrier, I see. Time and the onset of middle age haven't changed that."

"I'm serious, June. It's a worry. I don't know if I should mention it to Clarissa or not?"

"Definitely not," said June firmly. "Goodness, it's like being back in nineteen-sixty-four. I'm sure we had a very similar conversation then. We said if I remember correctly, that the father could well be Mike. I know he said he wasn't and you always thought it was Enzo, but in the end Mike allowed you to name him as the father on the birth certificate, so as far as the law is concerned Mike Bennett is Clarissa's father. Just leave it at that. Least said soonest mended, as our mothers would say. Anyway, I can't see anything remotely Italian about Clarissa."

"She's a brunette, well more than brunette. Her hair is definitely black, and she's got Enzo's incredibly dark blue eyes!"

"Well, half the population of the British Isles is brunette and so was Mike, well, brown-haired anyway. So, please stop your fretting and just enjoy the fact that you've got your daughter back."

June held out her hand. "Come on, let's go and see if our respective husbands and your dad are ready for a coffee. I'm gasping!"

★★★

Back in the house, the conversation about adoption continued. Dennis, who had recently had lunch with Clarissa in London, was saying what a lovely girl she was. "And she seems really happy to have discovered she's got a whole new family."

Handing round coffee cups, Juliet said: "I was worried that

she might be disappointed when she met me. She said that when she was a little girl, she always told people that her real mummy was a princess. I thought I might have been a bit of a let-down, but I remember Mrs M telling me that Adele always said her mummy was a princess, so perhaps that's what all little girls who have been adopted say."

Ted patted her hand: "You'll always be a princess to me, sweetheart."

"Thank you, darling," replied Juliet, "but Moira – you know, the woman who used to be the Morrison's cleaner – found her birth mother after a huge amount of effort and then wished she hadn't bothered."

"Really?" said June with interest. "Mmm. Apparently, they were completely different in every way, looks, religion, class, beliefs, you name it. She said she had built up a picture in her head of how her mum would be, and she was nothing like it, a real disappointment.

The saddest thing Moira said was, if they had met in other circumstances, they would have had nothing in common and probably wouldn't have liked each other very much."

"Golly," said June. "I wonder if I would have liked Annie Brent if I had been allowed to get to know her?"

"Chances are you wouldn't," said Brian. "I gather stories with happy endings like Juliet and Clarissa are few and far between. There's usually too much baggage on both sides to make these adoptive relationships a long-term success."

"I was going to say that Kathy, the groom who was my friend at Western House, was also disappointed when she tracked down her birth mother," continued Juliet. "She told Mrs M that she felt as if she had opened a can of worms and was worried about where it might all lead."

"How horrid," said June. "What was wrong with the birth mother?"

"I don't really know the details," said Juliet vaguely, "but Mrs M said that once Kathy had met her mum and found out about her birth family, she'd had enough and just wished she could put her back in the box again and walk away. Unfortunately, once you've taken that step, there's no going back. You can't pretend it hasn't happened."

"So, it's not always sweetness and light, then," said Dennis. "I suppose that's why they encourage adoptees to have counselling before they embark on that journey."

"But don't you think," said June, "that Juliet and Clarissa have hit it off so well because neither of them was looking for anything from the other?"

"What do you mean?" asked Ted with interest, "money and stuff?"

"Well, I suppose there could be a situation where one half is hard-up and hoping for financial support from the other," said June slowly. "I was thinking more of emotional support. Juliet, as we know, has a happy marriage and three wonderful kids and wasn't really looking for another child. She just wanted to know that Vittoria, I mean Clarissa, was alright. And Clarissa has a happy family set-up and wasn't looking for a mother; she just wanted to know about her background." Dennis nodded. "Yes, I see, and the fact that when they met, they jelled, so to speak, is a bonus?"

"Absolutely," agreed June.

"Well, I must say that Juliet has been very fortunate it's all worked out so well. Clarissa is a great credit to her parents, and they must be very proud of her. She was telling me what a close family they are and how well she gets on with her mother," said Dennis.

Brian looked up from the *Sunday Times*, which he had spread all over the coffee table and onto the floor. "That is all very well and good, but surely we cannot get away from the fact that Juliet is also her mother," he said. "Birth mother, my love," replied June.

"Well then, she now has two mothers, lucky or unlucky, depending on how you look at it. Personally, I would say it is rather unfortunate if her other mother is anything like mine."

June giggled, but Juliet said seriously: "No Brian, Clarissa has only one mother, and that's the woman who adopted her and brought her up, the person who was there to look after her when she was ill, who took her to school for the first time and cuddled her when she was unhappy.

"Clarissa will always be my daughter, and I love her. Nothing can change that. But I won't ever be her mother because she has one already, and whatever you say, we can only truly have one mum. After all those years of thinking I would never, ever see her as long as I lived, I feel extremely privileged and grateful that I can now be her friend."

There were tears in Juliet's eyes, and Ted jumped up and went over to put his arms around her. "Don't cry, Smudge. It's all worked out far better than we could ever have hoped."

"They're tears of happiness," sobbed Juliet, and hugged him.

Part Eleven
The Two Js

(Many years later)

Reflection

"Yesterday is history, tomorrow is a mystery, today is a gift. That's why we call it The Present."
Eleanor Roosevelt, former First Lady of the United States of America, diplomat, and activist

HERE I am, an old woman, constantly dreaming and reflecting on a long life. Many beliefs have changed over seven decades, most for the better; things that were taboo for generations are now an accepted part of life. Not just unmarried mothers and illegitimacy, but homosexuality, divorce, women's sexuality, and equality… the list is endless.

I can remember thinking that my mother was wrong when she said one must live life so that when death comes, there are no regrets. As a young girl, it seemed impossible not to have any regrets at all at the end of life. Nothing about which to say "I wish…"

For most of my happy and busy life, I have had little time for remorse. Overall, it has been a good life despite the ups and downs. Now I am elderly, I confess I do sometimes look over my shoulder at the past and wonder what would have happened if I'd taken a different path and made other decisions. I do admit to saying the occasional 'I wish…"

And I am constantly dreaming about the past. Even the events of half a century ago seem as if they happened only yesterday. They are still very fresh and real. Many of the songs that Enzo used to sing to me on Capri go round and round in my head, not only *Can't Help Falling in Love,* which is always playing in my mind, and *Quando, Quando, Quando*, but also *Que Sera Sera (Whatever Will Be Will Be)* and I am taking that as my mantra for the years I have left.

I can't change the past – that's done and dusted, and the future is a mystery yet to unfold. The present, however, is indeed a gift, and I am enjoying it to the full. *Que Sera Sera.*

Chapter One

TWO ELDERLY ladies sat beside the long open window of their seaside flat and dozed contentedly in the sunshine. Each had a cat curled up on her lap, while a small hairy dog of indeterminate breed snoozed at their feet. Following the deaths of their husbands, Juliet and June had sold their respective houses and bought a second-floor balcony flat on the seafront in Hove.

"Do you remember when we were girls, I always said that when I was an old lady, I wanted to sit in a rocking chair with a cat on my lap and a parrot on my shoulder?" said June, opening her eyes and squinting across at Juliet. "Well, you've got the rocking chair and the cat," said Juliet," but I draw the line at a parrot. I can't abide feathers!"

"Huh!" June laughed. "I'm quite happy with the cats and dear Florence and you, of course!" Hearing the mention of her name, the dog scrambled to her feet and looked hopefully at June. "Sorry, sweetie, no walk until later; now, settle down." With a huge sigh, Florence plonked herself down on the floor again, shedding a cloud of wiry hair as she did so.

"Thing is Jules, nowadays, I seem to spend an awful lot of time looking back. Thinking of how things used to be and about everything that has happened to us through the years."

Juliet fondly regarded her old friend and stretched out a hand to pat her knee. "That's the work of old ladies," she smiled. "The past seems to constantly catch up with us. We're always going back in time."

"I find it so hard to accept that we are old," said June a trifle peevishly. "Where has all that time gone? How did it all slip past so quickly?"

"While we weren't looking," laughed Juliet.

"I know it sounds silly," said June, "But in my head, I'm still eighteen. I sit here and watch a handsome young man walking along the promenade, and I still get a thrill creeping up my spine and think, 'Gosh, he's nice!' I forget I'm old and that he wouldn't give me a second glance or even a first one."

Juliet laughed. "The truth is he is young enough to be your grandson, and the only interest he would have in you is to politely offer his arm to get you safely across the road. Yes, I know, I do it too. I still have an eye for an attractive Italian, and I also fondly imagine that I can put on a mini-skirt and long boots and do the Twist at the Regent Ballroom or go for a jive down in the basement at the Starlight Rooms."

"What, a mini with legs like yours? In case you've forgotten, the Regent is long gone, and the Starlight is now a block of flats. Anyway, you'd look truly dreadful in a mini. Mutton dressed as lamb, as my dear mother would have said."

Juliet closed her eyes and leaned back in her chair. The tabby cat shifted on her lap, wriggling into a more comfortable position as Juliet stroked his broad, stripy head.

"Years ago, when you and Brian were in the States I think, I saw this old man dancing with a beautiful young girl. She was tiny and wafer-thin, with long blonde hair down to her waist, wearing a black mini dress and showing off the most perfect legs. She was on the other side of the dance floor with her back to me, and I idly assumed the old man was with his granddaughter. Imagine my horror when they danced round towards me, and I saw that the beautiful young girl was, in fact, an old, old woman. She was heavily tanned and all wrinkled like a prune. It was just like a horror film; she had the figure and looks of an eighteen-year-old from behind and the face of an eighty-year-old. I guess she was the man's wife and just as old as he was."

Juliet shuddered. "That memory has stayed with me throughout the years, and it still unnerves me, constantly reminding me never to try and look younger than I am."

June laughed. "At least we are happy to grow old gracefully, or maybe disgracefully. It's the only way, I always think. I know you still dress rather eccentrically, compared with my rather classical look, I mean, but that's you. The thing is, we dress age appropriately. Life goes on, and we are getting older with it. No point fighting it."

Juliet sighed: "When Ted died, I thought my life had ended. Being a heart attack, it happened so suddenly that I had no time to prepare. We had been together so long, more than half a century, and I really didn't think I could carry on without him. But I recovered, thanks to the children, grandchildren, and good friends. While life will never be what it was with Ted, it is still good. It is a different life, but I feel very blessed."

June regarded her steadily. "Of course, you loved Ted. Whereas, as I am sure you know, I never loved Brian. Oh, I was very fond of him, and we had a steady marriage and wonderful Ned, but I sometimes do feel slightly sad that I have never, in my whole life, experienced a deep and abiding love. Not even for my child, to be honest. Which, I suppose, makes me a very selfish person."

"Oh, June, you......"

"No, don't say it! What goes around comes around. You know better than anyone that I got what I deserved, what I wanted, I suppose. From an early age, I played the field, pitted all the boys against one another, had fun and didn't really care about anyone's feelings or about people getting hurt. I just had a good time and moved on. Oh goodness, Juliet, I can see now that I really was the most awful little tramp. What must people have thought of me?

Before Juliet could say anything comforting, June continued:

"I married Brian, not for love, but for money, and position, and jewellery, and property, and an easy life. Once I discovered that his parents were loaded and saw what money could achieve, I wanted that wealth and privilege myself. I also married to get away from my parents, whom I never really forgave for not telling me I was adopted.

"To this day, I don't know if Brian really loved me. He said he did, but I do wonder… He was such a complex character. Of course, we settled down happily enough and rubbed along together. I gave him the son and heir tradition demanded, and I was content but never in love. The secret of our marriage was politeness."

"Politeness? That's a strange thing to say."

"I've never admitted it to anyone, not even you, but I quickly discovered that to make a success of a loveless marriage, you need perfect manners. Brian and I respected each other and rarely rowed, mainly because I usually got my own way. He spoilt me and I stayed with him; he had a mistress, and I had affairs. Divorce would have finished him; people like us did not get divorced. We were life partners and, therefore, in it for life. So we presented a united front; it was a mutually advantageous situation. A trade-off"

"Ohh…" breathed Juliet, puffing out her cheeks on a long note of discovery, staring at her lifelong friend with speechless amazement. They had been The Two Js since they were five years old and had shared their deepest secrets, but she never had the smallest inkling of this hidden part of June and Brian's marriage.

"Then, of course, he had his clubs and male friends," continued June.

"Clubs?"

"Well, yes: you know he was a Freemason. It was a family tradition; both his father and grandfather belonged to the same Lodge, and Brian was there more often than he was at home. Then there was Whites, where he spent most of his time when he was in London, so really, it all worked out very well. I had no idea what he got up to on those numerous business trips and frankly, I didn't want to know. On the few occasions Brian was at home, it was a pleasure to see him. There was an element of rarity, which was incredibly exciting and we almost went into honeymoon mode."

June stared silently out of the window, remembering the past, and Juliet said nothing. She was shocked to the core. June and Brian had been her closest friends for decades and there had never been a hint that they had anything but a quintessential marriage. "I had no idea," she told June. "You were both very discreet."

"We were," agreed June. "Goodness knows how we got away with it; I wasn't aware that there was even any gossip. Mind you, there are a lot of couples who live in the shell of a marriage while keeping up the appearance of normal family life.

"When we found out Brian had cancer, and then later, when we knew he was not going to get better, we used to sit and talk about life," June continued, her voice cracking slightly. "But neither of us mentioned love; it would have seemed dishonest somehow. Now I often wonder what love would have been like, what I…what we…missed. We both had loads of sex but never love. Sometimes I feel I've been cheated, that I have been denied something fundamental." June's voice was steady, but there were tears on her cheeks.

Juliet jumped up, tipping the cat unceremoniously off her lap. The tabby stalked off, tail in the air, as Juliet went over to put her arms around her old friend. "No one who saw how devotedly you cared for Brian could doubt how fond you were of him," she said quietly. "Fond, yes," said June, "but never in love. You and Ted had the real thing. And I'm quite envious of that."

"Yes, I did love Ted," agreed Juliet, sitting down again, "but I never stopped being passionately in love with Enzo, who I still think about a great deal, even though it was so long ago, especially as I still believe he was Clarissa's father. Really, though, Ted was my other half. He was the one who was with me all through the years and I never really fancied anyone else after I met Ted."

"Apart from Enzo," said June naughtily. "I never stopped fancying him," retorted Juliet, "even after I met Ted."

Frowning as she recalled the past, she said: "It seems odd, thinking about it now, but I could never bear another man to touch me. Romantically, I mean, and certainly not sexually. When we went to those awful Band of Brothers dinner dances, I would never dance with anyone but Ted. I must have spent hours in the powder room, keeping out of the way while the slow dances were on. Unfortunately, he wasn't that keen on tripping the light fantastic and preferred talking business in the bar, although I did occasionally manage to drag him onto the floor for a smooch."

June pursed her lips but said nothing as Juliet stared into the distance, thinking about the way she had felt all those years ago. "I hated men putting their arms around me, and I was always amazed that most girls, even Cindy – you remember her and Dave? – well, even Cindy could be quite intimate on the dance floor with a man who wasn't her husband.

"Things often used to get quite out of hand back then as well. There were quite a few couples I knew who swapped partners. Do you remember those key parties?" June smiled wryly. "Certainly, I remember. I think I've got the T-shirt somewhere!"

That's right, June had told her about going to the so-called cheese and wine parties in the sixties and seventies when couples would put their house keys into a pile on the table. When everyone had reached the required level of inebriation…"enough not to care and not too much so you couldn't perform," said June…each man would pick up a key and go off for an hour or so with whichever woman the key belonged to. It was looked on as harmless fun back then, but Juliet knew that occasionally, it had caused a great deal of misery and trauma, particularly when children got caught up in the emotional mess that sometimes followed.

"I know a lot of people really enjoyed them, but I would have been hopeless at anything like that," said Juliet. "To be honest, I just couldn't imagine being in bed with another man, other than Ted – or Enzo, of course. That's the litmus test for me. And that's why, after Ted died, I just knew I would never marry again. She shuddered: "Just the thought of someone else touching me."

"Did you never love any of the others?" asked June with interest. "Gosh, you make it sound like there were dozens. The boys when I was young didn't really count. There was Italian Mario who was never serious, we were little more than children, and the kisses were very chaste, and my first real boyfriend Rob, remember him?" June laughed: "As if I could forget. I never understood what you saw in him."

"Well, I think that was what's called puppy love, and there was absolutely no sex involved, although I remember we did do a bit of rather unsuccessful French kissing. There were also a couple, or was it three, casual boyfriends I was infatuated with for a short while, but none of them were very exciting – not a tongue in sight.

"Then Mike, who I met just before you and Brian got married, before I went to Italy. Juliet frowned. "I do feel slightly guilty that Mike paid for me to go on that trip to Capri where I met Enzo. As you know, I was hopelessly in love with Enzo, but sadly, it turned out that it wasn't meant to be. Pity though. I wish I had been braver and taken a chance, but then, I would have had a very different life."

Juliet paused as she looked back across the years. "The first time Enzo took me to The Island I remember thinking that the decisions we make can change the course of our lives. Very prophetic as it turned out."

June was about to comment, but Juliet continued before she could speak. "After that, Mike again. It was very strange because for months our relationship was almost platonic except for a few kisses and cuddles. I certainly *didn't* love him and frankly sex, when it happened, wasn't up to much either.

"The one time he made love to me, I hardly realised it had happened, and as it was immediately after Enzo, the poor man really didn't stand a chance, there was no way he could compete with a sexy Italian. I am ashamed to admit it, but on that disastrous occasion when Mike made love to me, I was thinking in my head that he was Enzo; that's why I didn't realise what he was up to."

"Oh, my dear," said June with an amused smile, "don't feel guilty about that; more women do it than you would imagine. I have often been in bed with Elvis Presley or Sean Connery, only to wake up in the morning to find I was with a completely different man, occasionally my husband."

Juliet gave her a considering look with the faintest hint of a smile. "To my lasting shame, even though I didn't love him, and the sex was mediocre, I *would* have married Mike just because I was pregnant, and I wanted to avoid the shame and problems of being an unmarried mum. Thankfully, Mike was wiser than me and put a stop to it. To be honest, I am pleased it worked out the way it did. Mike really did deserve better. I do hope he eventually found love with someone who appreciated him. And then, finally, Ted. So that's my love life summed up in a few sentences."

Catching sight of the engagement ring Brian had given June, with its enormous diamond glinting in the sun, Juliet held out her hands, spreading her fingers which were bare except for her grandmother's wedding band. "Three proposals and one husband, and not one of them ever gave me a ring. Even my wedding ring belonged to Granny."

"There's more to marriage than a ring," said June sagely. "I kept this, not for sentimental reasons, but because it's such a gorgeous diamond and quite valuable. I haven't worn a wedding ring for years. I took mine off when I knew Brian had a mistress;

it seemed pointless to wear it, really. It was platinum and worth a bit, so I hocked it."

"Gosh, something else you failed to mention!"

"It was while we were in the States, and it wasn't that big a deal. I guess I just forgot about it." Juliet recalled Ted's promise to one day buy her a diamond. "When we were getting married, Ted promised to buy me the biggest diamond in the world once he had made his fortune."

She laughed: "Of course, it never happened, not the fortune or the ring! There was the wedding ring I wore while I was pregnant with Clarissa, but I bought that for myself. I've still got it in a drawer somewhere."

Juliet leaned back in her chair. "Nothing I did throughout my life pleased my mother, but I knew I could either live the life my parents had mapped out for me or a life based on my own truth. Whether I was right or wrong, in the words of Frank Sinatra, *I Did It My Way*."

June sat in silence for a while. Eventually, she said: "But if you remember, Jules, even Ol' Blue Eyes said, '*Regrets, I have a few…*' tell me honestly, we can no longer have secrets at our age, do you regret not going back to Enzo? You did tell me all those years ago when you returned from Capri that Enzo might turn out to be your one regret. I've never felt I could ask before, but is he?"

Juliet looked stricken, her eyes sparkling with unshed tears and her voice husky with emotion. "Not long after I had written to tell Enzo I wasn't returning to Capri, I suddenly knew beyond all doubt that I had made a mistake of gargantuan proportions," she admitted haltingly.

Ignoring June's gasp of disbelief, she said: "I knew I would never ever find anyone else like him and recognised that I had carelessly walked away from something unique and special. Sadly, that knowledge came too late; I found out I was pregnant…and I just couldn't be certain whether Enzo or Mike was the father.

Although deep down inside, I always knew it was Enzo, I had no way of proving it. You can have no idea how bitterly I still regret that foolish, casual sex with Mike. It changed the course of my life.

"Of course, I couldn't turn up on Capri and say, '*Ciao,* we're having a *bambino.*' It really wasn't an option. Suppose the baby had turned out to be Mike's after all. And as you said all those years ago, there was a chance Enzo might not have wanted to know. I also knew that he was going to Rome and then to the States, so there was a good chance I wouldn't have found him." She looked so bereft that June began to wish she hadn't broached the subject.

Juliet ploughed relentlessly on, her mind firmly fixed on the past. "With the wisdom of age, I know I should have defied my parents and refused to leave Enzo and Capri in the first place; then, Kismet would have decided the outcome. If I was *not* pregnant while I was on Capri, we would have gone to America together, and my life would have taken its destined course; and if I *was* pregnant, then Enzo was the father, and I would soon have found out if he really loved me. But I did leave, and I was too scared to return, lacking confidence and totally unsure of my ability to hold him. So, I will never know absolutely if Mike or Enzo fathered Clarissa. And I may have recklessly thrown away years of bliss."

"I have always believed," said June, "that a decision once made is the right decision. Hindsight is a wonderful thing. But if the decision to leave Enzo seemed the correct thing to do at that particular time, then it was the right decision for you, regardless of what happened afterwards.

Juliet considered for a while, shifting in her chair and looking at June with sad eyes. "I honestly did love Ted very much, but he could never be Enzo. What Enzo and I had was alchemy; I would never find anyone else in my whole life who would make me feel the way he did."

She broke off and stared out of the window at the dark

waves of the English Channel, restlessly rolling up and down the shingle beach in front of them, so different from the calm, warm, turquoise waters of southern Italy.

"I'm not saying that Ted was second best because he wasn't," Juliet said firmly. "I loved him, and he gave me years of happiness. But what I had with Enzo was unique and irreplaceable; once I had walked away from that, my life had to continue as if he had never been, or I would have gone completely mad. So, I married Ted as soon as I could and had a very different life."

She screwed up her face as she squinted down the years at a time long ago when she was a girl with long red hair streaming down her back, and a stunningly handsome Italian wanted to marry her.

A huge silver moon floating in the night sky above the Faraglioni rocks appeared unbidden in her mind. Juliet had known beyond doubt that the memory of that first night at Bar Russe, when Enzo had taken her to Marina Piccolo, would stay with her forever. It had arisen many times over the years and now, half a century later, the image was as clear as it had been at the time: it was as it had happened yesterday.

Juliet gave a huge sigh that came from the very depths of her being. "I know now that I am old, that it is impossible to wipe out an experience like the one I had with Enzo on Capri. Because our relationship didn't last forever, it doesn't mean its importance was any the less. What Enzo and I had during four short months has stayed with me in my dreams and my memory and has shaped me for the rest of my life."

She was openly crying now, huge sobs wracking her body. June started to move towards her, but she put up her hands as if to fend her off. "No, no, I'm alright. Really. This is good therapy for me. I needed to say it all out loud, so I know it is true, that it really happened; that a gorgeously sexy man like Enzo loved me and wanted to marry me.

"I stare into the mirror and see an old woman with grey hair, looking very much like my mother, and I wonder…if I'd gone back to Enzo, would we still be together? Would he still love me? Because I still love him. It's been going round and round silently in my head for over fifty years. After all that time, I still have the ache deep inside me."

The tears began to pour down her cheeks and she took the box of tissues June thrust into her hands. "Goodness, I seem to have spent most of my life crying or blushing for one reason or another."

Trying to lighten the atmosphere, June said: "It must be something to do with red hair." Juliet gave a watery smile. "Well, it's grey hair now, but the tears still come very easily."

She paused for a while before adding unsteadily: "My short time with Enzo was four months of passionate madness, a once-in-a-lifetime affair that could never be repeated.

I was so young, and I truly feared that I would not be enough for him. I was terrified that Enzo would eventually leave me for someone far more glamorous, and I would die of a broken heart. So, I gave him up rather than face any trauma the future might bring. Luckily, I met Ted, so my life wasn't ruined. I didn't become a Miss Haversham!"

June looked at her with real compassion. "I think it was Cecil Day-Lewis who said, 'Love is proved in the letting go.'"

Juliet, her mind still nostalgically in the past, didn't hear her. As if talking to herself, she said very softly: "That song, *Can't Help Falling in Love,* sums up my relationship with Enzo. It became our song, the one he always sang to me after we had made love. Although he beguiled me by singing *Quando* in Bar Russe, it was my favourite Elvis song that became uniquely ours. I can't listen to it, even now, without all those deeply buried feelings rushing to the surface. It was the only song I could never dance to, not even with Ted. It was too evocative of Enzo. It meant too much."

June stared mutely at her lifelong friend. She had never felt so passionately about anyone or anything in her life. Nor had she realised that Juliet, who had been as close as a sister since she was five years old, had been harbouring these emotions for half a century.

I suppose nobody divulges everything; we must all have a secret part of ourselves that is never shown to anyone, she thought. Can you ever *really* know another human being, however close you are to them?

After Juliet's revelation, June felt her life had been very shallow and hedonistic in comparison. There was nothing left to say.

★★★

The two old ladies sat quietly, each lost in their own thoughts of the past. Eventually, June said: "Neither of us has had a perfect life, but then, perfection is an impossible goal.

"Our lives have been perfectly imperfect and all the better for it. We've known each other for almost seventy years, and we've lived contrasting lives side-by-side throughout that time. We've both been happily imperfect in our own ways and…"

"And we're happily imperfect now," said Juliet firmly, wiping her eyes. "We're happy to be alive and have our wonderful memories, living in this beautiful spot with our families and friends and our animals around us.

She stood up and stretched languidly. "Talking of which, it's time to take poor old Florence for a walk. She's been waiting patiently enough!" June smiled, grabbed a cardigan from the back of her chair and, picking up the dog's lead, made for the door. Florence was there before her in a shower of hair, her claws rattling on the wooden floor as she happily shook herself, joyous at the prospect of the walk to come.

As they went out, Juliet laced her arm through June's and

said: "We may be old, but there's still time for new adventures and good things to happen. *Carpe diem*, seize the day. Let's make the most of the years to come."

★★★

MY NAME is Juliet, and I'm an old woman. My perfectly imperfect life has been both a gift and a blessing despite being occasionally tinged with tears. I am thankful and content. Life is a collection of memories. I am grateful to have had so many good ones.

Finally...

My deepest thanks go to those who have told me their stories and allowed me to weave them into this book. Sadly, some of those who inspired me to write are no longer with us, but my gratitude goes to them, nonetheless. My inspiration came from Georgina, Sandra, June N, the Carter family, Ray, June H, Alison, Lorna, the Bell family, Michelle, the endless succession of girls at mother and baby homes, and last but by no means least, the wonderful couple who adopted my baby.

www.ingramcontent.com/pod-product-compliance
Lightning Source LLC
Chambersburg PA
CBHW020351080526
44584CB00014B/978